Wilderness and Waterpower

Energy, Ecology, and the Environment Series

ISSN 1919-7144 (Print) ISSN 1925-2935 (Online)

This series explores how we live and work with each other on the planet, how we use its resources, and the issues and events that shape our thinking on energy, ecology, and the environment. The Alberta experience in a global arena is showcased.

Wilderness and Waterpower

How Banff National Park Became a Hydroelectric Storage Reservoir

Christopher Armstrong and H. V. Nelles

UNIVERSITY OF
CALGARY
PRESS

ENERGY, ECOLOGY, AND THE ENVIRONMENT SERIES
ISSN 1919-7144 (Print) ISSN 1925-2935 (Online)

University of Calgary Press
2500 University Drive NW
Calgary, Alberta
Canada T2N 1N4
www.uofcpress.com

LIBRARY AND ARCHIVES CANADA CATALOGUING IN PUBLICATION

Armstrong, Christopher, 1942-
    Wilderness and waterpower : how Banff National Park became a hydroelectric storage reservoir / Christopher Armstrong and H.V. Nelles.

(Energy, ecology, and the environment series, 1919-7144 ; no. 5)
Includes bibliographical references and index.
Issued also in electronic formats.
ISBN 978-1-55238-634-7

    1. Water-power—Alberta—Banff National Park—History. 2. Bow River Watershed (Alta.)—Power utilization—History. 3. Reservoirs—Alberta—Banff National Park—History. 4. Wilderness areas—Economic aspects—Alberta—History. 5. Electric power consumption—Alberta—History. I. Nelles, H. V. (Henry Vivian), 1942- II. Title. III. Series: Energy, ecology, and the environment series ; no. 5

HD9685.C33A43 2013   333.91'409712332   C2012-908282-1

The University of Calgary Press acknowledges the support of the Government of Alberta through the Alberta Multimedia Development Fund for our publications. We acknowledge the financial support of the Government of Canada through the Canada Book Fund for our publishing activities. We acknowledge the financial support of the Canada Council for the Arts for our publishing program.

This book has been published with the help of a grant from the Canadian Federation for the Humanities and Social Sciences, through the Awards to Scholarly Publications Program, using funds provided by the Social Sciences and Humanities Research Council of Canada. This project was also funded in part by the Alberta Historical Resources Foundation, using funds provided by the Alberta Lottery Fund. The Wilson Institute for Canadian History at McMaster University also provided financial support.

Government of Alberta ■   Canadä   Canada Council for the Arts   Conseil des Arts du Canada   ALBERTA LOTTERY FUND

Printed and bound in Canada by Marquis
♻ This book is printed on FSC Silva Enviro paper

Cover Photo: Bow Falls in Canadian Rockies © g01xm (istockphoto.com)
Cover design, page design, and typesetting by Melina Cusano

Table of Contents

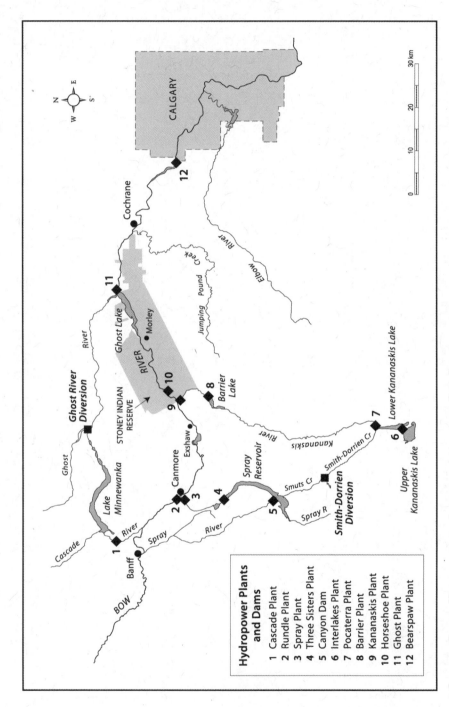

Hydropower Plants and Dams

1 Cascade Plant
2 Rundle Plant
3 Spray Plant
4 Three Sisters Plant
5 Canyon Dam
6 Interlakes Plant
7 Pocaterra Plant
8 Barrier Plant
9 Kananaskis Plant
10 Horseshoe Plant
11 Ghost Plant
12 Bearspaw Plant

CALGARY POWER HYDROELECTRIC INSTALLATIONS ON THE BOW RIVER

Introduction

We do not often think of the iconic Banff National Park being made to serve mundane corporate functions such as storing water for hydroelectric stations. But it does. By the same token, we do not think of electricity as being a major force in the development of national parks policy. But it was. It might be ventured that electricity was as much a factor in the history of Banff National Park as was the CPR.

Why did Banff National Park have to be significantly altered to accommodate hydroelectric storage? More broadly, how did the production and consumption of electricity in southern Alberta shape Canada's premier national park? This book attempts to answer those questions in a narrative of hydroelectric development in the Bow River watershed.

We do not mean to imply that the Banff we know is the result of something simply being plugged in. Rather, we offer an account in which path-dependent technology and hardening public policy continuously collided, driven by a relentless urban demand for electricity. But this is not a story of technological determinism. There is nothing automatic or predetermined about our story. At every point in the narrative, people made choices.

Almost from the beginning of the electric age, Banff National Park came under continuous pressure to accommodate the Calgary Power Company's need to modify the Bow River watershed to make electricity. That pressure was not absolute, but relative. It was not so much electricity itself as the method of its generation that led the power company to cast covetous eyes upon a national park. Calgary Power made a strategic decision at the outset to generate electricity using hydroelectric power. There were other ways of generating electricity. In a coal-rich region, thermal electric power represented a viable alternative. But the company chose instead to rely upon falling water in the Bow River for its energy, primarily because hydroelectricity was cheaper to produce over the long term. But as it turned out, the Bow River – a glacier-fed mountain river in a region of hard winters – experienced dramatic seasonal streamflow changes. As a result, it was not ideally suited to the efficient production of electricity on a constant basis throughout the year. To produce enough electricity to meet its commitments in all seasons, and to earn a profit, the company had to redesign the river to make it a better source of power. That is what led Calgary Power into a series of negotiations to create storage and generating facilities upstream in, as fate would have it, a national park.

The phrase *path dependence* describes a familiar predicament: early choices in system design virtually determine downstream incremental change. Or, in a more elegant formulation, path dependence exists "when the present state of a system is constrained by its history."[1] Familiar examples of this phenomenon include the gauge, or track width, of a railroad; the choice between 25 and 60 cycles, or 110 and 220 volts in electricity delivery; the QWERTY keyboard; and combined or separate sanitary and drainage sewers in cities. Once these initial choices have been made, it becomes increasingly difficult to make fundamental changes. Major change requires retrofitting or replacing the entire system, and usually it is easier and cheaper to continue on down the path selected at the beginning. The path dependence of hydroelectric generation impelled the Calgary Power Company as it searched for more capacity and more reliable power on the Bow River. And that brought Banff National Park into the crosshairs of hydroelectric engineers seeking to maximize output.

Path dependence may be a demanding master, but it is not necessarily a tyrant. It is a force exerted by the imagination and calculations of relative current cost, not by the machines themselves. It expresses itself through inertia and following the path of least resistance. Its grip can be broken, usually when incremental change no longer accommodates demand or when a new transcendent technology overshadows the legacy system. That too would happen to Calgary Power. here were always other ways to make electricity, but whenever the need for additional power arose, it seemed easier, cheaper, faster, simpler to extend the existing system rather than shift to another basic platform. Calgary Power eventually ran out of river to manage, at which point it redesigned its system around another method of power generation. This, in turn, took pressure off the river, but what would happen to those sunk hydroelectric investments on the Bow and in the park?

There is no necessary incompatibility between power generation and a national park. We may find the two contradictory now, but that depends largely upon our notion of what a park should be, an idea that has changed over time. The concept of a national park in Canada, following the development of the institution in the United States, evolved as a hybrid of several inherited notions of "park," among them the royal game park as a preserve, the park as a restorative spa, and the park as a place of public amusement and enjoyment. Banff, of course, was originally reserved to preserve its hot springs so that it might become a health resort or spa. The addition of recreational and aesthetic rationales for "emparkment" led to the progressive expansion of the park boundaries to include scenic and wilderness terrain.

The idea of what the park should be was as expansive as its territory. In a frugal, limited state, parks were fragile creatures competing for resources against well-established departments. Acknowledging this bureaucratic disadvantage, the early administrators of the national parks adopted an accommodating plan of growth and survival that has been called the "Doctrine of Usefulness."[2] Parks existed to be used and enjoyed by the people. The greater the usage, the logic ran, the greater the income and public support. It was under this latitudinarian management policy that the Calgary Power Company turned its attentions toward Banff.

Nor had the idea of what a park should be coalesced into a coherent perception or policy. For example, the railway predated the park. Whatever Banff might want to become, it would always have trains thundering through. Similarly, the territory encompassed by the park included coal mines, silver mines, logging operations, and considerable private property. And of course, the railroad and the government-built hotels, spas, a town, and leased large lots for the rich to set the tone of conduct by their presence and taste for architecture. Under such a regime, turning shallow Lake Minnewanka – formerly Devil's Lake – into a storage reservoir did not, on the face of it, violate any principles.

But over time that would change, a phenomenon that we call "policy hardening," a phrase of our own invention. In part because of experience with these "uses," park managers began to develop a more restrictive notion of park policy. The park idea itself had evolved into a purer form.[3] Seen from this perspective, coal mining, private property, and hydroelectric development were incongruous activities within the bounds of a national park dedicated to the preservation of nature and outdoor recreation. Policy hardening might be thought of as the opposite of "clientalism," the tendency of state regulators to take on the world view of their clients or to be "captured" by their clients. By contrast, policy hardening describes a process whereby state actors discipline their citizen clients by restricting permissible action in accordance with an abstract principle.

Over time, parks managers would change their minds about the need to accommodate economic activities within their mandates and would write increasingly restrictive regulations. The bureaucrats, in turn, were supported by a small but vocal interest group of park users who amplified their concerns and sometimes stiffened their resolve. As the Calgary Power Company returned again and again to government to find new ways of wringing more power out of the Bow River, it encountered a hardening policy, an ever more resolute bureaucracy, and an external lobby insisting that its aims were incompatible with those of a national park. What would happen when an irresistible force encountered an immovable object?

This struggle between the power company and the Parks bureaucracy of the Government of Canada was not played out in a vacuum. An apparently insatiable demand for electricity in burgeoning southern Alberta sometimes propelled the company to near desperation in its need to expand production. At the same time, it presented the Parks Branch bureaucrats and nature preservationists with a countervailing public good that could not be readily dismissed. At the beginning, electricity had only a few uses, street lighting and commercial illumination foremost among them. But electricity infiltrated all aspects of modern life: public transportation on the street railway and industrial power as well as, in the home, heating, lighting, cleaning, ironing, and, with the spread of radio, entertainment. Getting more electricity was not simply a corporate imperative; thousands of bill-paying consumers put a voters' face on demand and imparted an implicit political menace to their desires. Popular North American campaigns for electrification – from the Ontario Hydro-Electric Power Commission, to the Tennessee Valley Authority, the Hoover Dam, and the Columbia River development, to programs of rural electrification – had taken on a tone of religious revivalism. Electrification was as much a social gospel as an infrastructure project. The demand for electricity was a countervailing force that could also, like national parks, wrap itself in the high diction of social redemption.

Meeting the demand for electricity was also a forward-looking game: the electricity had to be there when the switch was turned on. Since it took years to get approvals and to design and build dams and generating facilities, installations had to be financed and constructed long before demand kicked in. Forecasting demand and anticipating it with installed capacity were inexact sciences, in part because demand – while highly predictable in some circumstances – could change dramatically in either direction. Wars and depressions would make a mockery of the most sophisticated plans, leaving the company in desperately short supply or with embarrassingly large surpluses.

Path dependence meets policy hardening in an atmosphere of unpredictably rising demand: in a nutshell, that is the essence of the story we are about to tell. But it takes more than bloodless abstract categories to make a good story. Strong characters are required, along with unpredictable plot shifts and some raw emotions. Our story has all of those qualities in abundance. The irrepressible and impetuous Max Aitken – later Lord Beaverbrook – sets our tale in motion. A stuffy, bumbling, and somewhat uncomprehending R. B. Bennett becomes the Ottawa fixer. He gives way to an archetypical gruff, hard-driving, square-jawed engineer-businessman, G. A. Gaherty. William Aberhart, Ernest Manning, Mackenzie

King, and C. D. Howe make cameo appearances and decisive choices. Earnest bureaucrats, lurking in their offices, struggling to be consistent within ambiguous policies and mindful of shifting political currents, lob convoluted, often turf-defending memoranda into the maelstrom. They can also be counted on for the occasional, if unintended, light comic turn.

Other actors in our story appear more often as collectivities than as individuals. The Nakoda (Stoney) Indians, whose reserve contained the most promising energy resources, had to come to terms with the prospects of hydroelectric development and then had to fight (almost literally) to obtain the compensation that they had been promised. The City of Calgary, as owner of a municipal electric utility and voice of the citizens and electricity users, volubly asserted those not-always-identical interests. The Government of Alberta had to make up its mind over policy within a provincial frame of reference in dramatically shifting economic and political circumstances through the Depression, World War II, and the Cold War; over time, shared jurisdiction of lands and waterpowers with the federal government eventually changed the power dynamic in the provincial government's favour. Then there was the mythical East, home of two of the most powerful players: the Montreal-based Calgary Power Company, and, of course, Ottawa, the seat of the bureaucracy and the federal government. If it seems that the only key player missing from this list is the CPR, let it quickly be said that it also weighed in at key moments on the hydroelectric question.

The story of a decades-long battle between wilderness preservationists and hydroelectric developers would, in other hands, be a simple moral tale in which greedy businessmen try to despoil a pristine wilderness in search of higher profits against the resistance of nature lovers. In such a Manichaean view, Indians are victimized, civil servants strive to uphold the public good, and nature is despoiled. That is not our reading of the evidence. The moral tale quickly becomes blurred. We see no consistent heroes or villains in this piece. Rather, we see largely honourable people on all sides striving to achieve legitimately conflicting versions of the public good as seen from their perspective. But like all of us, in the heat of the moment, they surrender occasionally to their human frailties. And in this struggle, they sometimes unexpectedly exchange black and white hats.

Irony resides, too, in the often-noted ambivalence that Canadians have always exhibited toward the landscapes that surround them. There is so much "nature" in Canada – so vast, so lovely, so challenging, and yet so foreboding – that to tame its resources for their economic rents remains a national obsession. Canadians have expended huge amounts of energy assaulting and destroying the ecosystems in which they live, while at the same time busily celebrating the beauty and importance of unspoiled nature in shaping the national character. But this story raises the question of whether this kind of development is an either-or proposition. Now that these hydroelectric structures have largely outlived their usefulness, who would propose pulling them down? They have become, in a strange way, part of the nature to be preserved.

A word or two about our title. The first word, *wilderness*, will be a familiar and uncontroversial term to many, if not most, of our readers. It will, however, raise eyebrows among our academic colleagues. Wilderness has become, in the argot of scholasticism, a "contested" term. That is to say, its common usage turns out on close examination to be quite misleading. In ordinary speech, *wilderness* has historically meant wild, scenic, often rough uncultivated places, where raw nature rather than humanity is in command. It is, in short, a space where humans are absent. But a recent body of scholarship, to which we ourselves have belatedly contributed, argues that this separation of nature and culture in the expression *wilderness* is overstated.

In the first place, the wilderness frequently had people wandering around in it, often the most ardent proponents of the wilderness experience: hikers, mountaineers, tourists. But that is a minor irony. The fundamental problem is that wilderness is not an objective thing, something out there to be encountered, like rock or trees. Rather, it is an intellectual construct, an idea projected onto a landscape. And the problem with wilderness is that creating an imaginary separation between humanity and nature masks the essential humanness of its construction.[4] Wilderness, then, in the form of a changing ideal, is man-made. But wilderness is a social construct in another sense. Historically, humans have rarely been absent from the land. Their presence as hunters, fishers, trappers, and travellers has had a significant impact upon the landscape. What was first encountered in the wild at European contact was not simply the work of nature. Native fire, in particular, connected the culture of a people to the natural world in which they were embedded. Modern human activity – railroads, logging, tourism – has also had a profound impact upon wilderness environments.[5] The casual assertion of an empty landscape devoid of humanity conveniently erased, as has so often been pointed out, the dispossession of Native people that occurred at the point of creating a national park and the continuing police action that permanently excluded them as hunters.[6] Note in that last sentence how readily wilderness elided into national parks, a matter to which we will return.

But first, we have to defend ourselves for using a word to describe something that does not exist, or rather, that exists as a cultural artefact. We use the word *wilderness* in the full knowledge of the problem associated with it. Nevertheless, we use it because it has had vernacular meaning for generations of Canadians.[7] As we have repeatedly run into the word in speeches, reports, newspaper articles, books, and letters ranging over a century, we have come to see it not in an absolute sense, as a noun identifying a specific kind of thing, but rather as a relative term, as a statement about the distance away from a point of observation. Looking out from the city, wilderness was the other end of the imaginative continuum from urban-industrial, human-constructed landscapes. The concept did not imply something pure that could be identified simply by its attributes. Nor did it disappear when some of its supposed attributes were missing. Rather, wilderness expressed the relative absence of human-made things, although that absence need not be complete. Conservationists and wilderness defenders might deplore the presence of industrial installations, like hydroelectric dams, while at the same time building trails, setting up camps, patronizing luxury hotels, doing business with outfitters, golfing, shopping in stores, and opening museums, art galleries, and even zoos. They might resist the symbolic intrusion of industrial humanity rather than quotidian human presence.

In that sense, there was and still is quite a lot of wilderness in Canada: that is, land beyond urban, agrarian, and even mining and forestry frontiers. Wilderness advocates did not think all of it should be preserved. Indeed, even the most ardent proponents of wilderness preservation admitted that much of it should be exploited for human benefit. But certain special places, set apart by romantic conceptions of the sublime or natural wonders (like hot springs), deserved special protection by the state within the bounds of a national park. This was indeed an impulse shot through with contradictions, as the phrases most often associated with the idea of a national park suggest: pristine wilderness, wilderness playground, wilderness sanctuary. To work, wilderness had to be remote *and* accessible.[8] It was often referred to as a place of refuge from an alternative life space, but at the same time, it redeemed that other life, at least in Thoreau's formulation, amplified by John Muir and photographed by Ansel Adams: "In Wildness is the preservation of the world." As a sanctuary, wilderness inspired near-religious experiences; at the same time, it served as a gymnasium for extreme and often dangerous outdoor sports. In wilderness, humanity found renewal. The goal was not that human culture be absolutely absent from wilderness, but that it be reduced as much as possible. So, aware of the plasticity and contradictory nature of the term, we will speak of wilderness as this imaginary alternative space.

*Waterpow*er, also called *hydropower*, is, by comparison, a fairly straightforward word. Water as it falls releases energy. A high school physics equation summarizes the process: $P = hrgk$. The height of the fall (h) and the volume of the fall (r) under the force of gravity (g) combine to give an energy output (P). This hydraulic energy can be captured with water wheels and turbines with differing efficiencies (k) to produce kinetic energy, which, through ingenious mechanics, can be made to do work. However, this equation overlooks another very important element of waterpower – the variability of flow (v), and therefore the quantity of energy available on a permanent basis. The results of the equation in an applied world need to be divided by v to reveal the minimum quantity of power available at the site. Hydroelectric facilities are rated on their ability to generate a quantity of power on a continuous basis. Thus, the minimum flow determines the output of the equipment. This little factor, v, will be the driving force in our story. Reducing variability to increase minimum flow became a crucial element in improving the efficiency of hydroelectric production. We should, in passing, also draw attention to the cultural construction of even the term *waterpower*. Waterfalls in the world are quite widespread. They are not everywhere and always conceived as waterpower by those living around them. Waterpower exists in culturally specific contexts.

Continuing on into our subtitle, we encounter the phrase "Banff National Park." This is an entity that did not come into existence until 1930. Before then, it bore the name Rocky Mountains National Park.[9] In the title, we use the current name to cover the earlier period, but in the text, we use the historically contingent names.

What then is hydroelectric storage? Electricity cannot be stored in significant quantities; it must be consumed as it is generated or, alternatively, available when it is needed. However, the water used to generate electricity can be stored in lakes and reservoirs. Our story in these pages will revolve around the need to create or enlarge upstream storage capacity capable of holding back water at certain times of year for release later when it is most needed. As it turned out, the best sites for water storage were located within a national park. We do not contend that the boundaries of Rocky Mountains National Park and then Banff National Park were entirely determined by the need for hydroelectric storage, but we do insist upon it being a major factor. Finally, we do not mean to imply that Banff National Park in its entirety became a storage reservoir or that it only served in that capacity. What we will explain in this book is the way in which hydroelectric storage and generation directly reshaped the ecology of parts of the park and indirectly led to a series of boundary redefinitions on its eastern borders.

Historical narrative, in the interests of coherence, proceeds *seriatim*, one thing at a time. That is not necessarily how history itself plays out. Historical actors multi-task; they are capable of thinking and doing more than one thing at a time. Readers should be aware, then, that our narrative sometimes separates things that occurred simultaneously in time. Our single-minded approach does not convey the complexity or the whole way in which contemporaries viewed a situation. For example, in chapter 6, for the purposes of clarity, we concentrate on the row over the proposed development of the Spray Lakes, which led to their ultimate excision from the park. But in chapter 7, we show that while the endgame on that issue played out, company officials were also thinking about how to develop the Ghost River site in time to meet a new contract with Calgary.

Before embarking on our story, we should acknowledge the assistance of scholars whose work has influenced our interpretation of these events. To Joel Tarr[10] and Martin Melosi,[11] two scholars who over the years have shared our interest in the history of urban infrastructure, we owe our understanding of the concept of path dependence. The writings of environmental historian Donald Worster have sensitized us to the social and political power required to harness nature, especially water; the power, wealth, and social and environmental exploitation involved in that process; and the hubris underpinning the desire to control nature.[12] Readers will note our indebtedness to William Cronon's *Nature's Metropolis* for an understanding of the incorporation of nature into the city under capitalism and the impact of city's demand upon the natural world far removed from the immediate vicinity.[13] From William Cronon, too, we have borrowed and adapted the notion of second nature, the hybrid derivative of human interaction in the environment. Finally, our book is, in a sense, a coda to Richard White's Columbia River story: here we explain how those machines got inserted in the Bow and how the river in turn became one great natural machine.[14]

We conceived this book and did much of the research while we were working on what became *Monopoly's Moment*. Soon after, we even roughed out a first draft. But being preoccupied with other projects, the manuscript languished. That was probably just as well, because we uncovered a great deal of relevant material in the Department of Indian Affairs files as we were doing research for *The River Returns*, and we learned from subsequently published work. That environmental history of the Bow River necessarily contained a chapter on hydroelectric development and another on the development of Banff National Park. But given the many other topics requiring treatment, we had to ruthlessly compress our findings into a few pages. Indeed, two well-informed reviewers of that book chided us for not giving the conflict between hydroelectric development and park policy more extended coverage. We are happy to oblige. Our excursion into environmental history with co-author Matthew Evenden also tempered our original political economy approach to the subject. Research for the Bow River book also entailed following the documentary trail from Calgary Power to its successor company, TransAlta Utilities, through the good offices of our friend Bob Page, then a senior executive with the company. This permitted us to analyze annual reports and other internal documents relating to the transformation of the company in the 1950s, with which our narrative concludes. We have thus touched on certain aspects of this story in several previous publications.[15] However, in drawing these threads together into this focused account, we have considered evidence that has subsequently come to light and have completely rewritten the text – except for the occasional phrase or sentence that we found we could not improve upon. In *The River Returns*, we expressed the hope that someday we might publish a fuller treatment of these subtle and complicated matters. This book brings that hope into realization.

Water Falls

Falling water has always excited the emotions. Thundering waterfalls and roiling rapids have filled hearts with both dread and wonder from time immemorial. Such fearsome places, where a misstep led to certain death, were thought by many peoples around the globe surely to be the abode of the gods. In the Christian era, it was believed that these were sites of revelation where God made manifest his enormous power, casting human pretensions in pitiful perspective. For millennia, human beings approached waterfalls with a sense of fear, awe, and wonder.

In the modern era, the power of falling water has also stirred another human emotion, ambition, inspiring ingenious thoughts on ways of using some or all of that power for human purposes. The aesthetic of the sublime associated with sites of spectacular nature was gradually displaced in the case of falling water by utilitarian thoughts guided by mechanical engineers and, subsequently, hydroelectric technology. How could that energy, now perceived to be going to waste in conspicuous display, be converted to productive human ends? How could the genie bottled up in nature be released to be re-employed in the service of humanity?

Millers led the way, creating millponds and rechannelling flows in ever more efficient ways to turn their water wheels and crank their machinery. At the larger sites of falling water, millers could use only a small portion of the energy available with their mechanical technology, but at places like Lowell, Massachusetts, and Minneapolis, Minnesota, extensive hydraulic engineering works recovered a large proportion of the available energy to power textile mills, flour mills, and other manufacturing enterprises.[1]

Hydroelectric power – a more efficient process that could be developed on a larger scale, producing a much more adaptable form of energy that could be used at a distance – rapidly displaced mechanical technology at the end of the nineteenth century. After the physics of electricity was worked out in the late eighteenth and early nineteenth century, it was left to tinkerers like Edison and Tesla of the late nineteenth century, and then the electrical engineers and capitalist entrepreneurs, to work out, manufacture, and distribute the integrated system to produce, transmit, and then use electrical power. Long-distance transmission proved to be one of the key elements of this integrated technological system, allowing power to be generated in one place but consumed with minimal transmission losses dozens, hundreds, and eventually thousands of kilometres away. Previously, energy users had to locate themselves at sources of power, or power production had to take place close to sites of consumption. Long-distance transmission broke the bond between production and consumption. Henceforth, industry did not have to go to power; power came to industry.[2]

In Europe and the Americas, electrical power generation, either by steam power or by hydraulic means, was well understood and widely exploited commercially by the beginning of the twentieth century. Large corporations produced, sold, and installed the equipment to generate, transmit, distribute, and consume electricity for a variety of purposes: domestic, commercial, electromechanical, industrial, and traction. Following the relentless logic of returns to scale, electrical systems and generation facilities sought ever larger power sources to generate electricity at the lowest cost and maximum efficiency.

Under this new intellectual and commercial regime, the energy of falling water could gradually be rechannelled through machines all over the world. Waterfalls went silent, or were greatly diminished. Dams across rivers drowned rapids in slack-water lakes as vast quantities of hydraulic energy were converted to electricity to light up the night, energize factories and transportation, and perform a host of mundane domestic tasks. The subdued hum of whirling turbines and generators replaced the thunderous roar of waterfalls and rapids. This new hydroelectric doctrine, which subjugated falling water and transformed hydrology, took root nowhere in the world more firmly than Canada, with its abundant and widely distributed waterpowers. Canada quickly became one of the most aggressive developers of hydroelectricity in absolute quantities, on a per capita basis, and as a proportion of its total energy production mix – an international ranking that it retains to this day.[3] Canada got the hydroelectric religion.

And so, eventually, did southern Alberta. With the rise of a significant urban population at the end of the nineteenth century, hydroelectric thinking descended upon the Bow River with all of the evangelism, restless drive, and impetuosity characteristic of western ambition. Calgary's early experience with electricity mirrored in a microcosm the development of the technology more generally. The first steam-powered electric generators sprang up in the city, close to the hotels and businesses and street lights they served. Then, also in the city, a small dam across the river, primarily for a sawmill raceway, raised water levels to power a low-head hydroelectric-generating facility. With the advent of long-range transmission and under the inspiration of iconic projects at Shawinigan, Niagara, and many other Canadian waterfalls, the entrepreneurial search for electrical energy to empower a burgeoning urban industrial society turned toward the upper reaches of the Bow, where several spectacular cascades advertised its hydroelectric potential.

The first reasonably comprehensive survey of hydroelectric development in Canada in 1910, a heroic example of inventory research conducted for the Commission of Conservation by Leo G. Denis and Arthur V. White, helps us place the Bow River developments in their contemporary context.[4] This snapshot of the Canadian hydroelectric industry in its infancy counted 960 waterpower sites across Canada, not including an unknown number of unsurveyed locations in the far North. Denis and White identified hundreds of hydroelectric installations operating or under construction, with a total output of a little over a million horsepower (hp), or 740 megawatts (mw). Most of these were small, low-head stations producing a few hundred horsepower and serving mines, sawmills, factories, electric companies, and municipal electric utilities. A few, associated with pulp and paper mills, generated in the range of several thousand horsepower.

Two projects at Shawinigan and Niagara Falls were world scale at over 100,000 hp each. Scale mattered more than the sheer number of projects. Only thirty-three large projects (over 5,000 hp) accounted for 79 per cent of total Canadian output. In 1910, electric companies, mainly privately owned, distributed approximately 75 per cent of this hydroelectricity to towns and cities for commercial, industrial, municipal, and domestic uses. A few municipalities close to waterfalls operated their own small plants. Pulp and paper companies and other industries equally divided the remaining 25 per cent of the hydroelectricity. Provincially, Ontario led the way with 53 per cent of total Canadian output, followed by Quebec, British Columbia, and Manitoba. All of the other provinces had less than 10,000 hp under development in 1910. Alberta, with 1 per cent of the national output, was thus just getting into a game already well under way in the East and in British Columbia. Significantly for us, Alberta's total was accounted for by a single project located on the Bow River.

To look ahead just briefly, Canadian hydroelectric fever would continue unabated in the decades to follow. Despite World War I, hydroelectric capacity would almost double in a decade. It would virtually triple during the 1920s, creating, as it turned out, serious oversupply problems for the industry during the Depression, when hydroelectric development had to be severely reduced. During the 1940s, a global war hampered development, notwithstanding the fact that electricity had become a major weapon of war. Postwar economic growth unleashed another hydroelectric building boom during the 1950s, when capacity once again more than doubled. Hydroelectric capacity growth would ease off during the 1960s, as the engineers ran out of easily accessible rivers. Nevertheless, hydroelectric expansion would continue, albeit at a slower pace, to the present day by exploiting more remote sites in the far North.

The engineering of the Bow River for hydroelectric development would, to a large extent, mirror the broader Canadian experience. As the first run-of-the-river projects became fully operational during the second decade of the twentieth century, growth rates spiked above the national figure. During the 1920s, the system on the river doubled its capacity, but during the Great Depression, not one new hydroelectric project on the

Hydroelectric Development in Canada in 1910

Province	Output (hp)	% of Canada	Electric Cos	Pulp & Paper	Other Indust
Ontario	532,266	52%	75%	11%	14%
Quebec	300,153	30%	64%	26%	11%
British Columbia	100,920	10%	87%	8%	4%
Manitoba	48,300	5%	100%	0%	0%
Nova Scotia	15,272	2%	12%	79%	9%
New Brunswick	9,765	1%	35%	31%	34%
Alberta	7,300	1%	100%	0%	0%
Yukon	2,000	0%	100%	0%	0%
P E I	500	0%	10%	0%	90%
Saskatchewan	45	0%	0%	0%	100%
Canadian Total	1,016,521	100%			

Source: Leo G. Denis and Arthur V. White, *Water-Powers of Canada* (Ottawa: Commission of Conservation, 1911), 22a.

Installed Hydroelectric Capacity in Canada, 1910–1960
(in thousands of hp)

	Installed Capacity	Growth Per Decade
1910	1,011.0	
1920	1,754.1	173.5%
1930	5,114.1	291.6%
1940	7,576.1	148.1%
1950	11,029.8	145.6%
1960	25,019.3	226.8%
1970	38,793.6	155.1%

Source: *Historical Statistics of Canada*, 1st ed., Series P1-6; 2nd ed., Series Q81-4.

Bow River Hydroelectric Development, 1910–1970 (in kw)

1910	7,000	
1920	23,900	341.4%
1930	51,900	217.2%
1940	51,900	100.0%
1950	82,800	159.5%
1960	234,200	282.9%
1970	320,000	136.6%

Source: Calgary Power and TransAlta Annual Reports, see Appendix.

Bow came online. The contraction on the Bow was more severe than the national average. Expansion picked up slightly again under the stimulus of World War II, after which the 1950s witnessed a major explosion of developments that slackened off considerably during the 1960s. By then, the Bow, like many other rivers in Canada, had been dammed, plumbed, machined, and wired to its maximum, and Calgarians, along with other southern Albertans, would have to look elsewhere to satisfy their electricity dependence.

But all of this did not just happen passively. These facilities had to be designed, financed, and built, and their output sold. They were thus driven by a capitalist imperative. Similarly, powerful social forces lay behind the rising but variable demand for electricity, which the developers strove to meet. Technological necessities, especially the need to increase the output of expensive capital equipment to the maximum capacity, demanded further action. The energy of the river was also perceived to be the "property" of other actors; this property had to be politically re-appropriated in favour of the power developers. None of this would be easy, nor was any of it inevitable. Electrification of a city had profound environmental, social, and political implications far beyond its borders. In the process, Banff National Park became a hydroelectric storage reservoir. Such was the power of the hydroelectric religion, capitalism, and urban growth, and the momentum of path-dependent technological development. This story of hydroelectric development on the Bow River, a tale that eventually involved a replumbing of the river to meet the requirements of the technology and the demand for energy, takes us into the fundamental questions of power in a democratic society: Who gets what? Who decides? Who pays?

Blame it on Calgary. Without the mushrooming of a major urban centre in southern Alberta, the Bow, like the other rivers flowing off the eastern face of the Rockies, would not have been extensively engineered. For three decades after its founding in 1875 as a North West Mounted Police post at the confluence of the Elbow and the Bow, Calgary's growth from a handful of residents to 4,152 in 1901 was far from spectacular. The arrival of the Canadian Pacific Railway in 1883 reoriented activity to the more expansive real estate possibilities of the open prairie, but the town remained primarily an unremarkable regional distribution centre for agriculture and commerce. Its energy demands, mainly for street lighting and commercial and industrial power, were slight but not inconsequential and could, for the most part, be handled locally.[5] Typically, major industrial power users – hotels, retail stores, and of course, municipalities for street lighting – provided the main stimulus to the development of the electric industry and often organized the companies themselves. Within just three years of the time that Calgary secured municipal incorporation in 1884, its council approved a proposal to light the streets electrically from the small locally owned Calgary Electric Company. Employing a small steam-powered generator, this undercapitalized and badly managed business made more enemies than friends with its intermittent service. Antipathy to the Calgary Electric Company opened the door to competition.[6]

The Eau Claire Lumber Company, organized by itinerant Wisconsin businessmen who had moved to Calgary, had set up shop on the Bow River just north of the town in the mid-1880s. It conducted logging operations on its timber leases located in the mountains in the upper reaches of the Bow River system, and in classic Canadian fashion, it floated its logs in an annual spring drive to holding booms at its steam-powered sawmill in Calgary. To create the ideal ponding conditions at the mill, the Eau Claire Company acquired the right to build a dam across the Bow just upstream from Calgary in order to redirect water into a channel between Prince's Island and the company's mills on the south bank of the Bow. This dam created the conditions for a low-head hydroelectric installation at the outlet of this channel.[7] Needing power for their mill, the Eau Claire partners built a small hydroelectric plant with enough capacity to serve other customers as well. With its steam plant and this hydro installation, Eau Claire, under the name Calgary Water Power Company, took over electrical distribution from the moribund Calgary Electric Company.[8] By the beginning of the twentieth century, Calgary had recapitulated the history of the electric industry: first came a centrally located steam-powered direct current system mainly for street lighting; then, a small hydroelectric alternating current system exploited local power resources – the slight drop in the level of the Bow River as it passed through Calgary – to serve industry, commerce, and municipal power users.

After 1901, however, the explosive growth of Calgary and expectations of its future possibilities suddenly outstripped the capacity of the local electric utility. Population growth and commercial ambition unleashed a search for new sources of energy; the situation was sufficiently urgent that the city itself was moved to act. Railway construction, ranching, settlement, meat packing, brewing, financial institutions, and wholesale and retail trades combined to create a classic western boom. Population soared more than tenfold in the first decade of the century, reaching 43,704 by 1911 and over 50,000 by 1914. At the best of times – periods of high streamflow and low use by the sawmills – the 600 hp Calgary Water Power plant struggled to meet its existing customers' requirements. But with seasonal diminution of streamflow, the ill-named Calgary Water Power Company had to rely upon its thermal generating system, a relic of which – the chimney – still stands like an industrial menhir in the Eau Claire recreation and entertainment area. Urban growth simply overwhelmed the Calgary Water Power Company, a subsidiary of the Eau Claire Lumber Company, whose main priorities remained supplying building materials for all of this construction.

Inevitably, relations between the city, as a main user of electricity and as an agent for frustrated commercial and residential customers, and the

CALGARY WATER POWER COMPANY HYDROELECTRIC PLANT BETWEEN PRINCE'S ISLAND AND THE EAU CLAIRE LUMBER COMPANY (GLENBOW ARCHIVES, NA-1044-6).

Calgary Water Power Company broke down. Interest groups urged the city itself to enter the electricity business to provide the needed infrastructure to maintain growth. At first, local ratepayers, in 1903, turned down a proposal to invest in a municipal steam plant. However, when the Calgary Water Power Company, faced with the need to finance a major expansion of its system, insisted that the city sign a ten-year contract in 1904, the aldermen balked at a long-term continuation of an unsatisfactory relationship and recommended a municipal plant instead. This time, the voters agreed, and the new station started production in 1905.[9]

Here, too, Calgary was following a well-established political tradition witnessed in other parts of the country. When private capital failed to meet expectations, government stepped in to meet the need. Market failure leading to public ownership had occurred in many small towns and cities across the country, most particularly in Ontario, where this municipal empowerment gave rise to a unique trans-provincial, publicly owned hydroelectric system. Not only population but also social and technological change drove the rising demand for electricity. The City of Calgary operated a street lighting system and an electric street railway, both of which needed large quantities of power. Similarly, the taste for brightly illuminated shops, warehouses, and even homes increased the public demand for electricity. The municipal system, operating at a much larger scale and greater efficiencies than before, charged lower rates, which, of course, only increased the demand for more electricity. Rising demand vastly outdistanced readily available supply. Into this gap, the animal spirits of industrial capitalism charged, bearing a new elixir: hydroelectricity, to be extracted from the Bow.

Like a siren, the Bow beckoned entrepreneurial spirits. It was so close, so accessible – seemingly inviting use. There was nothing new in this. The river had always appealed to its human inhabitants in one way or another. Evidence of the first human habitation, following the last ice age, has been found on the upper reaches of the Bow above Banff. Native peoples traditionally valued the lower reaches of the river, where buffalo herds often sought shelter, water, and lush grasses, and where buffalo jumps could be situated on cutbanks. On the lightly treed banks – the only woods to speak of on the prairie – poles for travois and teepees could be cut and firewood gathered. Fords and flats offered venues for meetings and ceremonies. After contact, Native people often raised their horses on the meadows of the river flats. For Native people, the mountain reaches of the river served mainly as seasonal hunting grounds. Mountain passes leading out of the Bow valley also afforded regular communication for commerce, comity, and conflict between the people of the foothills and prairie, and the people of the Columbia River valley. In the treaty-making process, the Native peoples of the plains all sought reserve lands astride portions of the river.[10]

For fur traders, the Bow was something of a disappointment. On account of the forest composition in the upper reaches, beaver were not as abundant as elsewhere. Moreover, numerous rapids, shallows, and waterfalls made the river treacherous for navigation in its upper reaches. Downstream, the Bow meandered aimlessly, from a trader's point of view, into a no man's land of desolate prairie far from the more northerly system of posts. Yet ranchers, when they arrived, valued the abundance of fresh water for their stock on the open prairie and the meadows on the flats for their ranches. The North West Mounted Police built their fortified post at a river junction. Railroaders used the valley floor as a roadbed through the mountains and the river's water to get up steam. Lumbermen admired the river's forested banks and its log-driving capacity. For them, the rapids and waterfalls were regrettable obstacles to be overcome.[11] But this falling water was precisely what caught the waterpower developers' attention.

While the Bow River is not particularly big as Canadian rivers go, over the 645 kilometres from the glacier where it trickles into existence to its confluence with the Oldman to form the South Saskatchewan River, the Bow River falls twenty-six hundred metres.[12] Much of this descent occurs on the lower streamflow of its upper reaches. But where the Bow forces its way out of the mountains at Banff and where it carves its way through the sandstone shelves in the foothills, it plunges over three quite spectacular waterfalls that drew attention to its hydroelectric possibilities: Bow Falls (19.5 m), Kananaskis Falls (21.3 m), and Horseshoe Falls (21.3 m). The Denis and White 1911 inventory of Canadian waterpowers contained full-page photographs of each of these falls in full spate. In the eighty-eight kilometres between Kananaskis Falls and Calgary, the mainstem of Bow River descends a total of 230 metres through valley terrain, providing several potential dam sites. As the Bow descends, its tributaries add to the volume of its flow. Taking the measure of the river below Calgary as 100 per cent, on average that flow is made up of the following constituents:

At Banff, only 30 per cent of the ultimate Bow tumbled over Bow Falls, but at the Kananaskis and Horseshoe Falls sites, waterpower developers had at their disposal approximately 60 per cent of the downstream flow of the river and a respectable twenty-one-metre head. They were located, however, within the bounds of a reserve set aside for the Nakoda in 1885 subsequent to their signing of Treaty 7 in 1877.[13]

Of course, others besides waterpower developers and hydraulic engineers took delight in falling water. By the turn of the twentieth century, the upper reaches of the Bow River had become an international tourist destination, with the Bow Falls a centrepiece attraction.

Elements of the Flow of the Bow River

Bow River above Banff	31.2%
Spray River	11.1%
Cascade River	5.9%
Kananaskis River	12.1%
Ghost River	5.8%
Elbow River	7.6%
Bow Basin runoff	26.3%

Source: Environment Alberta, South Saskatchewan
River Basin Historical Natural Flows, 1912–1995,
CD-ROM version 2.02.

During the construction of the Canadian Pacific Railway in 1883, workers discovered hot springs in the region that would come to be known as Banff. William Van Horne, the vice-president of the CPR, inspired by the example of the Northern Pacific Railroad and Yellowstone, urged the Government of Canada to reserve the area around the hot springs as Canada's first national park. The government obliged with commendable speed, the prime minister himself playing a leading role. In 1885, the government declared, and in 1886, created Rocky Mountains National Park, a small twenty-five square kilometre reservation that included the springs and Bow Falls. The initial inspiration emphasized the hot springs as a health spa, but other rationales also crept in. Prime Minister Macdonald, speaking in the House of Commons, expressed the hope that the new park would become "a place of great resort." Government ownership would prevent squatting and tawdry commercial development and would thus attract well-off tourists. In Macdonald's words: "There is beautiful scenery, there are the curative properties of the water, there is a genial climate, there is prairie sport and there is mountain sport; and I have no doubt that that will become a great watering-place."[14]

To accommodate visitors, doctors and businessmen built spas, hotels and sanitoria in the park for the ill, the infirm, and the enervated during the late 1880s and 1890s. The railway quickly built a grand hotel on a ridge affording spectacular views across Bow Falls down the river valley. A small tourist village developed where the road from the railway station crossed the Bow River leading to the hotels and spas. Drawn by publicity brochures, advertisements, and colourful railway posters, tourists from all over the world, but mainly the eastern United States, began to descend on Rocky Mountains National Park, arriving and departing, of course, as passengers of the CPR. As the number of summer visitors steadily expanded, so too did the boundaries of the park and its identity. Although it was a small postage stamp presence in 1885, two years later, conscious of the attraction of the unspoiled mountain scenery of the region, the government enlarged Rocky Mountains National Park to 674 square kilometres. In 1892, the Lake Louise region was appended to the park. By 1902, with tourists flocking to the region by rail each summer, the park had expanded to an enormous 110,250 square kilometres encompassing a huge triangular area of southern Alberta between the BC boundary and the front range of the Rockies.[15]

The tourists, through their behaviour and the aiding and abetting by the railway and local businessmen, gradually transformed a health resort and spa into something quite different. It turned out that visitors came primarily for the magnificent mountain scenery, and a brave few for the mountaineering opportunities afforded by the surrounding peaks. The mountaineers branded Banff as the "Switzerland of Canada," an idea seized upon by CPR managers, who imported actual Swiss mountain guides to ensure the safety of their wealthy and influential guests. Less adventurous visitors sought more moderate outdoor pursuits – tally ho rides, hikes, trail riding, sightseeing, fishing, and boating, activities assiduously developed and promoted by local entrepreneurs. All of this outdoor leisure could be enjoyed in a sublime, bracing mountain setting and in luxury accommodation. The CPR and local boosters ensured that the word got out.[16]

By the first decade of the twentieth century, Rocky Mountains National Park (it would become the more familiar Banff National Park in 1930) had established itself as one of the world's premier tourist destinations and an object of Canadian national pride. The idea of what a national park should be continued to evolve in practice under the necessity of attracting more visitors to make the park self-financing. Amusements and distractions – such as wild animal zoos, curio shops, and eventually a Wild West–inspired Indian Days festival – were organized to entertain idle guests and draw new types of visitors. Through it all, the Bow River in its various forms played a starring role in the park production – as lakes, as a mirror to mountains, as a gentle curving stream, as thundering falls, and as a majestic valley. In passing, it should be noted that the hydroelectric engineers excluded Bow Falls from their waterpower calculations after applying the principle of highest and best use. In the words of Leo Denis and J. B. Challies, who surveyed the waterpower of the Bow between 1911 and 1914: "The famous Bow fall, on the Bow River, near the Canadian Pacific Railway Company's hotel at Banff, has been considered to have a far greater potential value from an aesthetic standpoint than from any possible use for power development purposes. For this reason no attempt has been made to consider it from a utilitarian viewpoint."[17] In other words, Bow Falls had the potential to generate more income from tourism than from electricity.

A powerful new cultural phenomenon, tourism, combined with corporate authority of the CPR and the power of the Government of Canada, conspired to drape a world-famous and much beloved national park upon the headwaters of the Bow River. As fate would have it, the falling water and hydroelectric potential of the Bow River thus locked the City of Calgary, the power developers, the Nakoda people, and the national park in an inescapable mutual embrace.

CHAPTER 2

Power Struggle

In a networked society, things are connected in surprising ways, often at a distance. The simple act of turning on a light switch or hopping on a streetcar can have far-reaching ramifications. The energy needs of cities usually have implications far beyond municipal borders.[1] The concentrated demands of a city effectively reorient activities in the region to serve that city's needs. Knowledge, engineering capability, financial capacity, and business acumen have to be attracted and applied to sometimes remote resources to create an integrated electrical system. Local capabilities are rarely sufficient in non-metropolitan settings, and the process of combining these disparate elements is rarely harmonious. Calgary's growing power needs over the twentieth century thus spun out a complex regional, national, and even international web of reciprocal relations that subsumed local interests in a broader net of opportunities, obligations, and conflicts.

Hydroelectric technology, capitalist enterprise, and the urban demand for electricity transformed the rivers and streams that snaked out of the eastern foothills of the Rocky Mountains from nineteenth-century transportation disappointments into valuable twentieth-century natural resources. An all-too-familiar struggle of animal spirits followed to possess, control, and exploit those resources. Calgary's quest for electricity to energize its burgeoning growth after the turn of the century engendered a struggle between four main sets of actors: the City of Calgary, an electric company, the Nakoda people, and the Government of Canada. But it was even more complicated than that. We should not confuse the descriptive utility of an abstract categorization with unanimity of purpose or goal.

Words like *city*, *company*, *people*, and *government* sound like singular, cohesive units. On close examination, in this particular but not atypical case, the unity within each category breaks down very quickly. Each of these groups was internally divided into subgroups with different material interests and outlooks.

The struggle within was sometimes as intense as the struggle between. Policy emerged from a sum of the balance of power and the differences within categories. Negotiations between the actors were thus messy, seemingly interminable, and unpredictable. The need for power roiled affairs within the city council and divided ratepayers. Bureaucrats in different departments thousands of miles away struggled in lengthy memoranda to understand the situation and come to decisions consistent with ambiguous public policy. Entrepreneurs and engineers jockeyed against one another to line up the necessary licences and contracts. The Nakoda people found themselves in a storm centre of economic development. They, too, were divided by the possibilities and the apparent dangers of surrendering their resources. Risks had to be calculated and uncertainties dealt with all around in this high-stakes game. Even nature turned out to have a surprising trick up its sleeve; power from the river would not be released without a struggle.

But in the end, two waterfalls would be subdued and silenced, their waters diverted through penstocks and turbines to provide Calgary with the electricity it demanded. An eastern corporation, a creation of Canadian high finance in its most gilded age, could, with some qualification, be said to emerge triumphant in this struggle for power. Inevitability, as we shall see, is an illusion of hindsight.

The inadequate service provided by the Calgary Water Power Company led the City of Calgary, in 1905, to open its own municipally owned thermal electric plant powered by coal from the Bankhead mine in Banff National Park. Within two years, the plant had to be doubled in size to meet the surging demand. As the city fathers contemplated the need to expand the plant even further in the near future and, at the same time, build roads, sewers, and water mains, municipal pride in owning an electric utility collided with financial necessity. Moreover, the city hoped to build its own street railway, both a capital-intensive project on its own and a major new consumer of electric power. The new street railway would certainly overtax the capacity of even the newly expanded electric plant. How could the electricity required to drive urban growth be acquired in sufficient quality and reliability, and at the lowest price, with the city retaining control over distribution? It was a question that both inspired local businessmen and perplexed the aldermen.

Two newly arrived businessmen involved in the development of the energy-intensive cement industry, W. J. Budd and W. M. Alexander, simultaneously incorporated the Calgary Power and Transmission Company, applied to the federal government for a waterpower licence on the Bow, and asked the city council for a franchise to distribute their hydroelectric power within the city. With waterfalls thundering away upriver and knowledge of other hydroelectric developments circulating, the idea of developing these waterfalls to meet Calgary's needs had for some time been the topic of conversation and, on one occasion, of a brief investigation, but the technical, financial, and organizational requirements of such an undertaking overwhelmed local capabilities.[2] Hydroelectric development remained a dream until the upstart Budd-Alexander proposal in 1907 brought the practical possibility into sharper focus. The Budd-Alexander bid, however, drew immediate protest from the existing private electric utility, Calgary Water Power Company, as well as a counterbid from the Alberta Portland Cement Company, represented by a young lawyer, R. B. Bennett, which also promised to deliver hydroelectricity from the Bow but at a lower cost. Both bids were, to some degree, fictions since neither group had the licences, financing, or technical capability in place at the time. After lengthy negotiations, and despite the backbiting of rivals, city council eventually chose to deal with the less well-connected newcomers, Budd and Alexander, in two contracts, one signed in the spring of 1907 giving the Calgary Power and Transmission Company the right to distribute its power (but not electricity for lighting) to industries in the city, and a second signed in the fall of 1907 providing the company with the right to supply the municipal system with wholesale electricity for street lighting and distribution to local retail customers. With these contracts in hand,

Budd and Alexander were thus positioned to raise the necessary money and obtain the essential waterpower licence.

Initially, Budd and Alexander remained a little vague as to where on the Bow the hydroelectricity would be generated. But in December 1906, as their negotiations with the city heated up, they applied to the Department of the Interior for rights to develop the waterpower of Horseshoe Falls.[3] This simple request reopened the thorny question of who "owned" the waterpower of the Bow, or rather, under what authority rights might be granted and who might benefit. Alberta had been created as a province in 1905, but the federal government retained control over its Crown lands. Furthermore, under the Indian Act, the federal government had ultimate responsibility for Indian reserves, and beyond that, the federal government had jurisdiction over navigable rivers. In theory, the federal Department of the Interior thus had threefold authority over the disposition of Bow River waterpowers since the river was deemed to be navigable, the sites were on an Indian reserve, and, even if they hadn't been, the federal government managed Crown lands in Alberta.

The federal government exercised its jurisdiction over the water resources of the West through the North West Irrigation Act of 1894. This legislation – drafted by the redoubtable William Pearce, the western lands manager for the Department of the Interior, and based upon the water law of Australia – was intended, as its title suggests, to regulate the use of water for irrigation purposes, but it covered all other water-taking activities as well. The North West Irrigation Act explicitly rejected riparian rights as the basis of water allocation in favour of the "first in time, first in right" principle more suited to arid landscapes. Unlike irrigation, hydro power generation was not a consumptive use. Irrigation withdrew water; hydro merely used water in passing.[4]

As it turned out, Budd and Alexander were not the first persons to apply for rights to this site. In 1903, when Edmonton lawyer Frank Oliver, representing clients who wanted to build a sawmill and flour mill, asked for a licence to use the waterpower of Horseshoe Falls, he was advised that since the falls lay within the Nakoda Indian Reserve, he would first have to purchase the necessary lands from the Nakoda.[5] Bureaucrats in the

Department of the Interior further informed Oliver, no doubt gleefully, that no waterpower licences had ever been granted on Indian reserves – a clear signal that even with a land purchase agreement, no waterpower licence would be forthcoming. Internally, the department legal officer even doubted that the Interior Department had the authority to grant a licence since the waterpower was situated on a navigable river.[6] When the Nakoda people themselves were approached directly by the power developers, some younger band members approved of selling land for waterpower development, but Chief Chiniquay and his family disapproved of parting with such a large piece of the reserve. Several other potential developers lost interest after making initial inquiries.[7]

Looming electricity shortages in Calgary led the opportunistic CPR, in the spring of 1906, to apply for rights to Horseshoe Falls, as well as Kananaskis Falls just upstream. Officials from the Department of the Interior Lands Branch refused the request on the grounds that these waterpowers lay in what the department now considered "unnavigable waters within an Indian reserve." Lands Branch authorities seemed to believe that the Nakoda possessed riparian rights in the falls and that they had the authority to sell the waterpower rights themselves.[8] They would subsequently change their minds.

Following this line of legal reasoning, the Indian Affairs Branch of the Department of the Interior took over the file and began discussion with the Nakoda, employing the Reverend John McDougall of Morleyville as interlocutor. In response to McDougall's prodding as to what terms they might demand should the CPR wish to negotiate, the Nakoda at first balked on the grounds that the railway had already surveyed the site without their permission and that sparks from passing trains had often set fires on their lands for which they had received no compensation. McDougall persisted nevertheless. In these negotiations, Indian Affairs officials instructed him to separate the issue of land sales for buildings and transmission towers from actual waterpower sales: "It is to be borne in mind in connection with the disposition of the water powers that there is serious doubt as to whether these are the property of the Indians, on account of the nature of the Bow River, and it is important that the question of the value of the land should be determined apart from the value of the water powers." In response, in mid-summer 1906, the Nakoda tentatively agreed that they might be willing to part with three thousand acres for ten dollars an acre, a per capita payment of twenty dollars ($13,000), and three hundred head of cattle ($9,000). The CPR, believing this to be too high a price to pay, walked away.[9]

Six months later, the Budd and Alexander application arrived in Ottawa. Following these earlier precedents, the Department of the Interior advised Budd and Alexander to negotiate a land purchase to accommodate their works with the Nakoda directly, but the department would have final authority over the land surrender. In a new twist, however, department lawyers now considered the possibility that the bed of the Bow, as it passed between the three parcels of land making up the Nakoda Reserve, might now belong to the recently created Province of Alberta. Not wanting to surrender this important power under ambiguous circumstances, the department nonetheless decided that it had the authority to issue an interim waterpower licence once the developers had acquired the necessary property from the Nakoda. After the works began operation, a final licence would be granted.[10]

When Alexander and Budd applied to the Department of Indian Affairs to purchase the necessary land, they were informed that Indian Affairs itself lacked the power to "grant land under water or permit diversions," but that it could help out with the land purchase issue.[11] In a remarkably short period of time for such a complex issue, on March 12, 1907, Alexander, Budd, and the Nakoda signed an agreement for the purchase of one thousand acres of reserve land. The band – represented by its agent, T. I. Fleetham, and Chief Moses Bearspaw, Chief Peter Wesley, and Chief Jonas Two Young Man, as well as Councillors James Swampy, Amos Big Stony, John Mark, Hector Crawler, and George McLean – surrendered what they considered "gravelly land" unsuited to agriculture. The power developers obtained the land they needed for their dam, powerhouse, head works, reservoir, and transmission line (and whatever rights might appertain to it) for $10 an acre, a one-time payment of $3,350 (distributed as follows: $5 per capita, $15 for headmen and $25 for chiefs), the purchase of fifty brood mares, and the promise to fence the property they had attained. The land purchase and waterpower lease were considered separately as the Department of the Interior legal advisors insisted. Budd and Alexander also agreed to pay $1,500 to the superintendent of Indian affairs annually as a water rental. An interim agreement with Indian Affairs was subsequently drafted in the name of the Calgary Power and Transmission Company.[12] Throughout these talks with hydroelectric power developers and the government, the Nakoda proved surprisingly willing to negotiate and conclude a deal, notwithstanding divisions of opinion among them. Moreover, they consciously demanded what they and their counterparts considered exacting but reasonable terms. They knew the market value of their land, and they got it.

The Native people on the site settled their differences over waterpower development, but the subterranean battle among the bureaucrats in far-off Ottawa continued unabated. The waterpower officer in the Lands Branch of the Department of the Interior, J. B. Challies, strenuously objected to not being consulted. He believed that neither the Indigenous people nor Indian Affairs had the right to lease the waterpower either under Treaty 7 or as riparian owners. They might authorize the sale of lands, he argued, but not the rights to waterpower. Challies insisted that the annual waterpower rental fee was being paid to the wrong party. His superiors agreed that the Department of the Interior alone (not Indian Affairs) had the right to issue a permit for the use of the water. Section 92 (24) of the British North America Act clearly granted the federal government jurisdiction over "Indians and lands reserved for Indians," powers to be exercised by the superintendent general of Indian affairs.[13] But as a result of a technicality, probably unique to the Nakoda situation, the waterpower bureaucrats may have concluded that the Bow River was not technically part of the Indian Reserve. The Nakoda reserve lands as actually surveyed and registered consisted of three separate parcels of land, two on the north side of the Bow and one on the south side. These parcels, as spelled out in the official documents and drawn on the surveyors' maps, were described as running from specified points in the interior to the banks of the Bow, not to the river's mid-point. This seemed to imply that the Nakoda were thus not

Stoney elders, circa 1908: (l. to r.) James Swampy, Hector Crawler, Jonas Two Young Man, John Bearspaw, Peter Wesley, Amos Big Stoney, John Mark (Glenbow Archives, NA-1263-13).

riparian owners, in which case administration rights to the riverbed and waterpower may have been thought to lie with the Interior Department rather than Indian Affairs. In any event, the waterpower bureaucrats in the Lands Branch (who were in the process of seeking their own divisional designation as the Water Power Branch) asserted their authority by demanding that the lease should stipulate the conditions under which the power might be used, the dates of the term, the obligations to continuous development owed by the lessee, the authority of government regulatory oversight of rates, and the conditions under which the licence would be suspended and the property recovered.[14]

By the end of 1907, Budd and Alexander had in hand important power contracts with the City of Calgary and the promise of a waterpower lease to Horseshoe Falls, subject to their agreement. But they could not command all of the financial resources or entrepreneurial skills required to complete the project. They retained professional engineers from the East to draw up detailed plans for a dam and powerhouse with a working head of seventy-four feet that would permit the initial development of about six thousand horsepower annually at a cost of some $600,000.[15] Yet, notwithstanding the contracts with the city and an agreement to sell bulk power to a nearby cement company, Budd and Alexander proved unable to raise such sums, and eventually, in 1909, with the deadline for commencing power supply to Calgary closing in, they surrendered control of Calgary Power and Transmission Company to their principal creditors: their engineers, C. B. Smith and W. G. Chace. But neither could the engineers raise the money required to finance a hydroelectric project of this size. Smith, therefore, immediately set about flogging this western property among the community of eastern Canadian hydroelectric financiers; he found an eager buyer in the Royal Securities Corporation of Montreal.[16]

Enter William Max Aitken, the impish wizard behind Royal Securities Corporation. Though not yet thirty years of age, Max Aitken had already ascended the heights of Canadian finance capitalism, earning a reputation along the way as one of its sharpest, most aggressive, and slightly slippery company promoters. As a personality, Max Aitken impressed everyone he met with an indomitable will to succeed, a salesman's counter-jumping enthusiasm, a rare zest for life, and a relentless focus on the business at hand. For example, he turned his Cuban honeymoon into a scouting trip for street railway prospects. His youthful appearance, raffish manner, and arresting physical appearance invariably drew comment. His round head was, by universal agreement, far too large for his body. A huge Cheshire cat grin permanently creased his cheeks; outlandish ears, a tight collar, and a porkpie hat perched casually atop his head did nothing to diminish first impressions of a boyish mischief maker. Nonetheless, it was his success in the cut-throat business world of company promotion and mergers that impressed his financial superiors, made him indispensable, and stirred mixed emotions of admiration, wariness, and betrayal among those with whom he did business. It turned out he knew a thing or two about Calgary.

Born the fifth of what would be nine children to the Reverend and Mrs. William Aitken in 1879, the young Max fled the patriarchal rectitude of the Presbyterian manse and its preordained career in banking or law. The truant of Newcastle, New Brunswick, set out for the far West, following his youthful idol and mentor, R. B. Bennett, to Calgary in 1898 to make his fortune peddling life insurance, running a bowling alley, selling real estate, and delivering meat. Dissipation and disappointment delivered him back home to Atlantic Canada – contrite, more sober, but all the more determined to make his mark. It was at this low point in 1902 that Aitken somehow scraped an acquaintance with John F. Stairs, the dean of Halifax finance and president of Royal Securities Corporation. Stairs put him to work raising money for the steel companies and utilities that he and his friends controlled. Max soon made himself indispensable. In this environment, he developed two remarkable talents: company promotion and securities salesmanship. Mentored by the Halifax financial community, Stairs's protege launched or rebuilt street railways and electric companies in second- and third-tier communities in Trinidad, British Guiana, Cuba, and Puerto Rico. Just as important, he developed an enterprising sales network to unload the securities generated by these company promotions on the doctors, lawyers, ships' captains, merchants, widows, and orphans of Maritime Canada.

After Stairs's sudden death in 1905, Max Aitken emerged as the guiding spirit of Royal Securities, turning it into an investment bank specializing in high-risk but also high-return enterprises that, for the most part, he controlled. By 1907, the Maritimes had begun to be too small for his ambition, and the region lacked the financial resources he needed for his ever more ambitious schemes. Moreover, the backbiting and squeamishness of his more staid and established associates, who perhaps resented his spectacular success, curbed his style. It was a messy divorce. But in the end, Max Aitken decamped, as the undisputed proprietor of Royal Securities, to Montreal, where he would be closer to the real action in company promotion, the A-team of Canadian capitalism, and the really big piles of money.[17]

Royal Securities, as an investment bank, needed a continuous stream of company promotions, mergers, and reorganizations. It was Max Aitken's responsibility to put together these deals and negotiate the purchase terms and the capital structure, whereupon his sales team would then have to flog the "stuff" – the insiders' argot for the various bonds, stock, and preferred shares generated – to institutions and private investors. Max Aitken

had to make rain. He was thus on the constant lookout for new opportunities – either new companies to promote, like the Western Canada Power Company in Vancouver, or, his preferred choice, "established and going concerns with good earnings which we can profitably capitalize" (read: load up with debt).

Recalling his not-too-distant youth, Max Aitken had already expressed interest in the prospects of the Calgary area. In 1908, he had suggested that his fellow New Brunswicker, Calgary lawyer R. B. Bennett, should "take up" the electrical situation in the Alberta city to see whether the two private companies might be merged. Bennett, having long been involved with the situation, urged him not to get involved. The same year, Aitken dispatched his brother to see whether he could obtain a street railway franchise in Calgary on favourable terms, his thinking being that he might work backwards from the electric demands of the street railway to acquire and merge the two electric companies into an integrated utility with bond sales and bonus stock all round. City council drove too hard a bargain, and besides, seemed determined to build its own street railway system. Max Aitken retreated from the encounter complaining bitterly to his brother: "I think the council is so socialistic that a satisfactory proposition cannot be obtained at the present time." His brother agreed, adding that he considered the councillors "a bunch of grafters of the meanest kind."[18] These negotiations also brought him into contact with C. B. Smith, who was struggling to make the Calgary Power and Transmission Company a going concern. Aitken initially dismissed all thought of taking over that company because he considered the contracts with the city disadvantageous to the company.

His Calgary excursion had also brought him into contact with Toronto financier E. R. Wood, the promoter of the Alberta Portland Cement Company, which had rights to the undeveloped Radnor hydroelectric site on the Bow near the confluence with the Ghost River. The two eastern financiers bruited about the possibilities of a grand merger of electric interest in the region during 1908, but the collapse of the street railway talks with the city put paid to that scheme for the time being.

The following spring, however, Max Aitken changed his mind after spotting a desirable-looking waterpower site from the CPR train en route to his hydroelectric development in British Columbia.[19] That summer, as he was coordinating the merger of all the leading cement producers in the country into the Canada Cement Company, Aitken realized that a power development in the Bow valley would fit neatly into his plans. First, if the merger were to proceed, only the manufacturing assets of Alberta Portland Cement would be valued. That meant the company would have to dispose of its Radnor hydroelectric site before the deal went through. Second, although Portland cement, a new product made from processed crushed limestone, was cheaper to produce than the old marl cement excavated from lakebeds, it required vast amounts of electricity, especially to crush the stone. A new company could serve the power needs of the Alberta Portland Cement Company. A Calgary Power and Transmission takeover would include the contract to supply the Portland cement company at Exshaw, a floundering property presided over by Sir Sanford Fleming and an American buccaneering entrepreneur, James Ivor, who also intended to be included in the Canada Cement merger. These two industrial power contracts and the Radnor site – combined with the Horseshoe Falls development, rights to upstream hydroelectric sites, and a contract to supply power to the Calgary municipal electric utility – made a Calgary deal look much more interesting to the mercurial Max.

At the height of the three-ring-circus Canada Cement merger negotiations, Aitken met with C. B. Smith and E. R. Wood in September 1909, and in two days, they reached an agreement. A new company would be created to acquire Calgary Power and Transmission Company and the waterpower rights from Alberta Portland Cement at Radnor. Aitken bought the company from Smith and Chace for $70,000 in cash and about $300,000 in stock in the new company, and Smith and Chace continued on as engineer-contractors of the Horseshoe project. The new company also assumed the Radnor site from Alberta Portland Cement as part of the cement merger deal and, along with it, a contract to provide electricity to this subsidiary of the merged entity. Aitken, of course, managed the financing of the new company, renamed Calgary Power. Royal Securities underwrote $3 million par value worth of its bonds at 85 per cent of their face value and received a generous bonus of common stock, probably in the range of a nominal $1.85 million, which, after taking his promoter's profits, Aitken aimed to resell to Royal Securities' clientele.[20] It seemed on the face of it a neat side deal, a tasty snack en route to the much larger Canada Cement feast. In this flurry of deals, a financial magician like Max Aitken could make things even sweeter (for himself) without anyone being the wiser. One of Aitken's minions, in examining the terms of the agreement, noted in wonder to Max that Royal Securities was owed a further $300,000 stock in Calgary Power as a result of the inclusion of the Radnor property in the deal: "I wish to bring to your attention that Royal Securities will be in effect receiving this $300,000 in stock for nothing."[21] Imagine that.

In a deal of this sort, the revenue from the bond sales would effectively purchase the properties and finish construction. The bonds themselves would be taken up by a promotional syndicate at the discounted price making payments in instalments. After the promoter had taken his cut of the common stock and payments had been made to the principals of the companies being acquired, the remainder would be parcelled out to the bondholders as a bonus, the proportion of stock to bonds varying with distance from the inner circle of the syndicate, although there were risks associated with having too many unconstrained participants. Eventually, the bonds and the stock would be resold at a higher price and with much less bonus stock as the company progressed. Meanwhile, the syndicate members would agree to pool their stock for a period, designating one of their number a market maker who would buy and sell from the market in such a way as to create the illusion of a stable and promising investment.

Then, the syndicate members would cautiously unload their high-yielding bonds and now monetized common stock to what they called "real investors" who would hold the securities and not dump them onto the market at the first whiff of trouble. The inner circle of the investment syndicate could then realize their profits on the transaction, although some would wish to retain significant holdings in a particularly good going concern. But for the deal to be successful, the bonds would have to pay interest and the stock would have to earn its face value through growth and sound management.

This refinancing allowed construction of Calgary Power's Horseshoe Falls project to forge ahead following C. B. Smith's design and under his supervision. However, for the math to work on the Calgary Power deal, Max Aitken believed that the company would have to sell a great deal more power in Calgary and on better terms than the existing two contracts with the city. He instructed R. B. Bennett, a director of the company and its local fixer, to wring a new contract out of city council for a longer period, in greater quantities but at a lower price than previously agreed. Meanwhile, as Bennett grappled with what turned out to be a Sisyphean task, Aitken, a promoter and financier rather than a utility manager, turned over direction of the company to Herbert S. Holt, well known as the president of Montreal Light, Heat, and Power. Aitken, preoccupied with other deals, gradually withdrew from company affairs, although he did take a lively interest in the negotiation of a new contract with the city.

Just when the company's future looked set, serious problems arose. In all the investigation of power sites in the Bow valley, nobody appears to have bothered to take systematic and detailed streamflow measurements. C. B. Smith had simply contented himself with observing that "a valuable feature of the water supply in this river is the fact that all the head waters above the power site are situated within the Rocky Mountain[s National] Park, ... which will be very slowly deforested if at all. The future constant flow of the river is thus ensured."[22] What that ignored, of course, was that these headwaters flowed out of mountains locked in ice half the year. Like all glacial streams, the volume of water in the Bow varied dramatically from season to season. As the snows melted in the spring, there was a spate

followed by a steady run throughout the summer, but as the winter freeze-up took hold at higher altitudes, the flow diminished steadily in the river's gravel bed until it was little more than a trickle. Visitors usually saw the waterfalls in summer, during peak flow. The photographs in the White and Dennis inventory of waterpowers, for example, showed Bow, Kananaskis, and Horseshoe Falls foaming white in impressive early summer display. In mid-winter, these waterfalls would present a more timid aspect.

Flow variation on this scale was a critical problem for a run-of-the-river hydroelectric station with only a small amount of water storage. Power production was measured on a twelve-month basis, and continuous output was a critical factor, especially for a city like Calgary, where cold, dark winters created high peak loads for electric lighting. Another engineer retained by Max Aitken in the fall of 1909 had warned that gauging of the Bow had not been carefully done to date and that it was well known that the flow was low at certain times of the year.[23] Just how critical the problem was became obvious in dramatic fashion during the first year of construction at Horseshoe Falls. In February and March 1910, the river practically dried up altogether, and then in June, it burst through the cofferdams and undermined the footings of the main dam. As a result, the spillways had to be redesigned to handle the late spring runoff, and the winter horsepower rating of the plant was revised downward. The company did not even have enough capacity to provide all the power already contracted for, much less to provide for future expansion. The directors of Calgary Power were so angered that they fired C. B. Smith as the project engineer on account of negligence and incompetence.[24]

Detailed hydrographic studies over the next few years revealed the unpleasant truth. Smith had estimated that the absolute minimum flow in the most extreme winter conditions would be 960 cubic feet per second (cfs) with an average flow of about 1,600 cfs, permitting annual average production of 10,000 hp. Federal government engineers discovered that the Bow at the mouth of the Kananaskis River just above the dam carried an average of only 725 cfs in March and 880 in April. During the second decade of the century, the highest flows ever recorded during these months were 1,080 and 1,340 cfs, respectively, in 1916, while in the dry winter of 1920, the river trickled along at only 550 and 530 cfs in March and April.[25]

With the company in these vulnerable circumstances, R. B. Bennett faced serious opposition in his attempt to negotiate a new contract with the city. With its expanded municipal steam power plant and growing distribution system, city council thought of itself as a competitor in the electricity business. Indeed some members of council urged the city to build a hydroelectric station of its own on the Bow. Once Bennett gave up on the idea of entering the city as an operating company and stringing the company's own wires alongside the two other sets already on the street, and began talking about supplying power wholesale to the municipal utility, city council seemed prepared to talk but remained wary. After the well-publicized problems with the Horseshoe project, councillors harboured quite justified apprehension about the quantity of power the company might deliver and its all-season reliability. Skepticism even led city council to encourage a locally promoted hydroelectric scheme on the upper Elbow River during this period. This distracting sideshow preoccupied city officials and even led the city to apply for and receive a waterpower licence from the Department of the Interior on the Elbow. Bennett thus had to face off against another hydroelectric enterprise as well as the city's municipal utility. Although this combined public-private hydroelectric project on the Elbow never came to fruition, it served its purpose as a stalking horse in the Calgary Power negotiations.

On the one hand, although Bennett was on good terms with the mayor and councillors, and could muster influential friends in the business community, city council members remained obdurate about negotiating a new contract, concerned as they were about the dependability of the company's power and protective as they were of their own electric utility. On the other hand, the city needed more power, even with a relocation and expansion of its steam plant in Victoria Park. Councillors could not be seen to be denying customers cheaper electricity by favouring their own pet project. So, after much toing and froing, the city and Bennett eventually cut a deal in August 1910, but not on terms Max Aitken would approve. The city granted the company a mere one-year contract for 2,000 hp at thirty dollars per horsepower, additional power to be supplied in 500 hp increments and at progressively lower prices. At 10,000 hp, the price would fall to twenty-four dollars. The new contract was for one year and could be renewed, but it gave no security to the company and it left the city open to either supplying Calgary's growing power demand from its own expanded plant or buying more power from Calgary Power when the need arose.[26] Max Aitken had met his match in the Calgary city council, but at least the company had its foot in the door.

For all of these reasons, the first delivery of Bow River hydroelectricity to Calgary from Calgary Power's Horseshoe Falls station on Sunday, May 21, 1911, turned out to be a rather low-key affair. Some municipal employees woke the mayor at 8:30 in the morning and drove him to the nondescript East Calgary substation, where he simply inserted a plug on a switchboard. "There was no demonstration of any kind," the Calgary-based *Weekly Albertan* commented, "no cheering crowd to witness this interesting event."[27]

There was no cheering in Montreal either, where the management feared the company would not be able to pay even its fixed charges,

Horseshoe Falls Dam and Powerhouse (Glenbow Archives, NA-3496-14).

Horseshoe Falls Power Station (Glenbow Archives, PD-365-1-93).

much less earn a profit. The Calgary Power promotion had not gone off as planned. Expensive construction overruns and delays complicated the financing, as did the failure to obtain a long-term contract with the city. A casual observer would have concluded that Max Aitken's second encounter with Calgary proved more successful and profitable than the first: he built a power company rather than a bowling alley. But to Max, both encounters ended in bitter disappointment. Burdened with an unco-operative city council and a rogue river, Calgary Power would not be the financial success that the man known as "the money spinner" had imagined.[28]

But by the time the company actually went into operation, Max Aitken was long gone and the problems were for others to fix. His bruising manner in putting together three of Canada's largest mergers in the cement, steel, and railway equipment industries had won him few friends and earned him many enemies. Even his application to the Mount Royal Club was blackballed – "pilled," in the local parlance. He made money for some powerful people, not the least himself, but his ruthless treatment of Sir Sanford Fleming – forcing his company into bankruptcy to get fire-sale terms for inclusion in the merger – deeply offended those same people.[29] In any event, Montreal, and even Canada, had become too small for Max Aitken's ambition. By the time the turbines of Calgary Power started spinning in the spring of 1911, Max Aitken, now just a shareholder with a sentimental interest in the property, had set himself up in London, England, to open a new phase in his life.[30]

CHAPTER 3

Doubling Down

Capitalism, in Canada's gilded age, could be a cruel taskmaster. Money easily raised and invested had to be paid back, with interest. Common stock would remain worthless as a bonus unless growth of the business drove up the market price; otherwise, bankruptcy loomed. For Calgary Power to succeed as a company flotation, or even to meet its outstanding contracts, it would very quickly have to produce and sell more power on a continuous basis. Thus, on the one hand, the company had to convince its principal customer, the City of Calgary, to purchase more of its power. On the other hand, the company did not have power to sell from its existing plant.

Survival, then, compelled the company to undertake two expensive projects immediately. It would have to build another hydroelectric station on the Bow River as soon as possible. But that plant, given the seasonal fluctuations in streamflow, would be as inefficient on a continuous yearly basis as the Horseshoe plant unless the company also addressed the imperfections of the river as a power producer by building an upstream storage reservoir to smooth out the flow of the river. However urgent these two projects were from a business point of view, both faced serious and legitimate objections. Financial necessity would compel the company to ride roughshod over these obstacles. Sometimes it would be its own worst enemy. The company would prevail, as this chapter and the next explain, but not without guile and, once again, not on its own terms.

When Max Aitken received the warning in 1909 from an engineer that severe seasonal fluctuation in water supply might be a problem, , he

KANANASKIS FALLS LOOKING DOWNSTREAM ABOUT 1913 (GLENBOW ARCHIVES, NA-3544-27).

took steps, even before the spring freshets swept away the cofferdams at the construction site in 1910, to try and rectify the situation by securing additional generating capacity for Calgary Power. A couple of miles upstream from Horseshoe Falls where the Kananaskis River flowed into the Bow, the river tumbled over a series of four low pitches totalling about forty feet in height as it flowed through a narrow gorge about one hundred yards long. Properly dammed, a head of seventy feet could be developed at Kananaskis Falls, which would permit the generation of 3,500 hp annually, even with a minimum river flow of 550 cubic feet per second (cfs).[1]

In January 1910, Calgary Power applied to the federal government for permission to begin a development at Kananaskis Falls. Officials at the Interior Department quickly recognized that the plans would create two problems: the lands flooded by the headpond were, in part, inside not only the Nakoda Indian Reserve but also Rocky Mountains National Park, whose boundaries had been greatly enlarged in 1902. As of 1910, the legislation governing national parks did not authorize hydroelectric development. The Nakoda Indians would once again have to be persuaded to sell

Kananaskis Falls looking upstream before dam (Glenbow Archives, NA-3802-8).

the land needed for development of the hydroelectric site. No development could proceed without a satisfactory settlement of these issues. Despite repeated entreaties from the company, a whole year passed without anything being done. Even the retention of a prominent Liberal politician and lobbyist, Senator N. A. Belcourt, failed to secure action. The waterpower expert at the Department of the Interior, J. B. Challies, was convinced that Calgary Power should receive no further concessions until the Horseshoe plant had begun production, which would not occur until May 1911. On the one hand, Challies could see the virtues of having a single company develop both Kananaskis and Horseshoe: it would permit the coordinated use of scarce water resources and eliminate the need for duplicate transmission lines and substations. On the other hand, he feared that Calgary Power lacked the capability to raise the large sums of capital required to finance both developments.[2]

Those concerns were reinforced by the appearance of a second contender for the development rights at Kananaskis Falls in January 1911. Heading the rival syndicate was Dr. Andrew Macphail of McGill University, a prominent essayist and political commentator who usually reserved his deepest scorn for the plutocratic businessmen who dominated turn-of-the-century society in Canada.[3] Despite the irony of having to do business with Canada's leading critique of finance capitalism with no previous experience in the hydroelectric industry, the government bureaucrats had to take Macphail's application seriously. First, Macphail had money of his own and could be reasonably expected to raise the amounts required by a project of this size. Second, within his family circle, he had the engineering expertise to design a professional hydroelectric facility. Macphail had also been shrewd enough to retain another Liberal lobbyist to put his well-conceived case for waterpower rights before the Department of the Interior.[4]

This competitive bid complicated the situation and made a speedy resolution to the licence less likely for Calgary Power. Both designs made effective use of the Kananaskis waterfall. The simplest solution – granting the power to the earliest applicant – was not available since neither had been first. The CPR had long ago applied for rights to develop Kananaskis and had been denied by the Department of the Interior, apparently on the grounds that the railway company was simply acting as a speculative monopolist of western waterpowers. Therein lay a further difficulty. Could a government department be seen, on its own, to grant a monopoly of the waterpower on the Bow River to one company since it also owned rights to the downstream Radnor site? The civil servants needed some cover. Time for outside professional advice.

Faced with these two claimants, the bureaucrats retained Canada's foremost hydroelectric engineer, C. H. Mitchell, to assess the merits of the rival schemes. He reported that there was little to choose between them, but concluded,

> Apart from purely technical considerations and on grounds of public utility (i.e. efficiency of public service and freedom from

possible interruption, etc.), there is a certain obvious advantage in the ownership and operation of a plant on this site by the same company which owns and operates the Horseshoe Falls plant. The interests, market and sphere of operations of the two plants would be similar and unless there were strong economic or political reasons for separate companies and fields of operation, a close cooperation, or at least working arrangement, would seem to be a natural consequence. This appears especially so as the sites are so near each other and closely interconnected by river conditions, and because it is quite feasible and economic to operate the two plants in parallel by the same staff and transmit the power to the market over the same transmission lines.[5]

In opting for monopoly control, Mitchell confirmed the views of other technocrats, such as J. B. Challies, about the greater efficiency of coordinated development.

Mitchell's endorsement effectively derailed Macphail's proposal and ultimately opened the way for the federal government to grant Calgary Power the Kananaskis site. The department quickly endorsed Mitchell's opinion although the terms of the final waterpower lease would not be ironed out for another year.[6] At this critical point in the life of the company, the presidency changed hands once again. With Horseshoe Falls finally delivering power in the summer of 1911, Herbert Holt took the opportunity to step down as president. "I consider that it is vitally important for the welfare and interest of the company that the chief executive officer should reside in the West," he reported to the board. This was persiflage. The Montreal directors had become disenchanted with the company and did not see the virtue of pouring good money after bad. By contrast, those directors closest to the scene remained optimistic, influenced perhaps by the boom town atmosphere of Calgary. This internal division had hampered decision making. Holt resigned in the interest of unified management. This also let someone else carry the can, in the event of failure, and assume the burdensome and risky responsibility of negotiating the licences, finances, and sales contracts needed for the company to succeed.

R. B. Bennett, the local legal fixer, was duly elected president, a doubly fortunate choice since he would soon become a Conservative member of Parliament from Calgary, well placed to exert pressure in the company's interest upon the new Conservative government of Robert Borden.[7]

By the time Horseshoe Falls began operations, several other obstacles to the development of power at Kananaskis had been removed. The company required nearly two hundred acres of land within Rocky Mountains National Park for its reservoir, but the act that had created the park in the 1880s contained no provision for the alienation of lands for such purposes. The Laurier government had already set about drafting a new Forest Reserves and Parks Act that gave the cabinet the power to make regulations covering the exploitation of natural resources, including waterpower developments and transmission lines. This legislation went through Parliament in the spring of 1911, attracting little attention.[8]

The interim licence to develop Kananaskis Falls, granted in October 1911, only conveyed the right of development. For its works, Calgary Power would also have to acquire more than two hundred acres of land on the Nakoda Indian Reserve. The company claimed to possess the same powers as a railway company to expropriate reserve lands when necessary, in case the band tried to hold them to ransom.[9] And to ensure that such a thing could not occur, the Laurier government also amended the Indian Act in the spring of 1911 to give railways and public utilities broader powers in this regard. In the debate, Interior Minister Frank Oliver made plain that Native bands were not going to be permitted to stand in the way of developments favoured by the rest of Canadian society:

> The Indian reserves throughout the country have been selected, one may say, with very good judgment; the reserves are probably the choice locations in the Dominion of Canada from one end to the other. Consequently with increases of population and increases of value of land, there necessarily comes some clash of interest between the Indian and the white man.... [I]t is not right that the requirements of white settlement should be ignored

– that is, that the right of the Indian should be allowed to become a wrong to the white man.[10]

The leader of the opposition at the time, Robert Borden, objected, arguing that these powers of expropriation could override treaty rights. Oliver reluctantly agreed and amended the bill to require cabinet approval before any such expropriation of Indian lands could take place.

Once more, the thorny issue of whether or not ownership of the adjacent land made the Nakoda the owner of the waterpower raised its ugly head. Whatever the government bureaucrats might think – and in this case, the Indian Affairs and Water Power officials in Ottawa disagreed – the Nakoda believed that their land and the waterfalls were connected, and they valued the land accordingly. In the subsequent negotiations, they steadfastly refused to give way to the demands of Calgary Power unless they received compensation that they considered adequate. Against the company's supposed powers of expropriation, the Nakoda had their own defences. In this struggle, though, they found themselves at something of a disadvantage. Late in 1911, the Interior Department was thoroughly reorganized and responsibility for hydraulic matters, which had formerly been dealt with by the Railway Lands Branch, was transferred to a new Water Power Branch. J. B. Challies, the new superintendent of the branch, was a strong proponent of hydroelectric development in western Canada, which gave the power companies subject to his authority a strong voice at court. The election on September 21, 1911, also brought the president of Calgary Power to the House of Commons as a Conservative MP.

The Indians wanted the same terms that they had received for the Horseshoe Falls development: a lump sum of $10,000 plus an annual payment of $1,500 to the band treasury. Challies insisted that they had no right to any waterpower rental and should merely receive payment for their lands as though they were located anywhere on the reserve.[11] Delay in settling this matter pinched the company where it hurt – its bottom line. In the fall of 1912, Calgary Power complained to Challies that if the company was not permitted to begin construction at Kananaskis at once, it would not be able to supply the power needs of the city of Calgary by

Moses Bearspaw, Stoney Chief, circa 1908 (Glenbow Archives, NA-695-40).

1913. Challies applied pressure to the Indian Affairs Department (which also fell under the minister of the interior) to grant an interim licence to the company so that work could be started. Eventually, J. D. McLean, the acting deputy superintendent general of Indian affairs, agreed, provided that an agreement to compensate the Nakoda could be worked out later. Immediately, construction workers moved onto the reserve, cutting trees, building roads, and erecting a bunkhouse at Kananaskis.[12]

This unilateral action understandably infuriated the Nakoda, who had not been consulted. Local Indian Agent J. W. Waddy had to try and placate the angry band members, who now demanded as much as $125,000 for 212 acres of their land and, in addition, sought other lands and more horses for their use. McLean, the deputy, advised Waddy to warn the Nakoda that if they made such unreasonable demands, the power company would simply apply to expropriate the necessary lands. Nonetheless, the band rejected out of hand Calgary Power's offer of ten dollars per acre. They reduced their demand to a cash payment of twenty-five dollars per head for their 660 members ($16,500) in exchange for the lands, plus a yearly rental of $1,500 for the water rights.[13]

Waddy considered the Indians' demands quite reasonable and wired McLean in Ottawa: "Whole trouble caused by power company going ahead [with] permanent work with authority only for preliminary; [I] think the Indians acted very decent[ly] in matter [compared] to what white people would have done." But R. B. Bennett considered the price of the lands (roughly seventy-five dollars per acre) "absurd" and demanded that McLean find some way "to adjust the matter." In June 1913, angered by the company's stalling, the Nakoda threatened to attack the power plant and destroy the works. Waddy took the matter seriously enough to inform the local Royal North West Mounted Police detachment at nearby Morley, and the company put a couple of extra men on watch against trouble.[14]

Eventually, the Department of Indian Affairs dispatched its chief in-spector of Indian Agencies, Glen Campbell, to the reserve to see if he could defuse the situation. Campbell ordered Calgary Power to stop work in an effort to cool things down, but company secretary V. M. Drury hurried up from Montreal to Ottawa, where he mobilized the sympathetic J. B.

Challies in the Water Powers Branch to help him persuade Frank Pedley, the deputy minister of Indian affairs, to countermand Campbell's order.[15] The company was desperate to get on with construction to meet its existing commitments and to have the power on hand to expand and extend its contract with the City of Calgary when it came due for renewal in 1913.

Chief Inspector Campbell's investigation led him to support the Nakoda demands: "I feel certain if this property was owned by any one of the shareholders of the Company that he would not even consider $100.00 per acre." If Calgary Power disagreed, he reported, then the whole matter should be referred to an arbitrator to be valued like comparable sites: "I cannot think any rich company expecting to gain immense wealth (as no doubt its prospectus will show) by obtaining this franchise would care to have its method of obtaining possession aired in court or newspapers, and I strongly urge the Indians be paid their price under the stipulations they make."[16] But the company made only a modest increase in its offer: it would buy the 25 acres actually needed for the dam and powerhouse for $625 and lease another 160 acres for $500 per year, which, taken together with the $1,500 each for the use of the Kananaskis and Horseshoe Falls, would mean an annual income of $3,500, or about $5 for every resident of the reserve. Chief Inspector Campbell complained angrily to Superintendent McLean,

> I think the Department is absolutely remiss in its duties to its wards in permitting the Company to trespass on an Indian reservation without permission from the Indians, and furthermore, that when asked by those Indians through their Inspector to hold up the work until a settlement is made, the Department does not take proper steps to do so.

Campbell promised to accompany the band leaders to a meeting in Calgary with Interior Minister Dr. W. J. Roche when he visited there early in September and to "fight out the matter with him."[17]

Roche promised them a speedy and generous settlement, provided the Nakoda agreed to arbitration of their demands, but Calgary Power

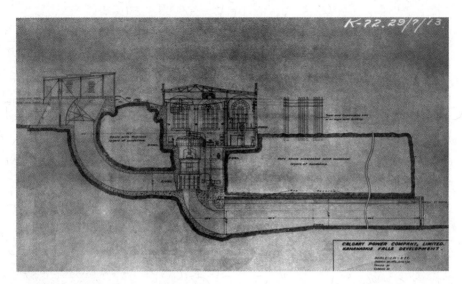

SCHEMATIC DIAGRAM OF THE KANANASKIS HYDRO-ELECTRIC PLANT (GLENBOW
ARCHIVES, NA-3802-2).

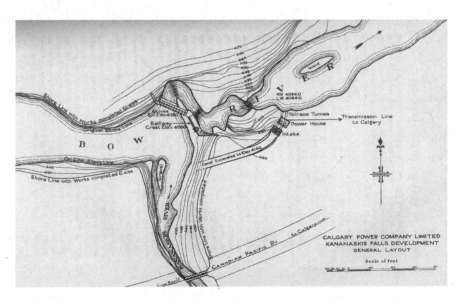

GEOGRAPHY OF THE KANANASKIS SITE (COMMISSION OF CONSERVATION).

procrastinated throughout the fall of 1913, refusing to "pay an exorbitant price for useless land."[18] At one point, the company claimed that it had power to expropriate an easement over the lands and did not have to buy them.[19] A few days later, they asked for an additional 290 acres of reserve lands along the Kananaskis River, which would be flooded behind a storage dam planned to try and further increase the water supply available. Superintendent McLean abruptly refused even to consider such an application until the ownership of the lands at the main dam site was settled.[20]

Construction on the dam and powerhouse continued at a frantic pace even though these negotiations dragged on due to the company's intransigence. Spring and summer passed without settlement. With no agreement in sight, the bureaucrats at Indian Affairs became increasingly nervous that there would be violence if the matter was not settled by the time the Nakoda returned to the reserve from the autumn hunt at year's end. Duncan C. Scott advised the company, "Unless everything completed by January first Department cannot hold itself responsible for the course of events." Even though the company had just signed a new five-year contract to deliver a minimum of 5,000 hp annually to the City of Calgary at $26 each, with provision for larger supplies in future, it refused to offer more than $2,500 for the ninety-odd acres it now wanted, a price characterized by Indian Affairs officials as "absurdly low for land enhanced so greatly in value as that in question on account of commanding the utilization of the power."[21]

In an effort to calm the situation, Indians Affairs decided in mid-December to advance the band $3,000 (or $5 per head) to be recouped from the ultimate settlement. Agent Waddy, however, had the unpleasant task of explaining to the angry Nakoda that it now appeared likely that their lands would be considered simply as arable, since the value of the adjacent waterpower was covered by the $1,500 annual rental that Calgary Power was offering. A valuator chosen by the band reported to Ottawa that the lands without the waterpower were of negligible value but suggested that lands and water rights together be given a nominal capital value of $67,000, which, at a rate of return of 6 per cent, would yield a total of $4,000 per year for the Indians. Despite repeated urgings by Agent Waddy, however, the Nakoda refused to budge from their demand of $25 per head ($16,500) for the lands plus an annual rental of $1,500.[22]

In January 1914, Calgary Power declined to agree to either figure, preferring instead to have an arbitrator settle the dispute. At the same time, the news that the company had already put one generating unit into service at Kananaskis Falls and expected to have a second in operation by February caused outrage among the Nakoda. Their chiefs informed Agent Waddy that the generating station must be closed down until the land claims were finally settled. Chief Inspector Campbell was again hastily ordered to Alberta to try and persuade them to do nothing while the arbitration proceeded. In March, a three-man panel was agreed upon between Indian Affairs and the company, and Agent Waddy reported about the Nakoda that if the panel went about its task quickly, "he thinks he can hold them down a little longer."[23]

But the arbitration quickly bogged down in technicalities, and after a month and a half, Chief Inspector Campbell reported from Calgary that he was "tired of loafing here indefinitely doing nothing." A visit to the reserve a few days later, however, alarmed him thoroughly:

Situation there so dangerous, that if there is no immediate prospect of settlement ... I advise you most seriously to arrange for immediate police protection to men at Kananaskis Falls. Indians determined to go to extremes to protect rights which they now believe are being sacrificed in favour of rich corporations. Waddy is holding them down hourly. Grave danger of trouble.[24]

Campbell's superiors in far-off Ottawa clearly considered him over-wrought. The general superintendent of Indian affairs, Duncan C. Scott, grandly ordered him to dispel the "myth" that the Indians were being sacrificed to the interests of the company and told him to warn them that they would be prosecuted if they took the law into their own hands. The power company had, after all, the ultimate right to expropriate their lands if no settlement could be arrived at. Campbell did as he was told but reported that these arguments cut no ice with the Indians. They had their own legal advice that they possessed the right to eject trespassers on their lands – by force, if necessary. "Stonies [sic]," wired Campbell, "really on [the] prowl."[25]

Eventually, a meeting of the band council was convened at Morley, Alberta, on May 12, 1914. The Indians delivered an ultimatum to Campbell, Waddy, and J. B. Challies of the Water Power Branch, who had been sent to advise on the value of the hydraulic site: they wanted a settlement on their terms approved by the minister of the interior within a fortnight or else the arbitration would proceed with instructions to determine the full market value of the waterpower. They were willing to send their three principal chiefs to Ottawa to explain their demands and sign an agreement. Challies endorsed Campbell's view that otherwise an Indian attack upon the power plant could hardly be avoided:

I submit that serious trouble costing thousands of dollars damage to Company's property will most assuredly result with Indians in their present mood, unless the Department either directs their chiefs to come to Ottawa or instructs the arbitrators to proceed....

The Indians have good cause to feel that they have not been dealt with frankly, fairly and promptly, and I am convinced that their attitude is reasonably fair and just.[26]

Duncan Scott, who up to that point had insisted that no good purpose would be served by a meeting in Ottawa,[27] hastily reversed himself and ordered Agent Waddy to accompany the three chiefs – George Maclean, Jonas Benjamin, and Dan Wildman – to the capital at once. The company seems to have recognized at long last that continued refusal to meet the Indians' terms posed a real risk to the plant at Kananaskis Falls. Representing Calgary Power at a meeting in Scott's office on May 20, 1914, corporate secretary Victor M. Drury signed an agreement conceding most of what the Nakoda had been demanding all along. A cash payment to the band of $16,500 ($25 per head) would cover the purchase of ninety-four acres for $9,000, plus an annual waterpower rental of $1,500 for the next five years. From 1919 on, the Indians would receive $1,500 annually as long as the company held the hydraulic rights to Kananaskis Falls.[28]

With the Indians en route back to their reserve, Scott sat down on May 23, 1914, and wrote a memorandum to the file analyzing the deal. This minor classic in the field of bureaucratic self-justification purported to demonstrate that the band had gotten a pretty good deal thanks to the activities of Indian Affairs. After all, the $9,000 that they had received for their lands was a few hundred dollars more than the sum suggested by their own valuator. Moreover, they had already received on account $5 per head out of the sum coming to them. Perhaps a more accurate light on the whole business was cast by a letter of gratitude from Victor Drury, thanking Scott for his "consideration in arranging the differences between the Indians and the Company."[29] The Nakoda had had to play on an uneven playing field, but in the end, they got their price.

Still, the company continued to display a rather cavalier attitude toward its obligations. It paid grudgingly and on a delayed instalment plan. When the deal was signed, Drury forwarded an initial payment of $2,500 on account, but Indian Affairs had to put up the balance of the $13,240 still owed to the Nakoda. In 1915, when the department requested another substantial instalment from the company, the company pleaded poverty owing to cost overruns on the Kananaskis plant and promised to send the money later.[30] Further pressure from the Indian Affairs superintendent, Duncan Scott, who reminded the company that this had been "a very difficult matter to arrange with the Indians," was deflected with the information that Bennett was off in England and would take it up on his return.[31] A year later, the company had still paid nothing. A warning from Scott extracted a cheque for another $4,000. A further $3,500 was paid over in the summer of 1917, and the final balance of $5,000 was received at long last that fall.[32]

The ruthless logic of capitalism, backed by the growing social dependence upon electrical energy, drove the company onward, in some respects against its own will. The most unlikely characters – even university professors – responded to this siren call of hydroelectric development. Calgary Power won its coveted franchise fair and square over its competitor, but its arrogance and intransigence in the subsequent negotiations over the lands were utterly unwarranted. The Kananaskis Falls story adds further evidence to the case of the state acting as handmaiden to capitalist development, aligning its powers and bureaucracy behind the developers. Yet it also shows, somewhat surprisingly, the countervailing influence of other elements of the state structure balancing development against other responsibilities. Indian Affairs provided consistent support to the Nakoda in their agonizing dealings, though that support was more resolute locally than in Ottawa. The Nakoda, too, demonstrated that there were other kinds of power that terrified bureaucrats and politicians, which they used quite effectively in these negotiations.[33] Finally, the whole affair raises the narrow technicality of whether the Nakoda sold something they did not own, a question that remains open to this day.

CHAPTER 4

Downstream Benefits

Connecting the lights and motors of Calgary to the turbines and generators on the Bow unleashed another powerful imperative: the need for technological efficiency. In order to be maximally efficient, hydroelectric installations must operate continuously and at capacity. For many months of the year, however, the Bow River provided only enough water to run the equipment at the Horseshoe and Kananaskis sites at a fraction of their capacity. Expensive capital equipment had to be paid for, even when it was not running: it could not be laid off like the human work force. Adding a second generating station provided some additional power but only doubled the scale of the efficiency problem. Paying the interest and principal on the debt required almost full plant utilization. Invisible filaments of financial obligation to investors across Canada and in Great Britain demanded that the Calgary Power plants be run at maximum efficiency: that is, continuously at their rated capacity day and night, year round. Not only did operating at optimum output make for a profitable corporation, but it also produced electricity at the lowest cost. Electricity consumers, therefore, as well as engineers and financiers, also had an interest in the efficiency of the Calgary Power system. Driven by this quest for technological efficiency, an alliance of consumers, producers, and capitalists conspired to make the river itself more efficient. Thus began a prolonged campaign of environmental modification for hydroelectric purposes that led to the redesign of the Bow River, and along with it, a national park.

The Bow River was anything but regular. A typical glacial river running off of mountains exposed to long, cold winters, the Bow was ill suited to the requirement of continuous operation of hydroelectric plants on account of its summer floods and its diminished flow in fall and winter. With full knowledge of the river's characteristics, the plants on the Bow probably would not have been built. No one else risked building other hydroelectric facilities on the rivers draining the front range of the Rockies in Alberta during the first half of the twentieth century.[1] But hydroelectric development of the Bow began with imperfect knowledge before the ups and downs of its flow were fully understood. As a result, the sunk investment had to be saved; Calgary needed the power.

The technological fix adopted to remedy the situation was upstream water storage. Dams in the watershed could impound water during periods of higher flow for release when the natural flow diminished. In that way, streamflow could be evened out: flood peaks could be shaved, and winter flows augmented. This, in turn, would increase the year-round capacity of the generating equipment and lower the cost of electricity. The concept was as old as the idea of the millpond. Canadian lumbermen had adapted the principle by building crude dams on upstream tributaries to augment spring freshets in order to create a surge strong enough to carry their cargo of logs downstream. The technique of upstream storage for hydroelectric purposes was already well understood, and the lakes and mountain valleys of the Rockies afforded many possible sites for storage reservoirs. The only problem was that the upstream watershed lay within Rocky Mountains National Park.

The original engineers promoting the project, lulled perhaps by years of above-average flow in the first decade of the twentieth century and spectacular summertime cascades, expressed more concern about the security of flow than its variation. Smith and Chace reassured investors that since the headwaters of the Bow River lay in a national park and were thus not at risk of being denuded of timber, the permanent flow of the river was more or less guaranteed. Nonetheless, the variability of the flow was a matter of common knowledge in Calgary. The developers knew it as well. Traven Aitken, in reporting on the street railway and electrical

Graph 4.1. Seasonal Variation in Streamflow on the Bow River 1908–15 (in cubic feet per second)

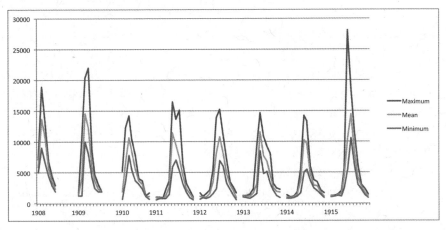

Source: Denis and Challies, *Water-Powers of Manitoba, Saskatchewan and Alberta*, 179–83.

situation in Calgary in 1908, reminded his brother Max of the seasonal differences.[2] Max Aitken's Western Canada Power engineer, called in to examine the Bow River situation in 1909, had warned of "poor water gauging" and "meagre supply at times."[3] Nevertheless, as we have seen, Max Aitken proceeded, not only on the advice of Smith and Chace but also, it must be said, on his own hunch that hydroelectric power would allow him to merge and monopolize the electric industry of Calgary.

Only after building had begun did the engineers and promoters discover, to their horror, the magnitude of their mistake. As noted earlier, the river displayed its extreme behaviour in 1910 when a flood washed out construction and in the subsequent winter when streamflow fell to a mere 600 cubic feet per second (cfs). The Horseshoe development had been built assuming a minimum streamflow of 1,000 cfs. Apprised of the seriousness of the situation by the developers, the Department of the Interior mounted an urgent scientific program to measure Bow River streamflow and to study the possibilities of upstream storage.[4] The chart above, compiled from data gathered by government waterpower engineers during Calgary

Power's construction of the Horseshoe Falls plant, documented for the first time the Bow's erratic nature and its unsuitability for hydroelectric development. The data, when analyzed in 1914 by C. H. Mitchell, Canada's leading hydraulic engineer, led to the following alarming conclusion: "The Bow River is peculiar, in that, in its natural condition, its summer flood discharge is upwards of seventy times its low water winter discharge, a condition which obviously renders its use, in its present state, unsuitable, inefficient, and commercially unfeasible for power purposes."[5]

Ironically, Mitchell was the engineer who, on behalf of Budd and Alexander, had first applied for the Horseshoe Falls waterpower. Meanwhile, the Calgary Power Company had installed generating equipment with a capacity of 19,500 hp at Horseshoe Falls and was in the process of adding equipment capable of producing an additional 11,000 hp at Kananaskis Falls. For much of the year – and especially during winter, when the city needed more power to light its streets, homes, and businesses – this equipment would lie idle. Engineers calculated that at best, the company could only produce on a continuous basis about one-third of its rated capacity.[6] In a dark moment, R. B. Bennett contemplated dumping the hapless company on its only likely purchaser, the City of Calgary.[7]

The predicament of the power company led the Department of the Interior to commission M. C. Hendry to undertake a serious study of the matter in 1911.[8] Data from his study, as it streamed in over the next several years, indicated that up to 280,300 acre-feet of storage could be created in the mountains. Engineers estimated that this could increase minimum streamflow at the power plants from 720 cfs to 1,500 cfs. The effect upon power production would be dramatic. Both the Kananaskis and Horseshoe continuous-wheel horsepower capability would rise from 3,820 to 9,545, almost a 250 per cent increase.[9] Calgary Power's first request to store water inside the national park was thus received sympathetically by the waterpower bureaucrats in Ottawa. By early 1911, the power company's attention had focused upon Lake Minnewanka, which lay just northeast of the Banff townsite and drained into the Bow through the Cascade River.[10]

This policy of upstream storage fit neatly with the hydraulic engineers' conception of "conservation." For them, conservation of natural resources

Lake Minnewanka, circa 1902 (Glenbow Archives, NA-4654-1).

Lake Minnewanka looking towards Devil's Gap (Glenbow Archives, NA-4564-5).

meant "wise use" and the avoidance of waste. The highest use of the Bow's falling water, they reasoned, lay in energizing the social and economic expansion of southern Alberta. They saw the river in its natural state as an inefficient producer of power – all of that energy going to waste in one season, when it could be usefully employed in winter. Thus, the conservation ethic of the hydraulic engineers regulating waterpowers harmonized with the financial imperatives of the promoters and the desires of Calgary's electricity consumers.

Chances of gaining permission to build a storage dam at Lake Minnewanka seemed good, because the Department of the Interior had already permitted the lake level to be raised by four feet in 1908 to accommodate the operators of steamboats that carried tourists on scenic cruises around the mountain-ringed lake.[11] In periods of low water, the steamers had been unable to land at the wharf, and the operators had persuaded the authorities to deepen the lake slightly. When local residents protested that raising the dam another dozen feet would ruin a prime tourist attraction and leave unsightly mudflats exposed for months while the lake refilled in the spring and early summer, the Interior Department's superintendent of forestry responded, "We would certainly like to save all the beauty spots we can, but if the development of the whole country demands the storage of some of the water supply I think we can hardly prevent it being carried out." All he could promise was that there would be a full examination of all possible storage sites before permission was granted.[12]

Parks Branch officials raised no serious objections to the proposal, a reflection of the attitude that they took toward development in Rocky Mountains National Park at that time. Parks officials themselves had been exploring the idea of developing their own hydroelectricity, both to supply the park and to produce revenue.[13] A memorandum entitled "Re Dominion Parks: Their Value and Ideals," composed by the new commissioner of parks, J. B. Harkin, soon after his appointment revealed his ambivalence.[14] Harkin began by asserting that "humanitarian" values were of the greatest significance:

National parks exist for all the people. They are the people's share of that natural beauty of mountain, lake and stream. Their mission is to serve that innate desire of every individual to seek relief and repose and refreshment of mind and body in the open air and sunshine, among the flowers and trees and hills.

Most of this document, however, was taken up with analysis of the "commercial" value of parks, which "attract in ever-increasing numbers an enormous tourist traffic from other lands." Note that Harkin thought of tourists as coming from outside Canada, a traffic that created an additional form of national revenue: "The tourist leaves large sums of money in the country he visits, but takes away with him in return for it nothing that makes the nation poorer." In Harkin's view, national parks had this dual role, preserving natural beauty for popular enjoyment and developing a revenue stream to sustain park development and enrich the country. In order to flourish, national parks would have to demonstrate their utility, a goal later labelled "The Doctrine of Usefulness."[15] Provided that no great damage was done to major scenic attractions, the park authorities were quite willing to provide such modern amenities as roads and electrical service for the tourists, many of whom would be Americans. In view of this attitude, it is hardly surprising that the national park's authorities accommodated Calgary Power's initial request for more water storage.

Early in 1912, therefore, Calgary Power received permission to build a sixteen-foot-high dam at the outlet of Lake Minnewanka, raising the water twelve feet above its then current level. Anticipating an increase in its capacity, the company signed a revised power supply contract with the City of Calgary in 1913 to supply 5,000 hp of electricity per year; in addition, a contract was signed to supply bulk power to the Canada Cement Company.[16] Park officials also required the company to install a thimble in its dam to deliver 150 cubic feet per second (cfs) of water for their use should they decide to construct their own generating station to supply the Banff townsite, which currently drew power from a thermal plant owned by the CPR at its nearby Bankhead coal mine. By 1913, such a development was being considered, and the commissioner of parks observed, "If a feasible scheme was discovered it would not only provide revenue for the Park, but would, doubtless, also redound to the credit of the Department throughout the province."[17] In considering whether diverting water from Lake Minnewanka to a power plant on the Bow might affect the scenery adversely, Harkin was sanguine:

> It seems to me that the only policy for the Department to pursue is to have the plan of the power development end of the work laid out, with a view to eventually using all the power. I do not anticipate that there will be any trouble with respect to the scenic end of the park in consequence of this power development.

In any event, with the department in full control of the scheme, "if necessary, steps can be taken later on to guard against any damage to the lake or its scenery."[18]

When the new dam at Lake Minnewanka was completed, however, Calgary Power found that even with the additional water during the winter months, it sometimes remained unable to produce 5,000 continuous hp at its Horseshoe and Kananaskis plants (which had a rated capacity of 31,000 hp). Storage worked, but the results were not as dramatic as the engineers had predicted. Comparing the average streamflow of the first and last three months of 1911 and 1912, without benefit of storage, with similar months in 1913, 1914, and 1915, when the Minnewanka storage dam was in full operation, streamflow at Calgary increased by 49 per cent in January, 9 per cent in February, and 24 per cent in March. The October, November, December comparison showed positive differences of 7, 24, and 50 per cent, respectively. However, not all of this increase could be attributed to storage alone.[19] Only about 20 per cent of the water released actually reached the power plant headponds a few miles downstream; the rest was trapped in narrow channels choked with ice or sank into the deep gravel bed of the Bow, which only worsened the spring floods.[20] From the Parks Branch perspective, the dam raised water levels, making a larger, in some senses more attractive, and certainly deeper lake for boating.

Building the new dock at Lake Minnewanka, 1912 (Glenbow Archives, PD-365-2-10).

Dam at Lake Minnewanka, 1912 (Glenbow Archives, PD-365-2-81).

However, for many years, debris and floating logs from the clearance of the raised shoreline posed a hazard to navigation.[21]

Thus, at the end of 1914, an application was made to remove the old four-foot high navigation dam (which had been left submerged behind the new dam) and to excavate the bed of the Cascade so that the lake could be drawn down six more feet altogether, or two feet below its natural level. The Water Power Branch was quite amenable to this proposal, and the Parks Branch seems not to have raised any objection, but the proposal ran into stiff opposition from federal fisheries experts, who predicted that such low water would prevent the trout in the lake from spawning. The application was, therefore, turned down, and Calgary Power had to manage without further storage capacity.[22]

Because Calgary Power's hydroelectric plants were often unable to deliver the power required in wintertime, the city maintained its thermal generating plant to meet the peaks. The municipal authorities even gave serious thought to trying to purchase the hydroelectric plants, but the difficulties of raising the necessary money during the First World War rendered that impossible. Thus, when the contract with the company expired in 1918, the city simply exercised its option to renew the contract for a further five years at the same rates.[23]

It should be noted that bad luck for the region – the collapse of the Calgary boom in 1913 – was, in some respects, good fortune for the power company. As the economic bubble burst, the demand for electricity levelled off. Because the pressure of galloping consumer demand was to some degree relieved, the company did not have to scramble to put in place the generating capacity to keep pace. For a time – it turned out to be a decade – the company could concentrate on getting the most out of its existing equipment to meet a fairly steady demand.

After the war, a group of Montreal financiers tightened their control over the management and operations of Calgary Power. When Max Aitken decamped for England in 1911, direction of his Royal Securities Company fell to his protege, Isaac Walton Killam, another former securities salesman from the late John F. Stairs in Nova Scotia and New Brunswick. In 1919, Killam and his junior partner, Ward Pitfield, bought control of Royal Securities from Aitken, now knighted and permanently ensconced in Britain. Along with Royal Securities came Calgary Power; two small Caribbean utilities in Camaguey, Cuba, and Demerara, British Guiana; and the Montreal Engineering Company.[24] Revived and restaffed in the postwar era, Montreal Engineering became not only prominent hydroelectric consulting engineers but also the effective manager of these three utilities. In a growing market for electricity in Calgary and southern Alberta, Killam's business strategy focused upon increasing production and making Calgary Power a more efficient and profitable hydroelectric power producer.

Calgary Power continued to face difficulties every winter in fulfilling its contracts with the city and large consumers like the cement plants, particularly in years such as 1920, when the flow of the Bow fell to only 60 per cent of the normal April mean. This required the Calgary municipal utility to retain a thermal generating plant with a capacity of 14,000 hp; the current that it produced was much more expensive than hydro (3.8 cents vs. 0.44 cents per kwh in 1919). When the war ended, the city renewed negotiations to buy out the company, in part to ensure service in the event of strikes by workers at the steam plant such as had occurred in 1919. Still, municipal officials were reluctant to take over the private utility without some guarantee that the city would secure adequate water storage to operate efficiently.[25]

When growth resumed in the 1920s, the company immediately sought to increase its generating capacity and, early in 1921, renewed its request to remove the old four-foot log dam behind its higher barrier at Lake Minnewanka and draw down an additional six feet of water. Once again, the Water Power Branch of the Department of the Interior gave its full support to the application. The hydraulic engineers argued that the additional water would produce at least 712 hp annually for Calgary and would allow the city to save $39,000 on steam plant operations. Not only that, but as the creation of Ontario Hydro had demonstrated, there were "the great indirect benefits which accrue to a community from an ample supply of cheap power." It was claimed that the lake would refill by the end of June in all but the driest years. If officials of the Interior Department were given authority to manage the refilling operation, the physical appearance of the lake might be "materially bettered" during the early part of the tourist season.[26]

Branch chief J. B. Challies even contended that by having had a thimble installed for its future use in the dam at Lake Minnewanka before the war, the Parks Branch had made a definite commitment in 1913 to the principle of a sixteen-foot storage range on the lake in the interests of the departmental power project: "In view of the former commitment of the Parks branch to the principle of the increased storage range, it scarcely appears logical to reverse the decision in the matter when a private interest is concerned." He urged quick consent by Parks Commissioner J. B. Harkin, or else the additional flow would be of no value in the low-water months that year.[27]

By that time, however, Harkin and his staff had nearly a decade of experience with the effects of a power reservoir upon the scenic beauty of Rocky Mountains National Park, and they had lost all of their enthusiasm for permitting Lake Minnewanka to be used as a power reservoir. This was the only such reservoir in the national parks system, and nearly two decades after the decision had been taken to permit the dam, Harkin ruefully admitted, with all the clarity of hindsight, "That was an experiment, made at a time when probably nobody realized the importance of the principle involved."[28] Beginning in the early 1920s, the Parks Branch started to object to the power company's requests to increase storage capacity within the park. Not only would the scenery at the lake be ruined by mudflats visible even during the high point of the tourist season in July, but the deleterious effects on the fish population of lowering the water two feet below its natural level remained a serious concern. The commissioner dug in his heels and stalled until the time had passed when any increased diversion from Lake Minnewanka would be useful to Calgary Power in 1921. Despite strong pressure from the Water Power Branch, he refused to agree to any such scheme.[29]

Thwarted again, Calgary Power decided on a new tack during the summer of 1921, proposing to construct an entirely new power plant at Anthracite on the Bow using water diverted through a canal parallel to the valley of the Cascade River, the natural outlet of Lake Minnewanka. When the final plans were submitted a year later, it was clear that this would be a major undertaking, involving a huge earthen dam to raise the water level forty-seven feet above normal to produce an average head of 320 feet for generators that could ultimately turn out 18,000 hp. The upper reaches of the Ghost River would also eventually be diverted into Lake Minnewanka to increase the supply of water.

Calgary Power was acutely conscious that the most serious objections were now likely to come from the Parks Branch:

> The only objection to the construction of this plant is the fact that it might be detrimental to the scenic beauty of the Park. This would have been a real danger had it not been kept in mind when the design was prepared, and every care taken to avoid disfiguring the scenery. The works are so laid out that they are mainly hidden from view, and each separate part is so designed that it will harmonize with the surroundings and in no way detract therefrom.

The power canal would be hidden in another valley to the west of the Cascade, whose flow out of Lake Minnewanka would be maintained during the tourist season. The powerhouse on the banks of the Bow would admittedly be visible from the road and the railway, but its "simple and dignified" design would conceal the switching equipment, and the 110,000-volt transmission line stretching eastward toward Calgary would be largely invisible to travellers, avoiding long vistas of poles.[30] Such care, concluded the engineers, had "entirely eliminated" the danger to the scenic beauty of the valley.[31]

Concerns about the appearance of the new storage reservoir were blandly dismissed:

> That Lake Minnewanka has never been regarded as an outstanding beauty spot is shown by the fact that the C.P.R. have never featured it in their advertizing [sic]. The reason is that the mountain lakes in the Rockies which are famous for their beauty, such as Lake

Louise, are glacial cirques, while Minnewanka is only a flooded river valley. Although Lake Minnewanka is surrounded by lofty mountains, the general effect is spoiled by low-lying flats covered by stubby growth of stunted jackpine. By clearing these flats and raising the water levels as proposed, they will be submerged, and the general appearance of the lake very materially improved.[32]

The company argued that future industrial development in southern Alberta was dependent upon supplies of cheap hydroelectric energy, which would place Calgary on a footing to compete with other Canadian cities for economic growth. "Is the future of Alberta to be sacrificed to maintain the parks inviolate," asked Geoffrey Gaherty, the company's chief engineer, rhetorically, "or are the natural resources in the parks to be developed under restrictions which will adequately protect the scenic beauty? Considering the vast area of the parks and what a small part of it would be affected by any conceivable economic use, and the importance of such use to the community, there can be but one answer to such a question."[33]

The responsibility for dealing with the application fell ultimately upon the minister of the interior, who possessed very broad powers over the development of waterpowers on federal Crown lands. The reorganization of the department in the spring of 1912 had created a separate Water Power Branch headed by J. B. Challies, whose staff soon came to the conclusion that the 1909 regulations governing such projects ought to be revised.[34] The object was to sever the title to the waterpowers from the adjacent lands so that the federal government could continue to exercise control after the lands were alienated, whether to individuals or to those provinces in which they were located. In addition, the Interior Department aimed to regulate the rates charged to power consumers. H. W. Grunsky, the legal expert responsible for drafting the revised regulations, explained to Challies why these changes had become necessary :

Public sentiment regarding the preservation of natural resources has grown rapidly in recent years. In particular, this sentiment has expressed itself strongly in respect of the water powers, which are so closely interwoven with public utility enterprises such as street railways and municipal lighting systems, that enlightened supervision and regulation on the part of the administrative authority has been demanded.[35]

After extensive consultation with waterpower experts in the United States and Canada during the First World War, Grunsky eventually drew up a set of new draft regulations.[36] In the end, it was decided to introduce a new piece of general legislation declaring all undeveloped waterpowers to be "works for the general advantage of Canada," thus ensuring permanent federal jurisdiction over them.[37] The Parks Branch, unhappy that the new legislation did not provide for special treatment of waterpowers located within the park system, evidently found itself outmanoeuvred. When the detailed regulations were finally proclaimed under the new act in October 1921, the Parks Branch complained that once the minister of the interior had given his approval to any hydraulic development inside a park, administrative control over the project passed entirely out of the hands of the commissioner of parks to the Water Power Branch, a situation the Parks Branch people viewed as "decidedly serious."[38]

Calgary Power's application in 1922 seemed to demonstrate the validity of these fears. The proposal set off some fierce bureaucratic infighting within the Department of the Interior between the Parks Branch and the Water Power Branch. J. B. Harkin and J. B. Challies vied for the attention and support of the deputy minister, W. W. Cory. The final decision had to be made, of course, by Cory's political superior, Charles Stewart, who held the Interior portfolio for the Liberals throughout the 1920s. As a former premier of Alberta, Stewart was well informed on the power situation in that province.

The staff of the Water Power Branch remained sympathetic to the company. J. T. Johnston, the branch's chief engineer, noted that careful study of the water resources of the eastern slopes of the Rockies in Alberta had revealed that there were few sites that could be used to store water for power purposes; the only ones that could be developed to provide a sizable block of power for Calgary at a reasonable cost were in the Bow River watershed. Johnston accepted Calgary Power's contention that schemes like the damming of Lake Minnewanka were inevitable in the long run:

> Insofar as the power and irrigation phases are concerned both this [Water Power] branch and the Reclamation Service have consistently maintained that this is ultimately unavoidable, since the total runoff from the eastern slope of the Rocky Mountains in southern Alberta is very limited, and since over 37% of this runoff has its origins within the boundaries of National Park areas, and since, furthermore, 65% of total runoff of the Bow River above Bassano comes from the Park areas.[39]

Largely because of their experience with the dam at Lake Minnewanka, Harkin and his staff in the Parks Branch had radically altered their views from the pre-war period about the compatibility of large hydroelectric developments and scenic preservation. After studying the plans for the new power plant at Anthracite, Harkin warned the superintendent of Rocky Mountains National Park, "So far as I can see, this is a proposition which the Parks Branch should strongly oppose." The transmission line alone running eastward down the narrow Bow valley would be, Harkin noted, "a very great eyesore" from the road and the railway.[40] In a memorandum to Challies, he argued that a power plant "in the heart of our most popular and developed park cannot fail to detract from its scenic value and that the power development in view is consequently opposed to the best interests of the park."[41]

When the minister of the interior visited Banff in the summer of 1922, Harkin and the park superintendent took him to see Lake Minnewanka; they hoped that the evidence of his own eyes would be sufficient to convince Stewart. Moreover, they had discovered that the company intended to raise the water level in the lake thirty feet initially (sufficient to generate 9,000 hp) and only use the other seventeen feet of water storage when power demand required it. That would make it virtually impossible to landscape the shoreline attractively in the meantime.[42]

In case more ammunition was needed, estimates were prepared showing that over forty-five thousand people visited the lake annually: "The Lake Minnewanka drive is, taking everything into consideration, the most popular drive in Rocky Mountains Park. The existence of this drive ... keeps tourists in Banff at least another half day." This generated revenues of $195,000 annually, making the scenic value of the lake, capitalized at 5 per cent per annum, $4 million. That information was fed to the Banff Citizens Council, which then registered a strong protest against the planned development.[43] This carefully orchestrated campaign had its effect, and the views of the Parks Branch carried the day with the minister on this occasion. In the fall of 1922, Charles Stewart announced that for the time being, no new concessions would be granted for power development inside the national parks and rejected Calgary Power's application to raise the Lake Minnewanka dam.[44]

An unvarnished episode of bureaucratic hypocrisy then ensued. To celebrate the victory in the combat with the company and its allies among the waterpower engineers in the Department of the Interior, the Parks Branch immediately announced plans to build its own 1,000 hp station on the Cascade River, since the CPR was going to close down its thermal generating station at Bankhead, which supplied the Banff townsite.[45] Not surprisingly, this proposal angered both Calgary Power and its backers in the Water Power Branch: it seemed simply to demonstrate the contradictions in the attitudes of Harkin and his staff toward development within the park system. What was forbidden to private entrepreneurs would be permitted to the Parks Branch itself.

Harkin's response to that kind of argument, of course, was that he and his men could be relied upon to protect the scenic beauty of the landscape as profit-oriented developers could not. The commissioner told company president V. M. Drury that "the established attitude of this branch is that the natural resources contained in the National Parks are more valuable in their natural state and attractiveness than they would be if developed for commercial usage." Calgary Power, by contrast, was "an ordinary commercial institution, and its aim is no doubt commercial not philanthropical. It is concerned in the wants of Calgary and district only insofar as it sees revenue for itself. It is looking for the cheapest development it can find."[46] The town of Banff required power, and the CPR was no longer prepared to supply it. In Harkin's view, the only alternative to a small and discreet powerhouse inside the park was a transmission line running westward up the Bow valley from the Calgary Power Company's plant at Kananaskis. With the support of the Water Power Branch,[47] the company, anxious to avert the construction of a small plant at Lake Minnewanka that might impede its plans for future development, offered to supply power from Kananaskis; the idea was rejected by the Parks Branch because the transmission line would be "very objectionable from a scenic standpoint." Moreover, it was noted that Calgary Power already had perennial difficulties meeting its contractual obligations to deliver current to Calgary during the winter. Most importantly,

> ... the Department has decided against the granting of power development concessions within the National Parks. In view of this stand the purchase of power from the Calgary Power Company would place the Department in an invidious position. The inevitable power shortage in Banff would be used by the Calgary Power Company as a means of exerting pressure towards obtaining further power concessions in the Park. As the power needs of Banff increased the Department would eventually either have to allow further power development within the Park by the Calgary Power Company or other private companies – in order to meet its own requirements – or build its own plant as is being done at the present time.[48]

Having won its battle in the bureaucratic infighting, the Parks Branch persuaded Charles Stewart to include in the Interior Department estimates for 1923 a vote of $200,000 to cover the cost of its new plant. Calgary Power lobbied as hard as it could to avert this, recruiting Liberal MP Walter Mitchell to put the case for the Minnewanka dam before the interior minister once more. On Mitchell's advice, the company did not seek

POWER STATION BUILT BY THE PARKS BRANCH AT LAKE MINNEWANKA (GLENBOW ARCHIVES, NA-841-396).

to arouse public opinion in Calgary about the possibility of power shortages but relied upon pressure behind the scenes.[49]

This procured the company one final hearing from Interior Department officials in the spring of 1923, followed up by a further plea to the interior minister from the company president. Noting that Stewart possessed "complete and almost dictatorial power" to approve or disapprove its application, V. M. Drury argued that rising power demand in southern Alberta would render the ultimate development of more power from the waters of Lake Minnewanka "inevitable." Calgary Power, he claimed, was earning only a small profit, and if the company was to develop more power and reduce its rates, it had to be permitted to add to its capacity at the lowest possible cost. The higher dam would actually improve the scenery at the lake by concealing the low-lying shoreline at the bottom end. Drury tried to put the best face on matters by claiming that even when the reservoir was at low ebb, the vast expanse of mudflats along the shoreline would simply "resemble a bold seacoast at low tide."[50]

This kind of persiflage no longer carried any weight with the Parks Branch: "It is quite true that power engineers seem incapable of recognizing [that] the filthy mudflats and bare shores without a vestige of timber or flower growth destroy scenery. But the average person who has seen what the small dam at Lake Minnewanka has done will … hold a different view."[51] Stewart's visit to Banff had evidently been sufficient to convince him, and he stood by his refusal to permit the raising of the dam at Lake Minnewanka. Decisive victory seemed to have gone to the Parks Branch in this round of bureaucratic infighting. The deputy minister was even persuaded to order the Water Power Branch to cease all exploratory work within the national park system in light of the minister's decision to ban all further hydraulic development there.[52]

The rejection of Calgary Power's application to enlarge its dam at Lake Minnewanka was, of course, by no means the end of the contest between park bureaucrats and power developers. Calgary Power still faced a pressing need to procure larger supplies of water in winter, and Rocky Mountains National Park remained the only feasible location for storage reservoirs in southern Alberta. As the chief engineer of the Water Power Branch noted, "The portions of the Rocky Mountain slope outside Park boundaries … are very remote and inaccessible and do not possess known power resources of sufficient magnitude to meet the needs of Calgary or adjacent markets."[53]

In the decade following the construction of the Lake Minnewanka storage reservoir, policy within Parks circles had shifted, or hardened, in our terminology. Some aspects of the formerly accommodating policy of social and economic usefulness had, in the light of experience, come into disrepute, to be replaced by a policy placing state protection of natural beauty as the highest priority. Still, this remained an ambiguous and, in some cases, hypocritical policy: it permitted zoos, tourist facilities, roads, Wild West shows, but not private power facilities. Furthermore, while the commissioner of parks and his staff might be opposed to commercial hydroelectric development within the national park system, that did not rule out development by the park authorities themselves.

Meanwhile, during its first full decade of operation, Calgary Power had managed to claw its way toward financial respectability. With more water in winter and new sales contracts with the City of Calgary and major power-using industries (mainly cement and milling), the company reported brighter financial results. These need to be taken with a grain of salt, however. The figures for gross income and net income are probably quite reliable, but the other numbers, especially the figure representing net surplus (profit), depend as much on accounting legerdemain as on performance. Nevertheless, the numbers support the view that the company became more profitable over time. Between 1912 and 1922, net income as a percentage of gross income rose from around 75 per cent to 82 per cent. Strict control over operating expenses left large sums of money available to pay interest on the debt, allow for generous depreciation charges, and reinvest in the property. The company's gross income, net income, and surplus rose over 150 per cent during the period. In the mid-1920s, the reported surplus surpassed 2 per cent of the book value of its assets. These better financial results, in turn, made it easier for the company to attract capital and to raise money at cheaper rates for expansion and renewals. Over time, the company's bonds and stock began to resemble the investment grade securities much sought after by insurance companies and other financial institutions. It might be said that in the 1920s, Calgary Power, its reputation redeemed, had become a fully paid-up member of the Canadian utilities club, which consisted of more than a dozen large operating companies in Canada and Latin America centred in Toronto and Montreal. The assumption of the presidency in 1928 by the now eminently respectable former protege of Max Aitken, Isaac Walton Killam, symbolically signalled the arrival of the company. No longer a frail supplicant, Calgary Power had grown into a powerful corporation in its own right, and with even more powerful friends holding its securities in the Canadian financial establishment.

In the process, the company established quite a different relationship with its local electricity market as well. After a renewal of its contract

with the City of Calgary in 1918, the company in effect took over supplying the baseload of the municipal utility. The city's Victoria Park steam
plant, which produced electricity at much higher cost, reverted to standby
and peak power duty. By the 1920s, Calgary Power had become deeply
entwined with the economic life of the region. As Calgary became more
heavily invested in the Bow River – through the company – for its electricity, Calgary Power's energy requirements became surrogate for the needs
of the entire region. Calgary Power thus spoke no longer just for itself but
with the implicit authority of the City of Calgary and thousands of electricity consumers. As such, the needs of the Calgary Power Company and its
customers could not be cavalierly or permanently dismissed.

Renewal of the application for development rights in Rocky Mountains
National Park was thus inevitable by 1923. The opposing forces – a bureaucracy with a more ideological notion of its mission and a company better
established in financial markets and in the region – girded their loins for
the next round in the contest of strength between them.

CHAPTER 5

Selling Scenery

Blocked in its efforts first to raise its dam at Lake Minnewanka and then to construct a large new power plant at Anthracite on the Bow River in 1922, Calgary Power nevertheless refused to drop the idea of constructing reservoirs in Rocky Mountains National Park. For its own financial well-being, the company simply had to make all the expensive generating equipment that it had already installed in its powerhouses at Horseshoe Falls and Kananaskis more efficient to meet steadily growing power demand in Alberta and to stave off possible competition. Indeed, with additional power, Calgary Power hoped to expand its service territory north to include Edmonton.

The provincial government found itself under increasing pressure to play some role in power development: two possible choices were to set up an integrated utility modelled upon the Ontario Hydro-Electric Commission, linking Edmonton, Calgary, and the smaller centres, or to opt for a more modest role as the holder of development licences, which the province could hand over to private interests. Either scenario would permit the provincial government to exercise control over rates and open the way for rural electrification in the long run. Seen from Calgary Power's perspective, the provincial government could either emerge as a competitor or, under certain circumstances, be recruited as an ally. With so much at stake, the battle pitting power development against wilderness preservation intensified after 1923.

Even before the interior minister had finally rejected Calgary Power's application to raise its dam at Lake Minnewanka, an alternative proposal surfaced that quickly sparked intense controversy. High up in Rocky Mountains National Park, east of Banff, lay the Spray Lakes, whose outlet, the Spray River, tumbled through the golf course at the Banff Springs Hotel before joining the Bow River just below Bow Falls. The company now proposed to turn the Spray Lakes into a huge reservoir linked by a tunnel to a new high-head power plant to be built on the Bow River near Canmore, east of Banff. That proposal sparked an outcry from mountaineering and conservation groups across the country. By mid-1923, this protest had coalesced into the Canadian National Parks Association, the first national lobby to decry the spoliation of wilderness preserves. The controversy generated an extra-parliamentary interest group desperately needed by the embattled Parks Branch bureaucrats.

As the debate over the fate of the Spray Lakes dragged on through the 1920s, the federal minister of the interior, Charles Stewart, found himself beset by angry power consumers in Calgary, ambitious provincial politicians in Edmonton, unhappy power company executives in Montreal, and angry nature lovers all across the country. The decision-making process was marked by the continuation of bureaucratic infighting inside the Interior Department between the Water Power Branch and the Parks Branch, two divisions that continued to hold strongly opposed positions on the question of power development inside the national park system.

When Calgary Power had first encountered water supply problems before World War I, it had commissioned studies that looked, among other things, at the possibility of developing the Spray watershed. The Spray River made the eight-hundred-foot descent from its headwaters to its mouth at a steady rate of about thirty feet per mile without any abrupt falls that would render hydraulic development easier, but the company concluded that as a reservoir, the Spray Lakes would be more expensive than Lake Minnewanka.[1] By 1920, however, Calgary Power's chief engineer, G. A. Gaherty, had begun to consider the more audacious possibility of damming up the Spray River, creating a much larger Spray Lake and then redirecting its flow through a tunnel over a cliff face to a pair of power plants in the Bow valley at Canmore, where the working head would be approximately eleven hundred feet. A relatively small flow could thus generate quite large amounts of power, and the set-up would be immune to problems created by the winter freeze-up. Yet the size and complexity of this development meant that for the time being, the alternative Cascade plant at Anthracite was more economically attractive.[2]

However, after the minister of the interior rejected the company's plans for a higher dam at Lake Minnewanka, interest in the Spray Lakes intensified. This would be the first major project for Geoffrey Gaherty, a thirty-three-year-old former artillery officer and now an engineer with Calgary Power's consultants, the Montreal Engineering Company; Gaherty would go on to have a long and distinguished career as an engineer, director, and ultimately president of both companies.

Geoffrey Abbott Gaherty ascended to the upper echelons of Canadian business and finance the old-fashioned way, through family connections. But for the fortuitous remarriage of his widowed mother, his career would certainly have taken a different course. He was born in 1889 to William Gaherty and Helen "Nellie" Bell in the small – now vanished – town of Dickinson's Landing on the St. Lawrence River west of Cornwall. After her husband's sudden death, Helen returned with her young son, Geoffrey, to her home in Almonte, Ontario, just outside of Ottawa. She probably met John F. Stairs through the matchmaking skills of a family friend – Conservative MP Bennett Rosamond, owner of Almonte Knitting Company in nearby Carleton Place. Stairs, a prominent Conservative and member of Parliament from Halifax and one of that city's "merchant princes," was the single father of seven children, having lost his wife nine years earlier. After a brief courtship, the two married in 1895. Stairs, Helen, and her son moved to Halifax following his retirement from federal politics that same year, and Helen took command of a large blended family and a stately home at 170 South Street. In 1902, their only child together, Margaret Rosamond, was born.

Back home in Nova Scotia, John F. Stairs embarked upon a disastrous career as leader of the provincial Conservative Party, but he also resumed his very successful business career as a merchant, banker, industrialist, and company promoter. It was at this time that Stairs took Max Aitken on as a trainee. With Isaac Walton Killam and A. J. Nesbitt also on the team, Stairs's Royal Securities Company peddled the stocks and bonds generated by Stairs's far-flung enterprises. In 1904, Stairs died suddenly at age fifty-seven while working on a bank merger deal in Toronto with Max Aitken at his side. His will generously provided for his widow, their daughter, his children by his first marriage, and his stepson. By the time he was a teenager, Geoffrey Gaherty was, through inheritance, effectively fixed for life. Nevertheless, Protestant ethics and bourgeois values drove him to make for himself a productive career. Having grown up in a house surrounded by talk of iron and steel industries, ships, railroads, electric utilities, and street railroads, Geoffrey chose engineering.

From private school in Halifax, Geoffrey was sent to Upper Canada College in Toronto. He returned to Halifax to study engineering at Dalhousie, where he resumed his friendship with his cousin by marriage, Denis Stairs. After graduating in 1909, these two long-time friends descended upon Max Aitken in Montreal looking for a job. Max, no doubt out of a sense of obligation to the Stairs family but also because of a desire to get them as far out of harm's way as possible, sent them to work on his Western Canada Power Corporation Stave Falls project in British Columbia. After gaining some experience with real work in hydroelectric construction, the two musketeers embarked in 1912 on what all young men with money in the Edwardian era desired: European travel. As legend has it, the two mates booked their return passage on the Titanic, but, lured to stay on by the attractions of London, they cancelled at the last minute.

When they returned, Royal Securities took care of them once again on the Western Canada Power project. When war was declared, Gaherty and Denis Stairs promptly enlisted. Gaherty served four years as an artillery officer, mainly in France, and returned physically intact. Stairs, serving in another unit, also survived but lost an arm. After the war, following a brief stint in the silver mines of Cobalt, Gaherty and Stairs once again sought out their friends at Royal Securities. Killam, a former employee of John F. Stairs and now in full command of the former family business and with numerous expansion prospects on the horizon, hired them both for the Montreal Engineering Company. Among his other tasks, Gaherty was given responsibility for improving the output and profitability of Calgary

Power. He was subsequently placed in charge of the reconnaissance, planning, design, and engineering of new storage, diversion, and generating works on the upper Bow River and was also responsible for seeking the necessary regulatory approvals. It would be a project that would occupy him for the next thirty or more years, with limited success for most of that period.[3]

The Spray Lakes diversion plan was intended to address Calgary Power's immediate and long-term corporate needs. Not only would the company be able to meet all of Calgary's normal peak needs, but the plan would also allow it to extend its transmission lines both northward to Edmonton and southward to Lethbridge. Most important was the fact that the new installation would also remedy the serious defects that had plagued the Horseshoe and Kananaskis stations from the outset. A "scientific combination" of the new high-head plant would supply the baseload in winter with the older run-of-the-river generators, which could be reversed in summer when the flow of the Bow swelled.[4] Although costly, the high-head plants at Canmore could greatly increase total output and help overcome the problems of lack of water downstream in the Bow. Gaherty frankly admitted that if accurate streamflow figures had been available in 1909, the run-of-the-river plants "would never have been constructed," but he contended that "it is only by the scientific combination of these two types [of power plant] that the maximum yield of power can be obtained from the water available."[5]

Calgary Power would have preferred to pursue the simpler and cheaper plan of developing the plant at Anthracite, using water stored at Lake Minnewanka, but with that possibility off the table, the company turned to the Spray Lakes development with enthusiasm, and it became Gaherty's pet project. The company knew that the plan would create controversy and encounter strong opposition from the Parks Branch. After Charles Stewart's announcement in the fall of 1922 that he would not approve the raising of the Minnewanka dam or the granting of any further power privileges inside the park system for the time being, Deputy Minister W. W. Cory privately told Gaherty in December that "in his opinion there was not the slightest chance of an application for power in the Spray basin being accepted."[6]

But the company refused to give up hope, pursuing its feasibility studies despite the opposition of the Parks Branch, which hastened to put on record its objections to a project that seemed objectionable in every way. First of all, there would be the flooding of nearly twenty-five hundred acres, which would prevent fish from spawning and drive away wildlife. The Spray valley was one of the prettiest near Banff, and turning the lakes into a reservoir would destroy them irrevocably. The economic arguments that had proven so persuasive in the fight over Lake Minnewanka were trotted out again. Pristine mountain scenery was a highly valuable commodity. In 1921, the national park system had earned Canada $18 million in United States currency. Ruining this natural beauty would destroy the appeal of the parks to American tourists.[7]

Parks Commissioner Harkin was particularly annoyed in the spring of 1923 when Calgary Power asked that the minister of the interior make no final, definitive ruling on raising the Lake Minnewanka dam until the cost of the Spray Lakes project had been established:

> The whole aim appears to be to get the department to mix up the Spray and the Minnewanka schemes and to have them considered together, not independently. In other words, the aim appears to be to get the department more or less committed to the idea that the company is entitled to further consideration in its Minnewanka application.[8]

Despite this opposition, the company persevered with its explorations of the Spray basin. Short of power in the winter and facing the need to renegotiate its power supply contract with the City of Calgary, the company felt that it had to have more water storage. By the spring of 1923, a proposal was ready to spend $6 million on a dam, tunnel, and power plant at the Spray Lakes, which would produce 16,000 hp initially and permit the generators lower down the Bow to turn out an additional 20,000 hp. With that reserve of power in hand, the company was prepared to offer to build trunk lines to supply Edmonton and the other cities in the northern part of the province as well. Ultimately, the development could be expanded to turn out over 250,000 hp in total, which could be expected to meet Alberta's needs for the next fifty years. The steam plants in both major cities could thus be dismantled, resulting in annual savings for consumers of $7 million, while industry would receive a major incentive to locate in the province, which, in turn, would greatly benefit the agricultural sector.

After studying the proposal, the Water Power Branch of the Department of the Interior reported upon it in highly favourable terms.[9] Chief engineer J. T. Johnston argued that since opportunities for water-power development in southern Alberta were very limited and so much of the eastern slopes of the Rockies was inside the national park system, it was "*inevitable*" that reservoirs would be constructed in the parks. The combination of high-head and low-head power stations proposed by Calgary Power was the solution to the power problems that had long plagued the region: "a balanced system ... offers that *only* basis which will provide for an adequate supply of economic hydro-electric power and ... *the key lies in the Rocky Mountains Park*." At stake, Johnston argued, was "*the right of the power consuming public in the Calgary district* to secure an ample supply of cheap hydro-electric energy if such is available." This de-velopment would place the city "on a plane" with other industrial centres in Canada where such low-cost energy was provided. Johnston contended that the discussion should not be wrongly allowed to resolve itself into an issue of Parks Branch interests versus Water Power Branch interests: "There is no such issue. The two interests are in no wise contradictory or in opposition to each other, but on the other hand may be considered as *complementary*." Recent debates in the United States had led to the ban-ning of hydraulic development within the national park system there, but Canadians should not be swayed by "the extreme result of carefully en-gineered and hysterical propaganda which represents the power interests as grasping monopolists determined to destroy the nation's beauty spots to serve the ends of private greed." In Canada, waterpower administra-tion was "*many years in advance*" of American expertise and could easily harmonize the competing interests. He urged that Canadians look instead to countries like Switzerland, where a *modus vivendi* had evolved.

Johnston was careful to refute each of the major arguments that he knew were certain to be raised by his bureaucratic rivals in the Parks Branch. National parks could never remain pristine wilderness: roads, bridges, sewers, and pole lines were essential. The Parks Branch itself was constructing a power plant near Banff: that constituted acceptance of the fact that dams and generating stations, if properly designed, could be "*features of added beauty and interest*" in a park. He rejected claims that visitors would go elsewhere:

> It is doubtful whether the development of water power in the Park would influence the route of a single tourist. The number so influenced would certainly be infinitely small – witness Niagara Falls, and Lakes Como, Garda and Maggiore in northern Italy – while the rights of the surrounding districts to their local natural resources should be considered in the balance.

Clearly, the power company had powerful friends at court, and their influence was quickly reinforced when Calgary's mayor and Board of Trade weighed in on the same side.[10] Company officials were given a full hearing by the minister of the interior. President V. M. Drury urged Stewart to issue the development licence immediately or else work would not be able to start for another year, and Calgary would be forced to start expanding its thermal generating station in order to avert a power shortage during the coming winter.[11]

Even if Charles Stewart had been disposed to move so swiftly, the whole matter was complicated by the fact that the Government of Alberta now began to express an interest in gaining control of the proposed power development. In mid-April 1923, the provincial legislature passed a resolution demanding that any development at Spray Lakes be controlled by Alberta. Premier Herbert Greenfield pointed out that as negotiations were already underway concerning the handing over of all Crown lands and resources to the province by Ottawa, it would not be appropriate for such a valuable grant to be awarded without his government's consent. Stewart, however, responded that these resources lay inside a national park and thus would remain under federal control in perpetuity.[12]

There the matter rested for the moment, but in early June, Calgary mayor George Webster met with the premier about future power planning. Webster pointed out that thermal power was six times as expensive as hydroelectricity (3 cents vs. 0.5 cents per kwh) and urged Greenfield to establish a provincial commission to oversee new development. In late August, Greenfield filed a formal application with the Department of the Interior for permission to develop the Spray Lakes.[13] Only in December, however, did the premier request the chair of the Ontario Hydro-Electric Power Commission to lend its chief engineer, Fred Gaby, to study the power situation in Alberta and suggest how future needs might be met.[14] Clearly, the United Farmers of Alberta government still had doubts as to how popular increased state activity in this sector would be with their rural, agricultural constituency.

By December, the development of the Spray Lakes had become the centre of a heated public debate that ultimately led to the creation of a national lobby group to defend the integrity of the national park system against encroachment and commercial development. When the news of Calgary Power's application became public in the spring of 1923, organizations like the Alpine Club of Canada quickly expressed concern. The chair of the Calgary branch was among the first to register a strong protest with the minister of the interior against using the Spray Lakes as a power reservoir: "'[H]ands off our national parks,' we say."[15]

Some of this public outrage was being quietly orchestrated by the parks commissioner and his staff.[16] While Harkin admitted that in this bureaucratic infighting, he ought not to "go outside and seek support for our side of the question," he told the president of the Calgary Automobile Club that he did feel it was proper for him to explain "the true significance of power applications of this kind with respect to the future of National Parks." Thanking the club for its support of the Parks Branch, Harkin set forth the reasons for opposing the conversion of the Spray Lakes into a power reservoir; in the process, he neatly summed up the ambiguities and contradictions in the attitudes of the Parks Branch toward commercial development inside the national park system:

> One of the most important aspects of the National Parks is the selling, or as we put it here, the exporting of scenery. Both the American Parks and the Canadian Parks seek business in the same market, namely the United States. The American Congress has tied up their National Parks system by legislation so that it is absolutely assured against any commercial invasion.… As we look to the American market for the bulk of our scenery selling business, it is obvious that unless we are prepared to sell them scenery which they look upon as ideal scenery, our sales cannot amount to very much.

Damming the Spray Lakes would ruin the appearance of the valley just as had happened with Lake Minnewanka.

Harkin challenged the economic justification for any power development in Rocky Mountains National Park:

> Quite apart from the other considerations we, in the Parks Service, are convinced that on purely commercial grounds the preservation of the integrity of the Banff Park will pay the city of Calgary and the Dominion of Canada much greater dividends than will ever be paid by the power scheme.

Oblivious to the irony, he added that the Spray Lakes lay on the route to Mount Assiniboine, along which the Parks Branch hoped to construct a motor road: "Once we get foreign tourists in our parks, our object is to make them prolong their stay, and the eventual opening up of a scenic highway by the Spray … will no doubt contribute very strongly in that connection." Harkin added a warning that any power concession would be a dangerous precedent that would ultimately permit lumbermen and miners to gain a foothold:

J. B. HARKIN, LONG-TIME
DIRECTOR OF THE PARKS BRANCH,
DEPARTMENT OF THE INTERIOR
(LAC E010951726_s1).

The Parks Service strongly opposes any form of commercial invasion of the National Parks. It feels that if a precedent like the Spray scheme is ever established it would be impossible to prevent the gradual disintegration of the Parks.... Certainly it would appear to be poor business to spend millions of dollars providing highways and other facilities for the tourists, if we are to destroy the value of such investments by ruining our scenery.

Harkin's argument found a receptive audience. Clubs, societies, and newspaper editors hastened to express their opposition to the Spray Lakes scheme to the federal government.[17] The executive director of the Alpine Club of Canada, Arthur O. Wheeler, reiterated the criticisms by the commissioner of parks concerning "commercial invasion" of the national parks:

> The Spray project is one particular case.... There will be assuredly in the course of time hundreds of other cases of varying types, all of which will have the same general grounds for argument as this particular one, and if not checked the ultimate result will be ruination to the National Parks of Canada.... There is no doubt in my mind that our National Recreation Parks are the best paying proposition that we have, and I sincerely hope they may be held inviolate as such.[18]

We cannot let the introduction of Arthur O. Wheeler into our story pass without a brief digression into his intimate, extensive, and conflicted relationship with the Parks Branch. The interruption in the narrative will, we hope, be more than compensated by Wheeler's astonishing chutzpah. The son of an aristocratic Irish immigrant in reduced circumstances whose position of harbourmaster in Collingwood was distinctly beneath him, Arthur Wheeler inherited his father's sense of entitlement and abrasive, imperious manners. As a surveyor for the Department of the Interior in the 1880s and 1890s, Wheeler laid out Indian Reserves and townsites, and surveyed the Selkirk Mountains using new photographic techniques. As a surveyor hauling his equipment over rough terrain, he developed an abiding love of the West, and of mountains in particular. As he rose in the bureaucracy, he would have been in line for the commissionership of the new Parks Branch, but he left the federal service in 1910 for a private consulting career and became executive director of the recently formed Alpine Club of Canada. Wheeler, an older, more experienced western hand, thus maintained a somewhat paternalistic, even patronizing attitude toward his junior, J. B. Harkin. And far from being in awe of government, he believed that he and the Alpine Club provided the Parks Branch with a reason for being.

It was in that spirit that Wheeler began what would become a long-standing relationship with the Parks Branch that focused on increasing utilization of Rocky Mountains National Park through a private business venture. Wheeler, reacting against the high cost of visiting Banff, proposed to organize inexpensive walking tours out of Banff to attract a new and more numerous clientele to the park. Wheeler's populism struck a chord with Parks officials, who readily agreed to accommodate and provide some financial support for this new form of tourism.

Wheeler first organized some walking tours as an experiment in 1920. Heading from Banff up the trail to the Spray Lakes, the walkers would skirt around the base of Mount Assiniboine and then go northwest along the Continental Divide to Healy Creek and back down to the townsite. A train of pack ponies was laid on to carry visitors' baggage. The Parks Branch gave enthusiastic support, clearing backcountry campgrounds and donating equipment, such as cots, worth $6,750. These outings attracted enough interest that the following spring, Wheeler spent $600 on producing a flyer entitled "Banff to Mt. Assiniboine, The Matterhorn of the Canadian Rockies via Spray Lakes Route," announcing walks departing twice a week

A. O. Wheeler, Alpine Club of Canada (Glenbow Archives, NA-4539-4).

from July through September. He persuaded the CPR to distribute ten thousand copies and to put a notice in their publicity bulletin, "Resorts in the Rockies," telling Harkin that for the railway, "it is evidently considered good business." Though Wheeler attempted to fudge the matter by heading his promotional stationary with "A Public Walking and Riding Tour, under the Patronage of the Alpine Club of Canada, Banff, Alberta," this operation was, in fact, a personal business venture from which he aimed to profit in his retirement. In order to keep going, in 1921 Wheeler sought $3,000 from officials to produce more leaflets and to improve the camps for the walkers. Even his friend Harkin found this a bit excessive, though he agreed to put up $600 (eventually raised to $900) for the improvement of the camps in the backcountry although he refused to fund either the advertising or improvements to the jumping-off point at Middle Springs.[19]

The scheme generated a good deal of favourable publicity; the *Calgary Daily Herald* described the scenic walks as a "magic spell" for people needing relief for jangled nerves created by their daily grind. Wheeler passed up no opportunity to play the populist card by condemning big interests like the CPR, and even the local outfitters, for jacking up prices and putting off ordinary people who wanted to enjoy the wonders of the mountains at economical rates. He complained to Harkin that Park Superintendent R. S. Stronach had no interest in "mountain people" and wanted to cater to the well-off rather than to every class of person. In his appeals for financial support, Wheeler emphasized that he was putting in all this work only out of a sense of duty and would quit if he could not make a go of it. By the end of the 1921 season, though, he was ready to pronounce the walks a definite success, since 250 people had participated over the past two years and word-of-mouth advertising was sure to bring in more paying customers in future.[20]

Eventually, however, the self-righteous Wheeler overreached himself and undercut his relations with officials. He allowed some "walkers" to ride on saddle ponies for four dollars extra per day. Before long the licensed outfitters began complaining about the government-subsidized competition for riders on the trails up to Mount Assiniboine. In the fall of 1921, Harkin had to tell Wheeler that he must stop offering saddle ponies if he wanted continued assistance for his walking tours. Serving the tourists was, after all, a business enterprise. Wheeler decided to pull out all the stops in an effort to protect his advantage: he organized prominent members of the Alpine Club of Canada to write to the federal minister of the interior endorsing his operation. On the first day of 1922, he followed up with a printed circular sent to all Alpine Club members denouncing the "transitory mountain outfitters" for challenging the club's work of "opening up" the Rocky Mountains. Claiming that the club represented the "large majority" of people interested in the little-known areas of the mountains, Wheeler called for an attack upon the "obstructionists" who only served the wealthy and ignored those who desired "access to primitive nature in the Great Hills of Canada for our revitalization and who do not desire artificial moonlight." The predictable result was a flood of letters to Ottawa from across Canada and the United States, obediently parroting Wheeler's line.[21]

Feeling bruised, officials complained to one another about this "vigorous propaganda," noting that despite all their generous assistance for the walking tours, only about two hundred people had ever taken them. The outfitters, who had their own influence, demanded a meeting with park officials in Banff. After that meeting, Wheeler was told that he could not expect a subsidy if he continued to offer mounted side trips for the walkers to places like Mount Assiniboine using his pack train as saddle ponies. He still tried to persuade officials to allow him to offer the side trips, provided that other outfitters offered them for the same price, but they realized that launching the riding tours from the subsidized camps would only generate continued criticism from important interests like the Brewster brothers. The quarrel presented Wheeler with abundant opportunities to expend his ample reserves of indignation, anger, and petulance toward any and all comers. Eventually, a compromise was worked out that permitted Wheeler to offer only one-day side trips, leaving longer saddle tours to the outfitters. On this understanding, the sorely tried bureaucrats agreed to grant him another $800, and the relationship assumed a more amicable tone.[22]

By 1923, Wheeler seems to have expected his subsidy more or less as a matter of right. He claimed that he was only breaking even on the walking tours and asked Harkin for another year's grant. The parks commissioner replied that he needed a formal application and report; Wheeler complied and again received $800. At the end of that year, the Calgary Power Company applied to dam the upper Spray River inside the national park and submerge the Spray Lakes. Wheeler helped organize strong opposition; he issued a veiled threat to tell prospective American walkers that he had discontinued the tours owing to the plan, warning that flooding the valley would "create a strong feeling of dissatisfaction in American centres where conservation of parks in their entirety is a vital question and one that has the full support of the public." He agreed, however, to continue the tours when Harkin offered a $1,000 subsidy for 1924.[23] Wheeler's walks and the subsidies would continue into the 1930s, when financial stringency finally brought an end to the relationship.

In mobilizing the Alpine Club behind the Parks Branch in its struggle against the Calgary Power Company, Wheeler occupied a somewhat anomalous position, to say the least. First and foremost, he *was* the Alpine Club, as he was happy to remind anyone, particularly when he was angry. Friends and opponents alike recognized that he regarded the club as personal property, a convenient cover for his personal interests. Second, he was a paid client of the Parks Branch, carrying out its work for a fee. Third, he was a private businessman enjoying his hobby on public land and profiting from it. Finally, he was simultaneously a fierce advocate of the "sanctity" of public parks and a part of the "commercial invasion" of the parks, though he did not, of course, see it that way. An uncharitable view of the matter would conclude that the Alpine Club of Canada's support of Harkin's Parks Branch in the Spray Lakes affair had been bought and paid for.

With that background information on the relationship between the Parks Branch and the formidable A. O. Wheeler, we return now to the Spray Lakes story. In the summer of 1923, a group of conservationists gathered at the Alpine Club's campground at Larch Lake, Alberta. Harkin was present and repeated his familiar argument:

From a straight commercial standpoint our parks are one of our most important resources.... I am referring to money brought into Canada from foreign countries by tourists.... There can be no doubt that the revenue the National Parks brought into Canada in 1921 was at least $15,000,000. That same year we spent $850,00[0]. That is ... we brought into Canada eighteen times the amount of money we spent on National Parks.... I emphasize the commercial side because I find that the general public persists in the idea that National Parks are simply frills and luxuries. Nevertheless, on the basis of cold-blooded commercialism I don't think there is an institution that pays as big a dividend as the Canadian National Parks.

A unanimous resolution was then passed forming a new Canadian National Parks Association and condemning any further alienation of natural resources lying inside the park system without a vote of Parliament.[24]

One member of the executive of the new association explained to the minister of the interior that the application to dam the Spray Lakes had brought about "a crystallization of public opinion generally throughout Canada against the franchise." Fears were expressed that the government had reversed its policy regarding parks "to conserve these areas from the national standpoint and for national purposes." While such a lobby would probably have been set up before long in any event, the move, according to A. S. Sibbald, a charter member of the new organization,

... was probably hurried forward at the present time by the question growing out of the proposal to develop power in the Spray Lakes basin ... and undoubtedly marks the reaction of the general Canadian public to the attempt involved to develop power within the Parks and incidentally to establish a precedent which would make it more difficult to refuse later franchises of that kind.[25]

The executive of the new association then started a campaign to put pressure on the interior minister and letters poured in from across the country.[26] During the next two and a half years, he received protests from hundreds of individuals and numerous organizations denouncing the Spray Lakes power project.[27] Among the most vocal and persistent of these lobbyists was Major Selby Walker, son of Calgary's founder, Colonel James Walker, and a sparkplug of the new Canadian National Parks Association. Walker, as imperious and self-important as Arthur O. Wheeler, whom he replaced at the head of the movement, favoured theatrical, sensationalist public relations tactics.[28] He hit upon several ingenious ideas to arouse Alberta opinion against the idea of damming the Spray Lakes. First, he suggested spreading a rumour in Banff that the rock footings of the dam would be unsound, creating the danger of a sudden collapse followed by a tidal wave down the Spray valley that would inundate the town. Later, he got in touch with the secretary of the Western Canada Coal Operators Association to see if the association would be interested in joining in the agitation in the hope of promoting the construction of more thermal generating stations.[29]

Rather surprisingly, this latter approach bore fruit. At first the coal operators simply responded that they did not know what to think about the Spray Lakes project itself, but they did oppose the provincial government "committing itself to an expensive hydro-electric system without at first investigating the possibilities of steam electric plants." Sensing an opportunity, Walker hastened to point out that approving one encroachment on the national park system would almost certainly lead to other applications, since "it is extremely difficult if not impossible to pick and choose between the different projected encroachments of water power interests within our parks."[30] In the spring of 1924, Walker put the common interests of conservationists and coalmen to them as plainly as possible:

> The National Parks Association desire[s], of course, to preserve the parks from commercial encroachment; your association desire[s] to mine as much coal as possible. The Spray Lakes concession, if granted, will, according to the Power Company's figures, save the

annual consumption of 2,000,000 tons of coal; and Alberta is not Ontario where coal must be imported.

That argument rang the bell. The Coal Operators duly registered their opposition to Calgary Power's plans (thus placing themselves in the somewhat unlikely company of the Toronto Field Naturalists Club).[31]

William Pearce, however, arguably one of the founders of Rocky Mountains National Park, raised his voice in favour of the Spray Lakes development. For him, the water requirements of prairie irrigation trumped other considerations. A torrent of letters poured out of his office, much to the embarrassment of his employer, the CPR, insisting that upstream storage would irrigate twice the amount of land presently under cultivation and would control flooding.[32] As for the scenic blight occasioned by reservoir drawdowns, he proposed clearing and laying down a gravel apron along the shoreline. But his was a weak and failing voice from the past, and it had little effect.

By 1923, the battle lines over the damming of the Spray Lakes had been firmly drawn. Ranged on one side were the Parks Branch of the Department of the Interior with the vocal alliance of conservationists in the Canadian National Parks Association. On the other stood the Calgary Power Company and the municipal government, which had recently signed another five-year agreement to take more power from the private utility.[33] Meanwhile, the provincial government hovered in the wings, increasingly interested in securing control of any further power development, either to provide the basis for a provincially owned utility or to give the province a firm regulatory hold over the electric industry.

Minister of the Interior Charles Stewart advised Premier Herbert Greenfield in December 1923 that Calgary Power had begun a forceful campaign to persuade him to grant their application.[34] When the question arose in the House of Commons in the spring of 1924, the minister seemed sympathetic to the company. He admitted that there was "no doubt" that additional power would eventually be needed. As for the route through the Spray valley, it was "not one of the most scenic" in the area although the higher terrain around Mount Assiniboine was very beautiful. As for the application to build a reservoir, he thought it might be possible to do it without marring the scenery "to any considerable degree." But, insisted Stewart, he knew how much the Parks Branch opposed the idea, so he was keeping "a perfectly open mind about it." That declaration brought Vancouver Conservative H. H. Stevens to his feet. Stevens was a fervent defender of the principle of maintaining the national parks against outside pressures. Would the minister, he asked, promise to do nothing to grant the application for one more year. Stewart, happy to let matters rest because of the noisy conservationists who were hounding him, eagerly agreed to this: "I am not in a hurry to deal with this particular question," he admitted.[35]

Stewart made it plain that if permission to dam the Spray Lakes were to be granted, the provincial government would have first refusal. Calgary Power, therefore, concentrated on persuading Premier Greenfield to press his application seriously on the understanding that Alberta's rights, once obtained, would be turned over to the company. President V. M. Drury wrote to the premier, who was visiting Ottawa, to suggest that he come down to Montreal for a game of golf.[36] But it soon became clear that the United Farmers of Alberta government was not yet ready to make up its mind about whether to proceed with a provincial scheme, at least until it received the report by the engineers from Ontario Hydro.

Despite Stewart's public commitment to delay the decision for at least a year, City of Calgary officials kept up the pressure in the hope that they would not have to operate their expensive thermal generating plant during the coming winter. But Stewart would not budge. All that he was prepared to do during 1924 was to formally reiterate his promise that the provincial government would be given first refusal on any grant.[37]

Early in 1925, the engineers of the Ontario Hydro-Electric Power Commission finally delivered their report to the Alberta government.[38] To the cabinet's dismay, this study estimated that taking over the Calgary Power Company's existing plants and completing the first stage of a new development at the Spray Lakes would cost between $12 and $14 million. Not only would such an investment tax the financial capacity of the government to the hilt, but in a province where rural electrification was almost non-existent, it was likely to be highly unpopular with the voters who formed the backbone of the United Farmers of Alberta. After this dose of cold water, all that Premier Greenfield could do was to reassert his government's claim to priority in developing the Spray Lakes and convene a meeting of municipal representatives to discuss cost-sharing for a province-wide system.[39]

Despite the enthusiasm for a provincially owned hydroelectric utility in Calgary (which had the backing of both the Board of Trade and the Trades and Labour Council),[40] the representatives of the other municipalities proved decidedly cool when they met in June 1925. Edmonton's representatives preferred to consider other sites nearer that city, while Red Deer was neutral and Drumheller, a large coal-mining centre, was openly opposed. "All municipalities definitely decline all financial responsibilities in connection with provincial electrical development," wired George Hoadley, the provincial government's representative at the meeting. All that could be agreed upon was to appoint two more engineers to review the Ontario Hydro report. This review, in turn, simply reiterated that the Spray Lakes project appeared to be the logical next step in developing provincial power resources and recommended that it go forward as soon as possible.[41]

In June 1925, the Spray Lakes development came up once more in Parliament. Stewart admitted that he continued to be buffeted by strong conflicting pressures both for and against it. In an effort to escape these, he proposed bringing in legislation at the next session that would put the natural resources that were inside national parks under the control of Parliament itself. Meanwhile, he asked for the views of the MPs on the application for rights at the Spray Lakes. In the absence of H. H. Stevens, the Parks Branch was without its strongest defender on the Conservative benches. Opposition Leader Arthur Meighen blustered that the government was abdicating its responsibilities but finally allowed that if the power was really needed in Calgary, the development could hardly be blocked any longer.

Other Alberta MPs endorsed that position, arguing that there was already plenty of land set aside for parks in the province. The Spray valley was not particularly scenic and, like other areas of commercial value, ought to be moved outside the boundaries of Rocky Mountains National Park. When nobody rose to challenge that point of view, Stewart announced that he would take this silence as an expression that Parliament favoured the development going ahead. Pressed further, the minister refused to say that he would definitely grant the development rights, in light of the opposition from conservationists; this was something for Parliament to decide. But, he added, if the Alberta government was "sincere" in its application, he would be "prepared to go forward with it."[42]

This was seized upon by the Calgary newspapers as "a definite surrender of the Spray Lakes for power purposes,"[43] but that was a misunderstanding of what Stewart had committed himself to. What he meant was that if Alberta was ready to press ahead with a formal application, he would set the bureaucratic wheels in motion. In fact, he knew that the government was not prepared to put up the money for a provincial hydroelectric system, and he still hoped to evade responsibility for any decision by introducing legislation that would require parliamentary approval for the alienation of any natural resources inside the national park system.

Certainly, Calgary Power Company officials were convinced that they would never persuade the Interior Department to grant them a licence, since the House of Commons was "prejudiced against them." Premier Greenfield simply renewed his demand that Stewart grant the development licence to the provincial government immediately so that it could be handed over to the company.[44] Stewart insisted, however, that nothing could be done unless the Province of Alberta gave a firm commitment to proceed with the development itself. As the commissioner of parks put it,

> ... the province is not yet convinced itself that the Spray scheme has enough merit in it to justify its proceeding with actual development, therefore there is no justification for the [Interior] Department granting any concession with the merit question still up in the air.
>
> The final inference in Premier Greenfield's wire is that if the province gets a concession it may proceed to authorize some other

institution to develop it. In other words he asks the Dominion to give it a concession which it can peddle.[45]

Federal officials believed in 1925 that the Government of Alberta would not proceed with direct development of the Spray Lakes project on its own, but in the absence of a clear statement to that effect, the provincial government's indecision justified further delay. In December, Charles Stewart responded to complaints about delay from the mayor of Calgary by telling the *Calgary Daily Herald* that he was

> ... still waiting for the provincial government to demonstrate its ability and desire to develop that project.... The federal government proposes to deal direct with the party that actually develops the scheme and cannot see why they should issue a license to any other applicant.

Although the new premier, John Brownlee, complained that this insistence made it impossible for him to bargain effectively with Calgary Power about the development of a province-wide hydroelectric system, Stewart refused to budge.[46]

At the end of 1925, then, it appeared that for the time being, the Parks Branch and its conservationist allies had won the day. The outcry against damming the Spray Lakes had caused the Interior minister to hesitate, then draw back, and ultimately seek a means to avoid bearing sole responsibility for the decision. The unwillingness of the United Farmers of Alberta government to commit itself to a publicly owned development of the hydroelectric potential of the Bow River valley provided a further excuse for stalling. By the end of 1925, matters were no further advanced than they had been more than three years earlier when the Minnewanka dam had been turned down.

Still, there remained a looming electricity shortage in Calgary in coming winters if nothing were done to increase the capacity of the plants in the Bow River valley. The editor of the *Calgary Albertan* probably spoke for many Calgarians who resented being dismissed as thoughtless vandals in supporting further development in Rocky Mountains National Park:

> Is it just and right that the people of the plains below should be deprived of light, heat and power at a price which they can pay, in order that the beauties of the park may be completely unimpaired? Is there not a beauty in well lighted houses, in better heated homes during the cold and cheerless winter nights, in power which will relieve the housewife of much of the drudgery on the daily round of household duties?

Many citizens regarded the failure to develop cheap hydroelectricity from the Spray Lakes as a bar to future progress: "We have plenty of scenery in western Canada," a *Calgary Albertan* writer declared.[47]

For the time being, however, arguments like those of Parks Commissioner J. B. Harkin carried the day. "Selling scenery" to the American tourists was too good a business to be risked by ruining the landscapes of the national park system. The Parks Branch officials and their lobbying groups continued to maintain that hydroelectric development had no place within a national park. That was an argument, they would subsequently learn, that cut both ways. Meanwhile, the standoff continued. Unless the Calgary Power Company could convince people that the Spray Lakes development was absolutely necessary, the Department of the Interior would continue to refuse permission for it.

CHAPTER 6

Political Logic

The stout defence of the integrity of the national park system put up by the newly aroused conservation movement kept the Spray Lakes out of the hands of power developers during the early 1920s. As long as the Alberta government temporized about whether or not to undertake its own hydroelectric development in the Bow River watershed, Interior Minister Charles Stewart appeared willing to bow to the arguments of the Canadian National Parks Association and his own Parks Branch officials; both groups urged him not to give way to the demands of the Calgary Power Company and Calgary's municipal politicians to convert the Spray Lakes into a power reservoir. But in 1925, the political fates turned against those interested in wilderness preservation when the Conservative Party rebounded strongly in the federal election and even briefly gained office. Thereafter, the Liberals were forced to pay close attention to the wishes of a small number of Progressive MPs from Alberta, who were closely allied with the United Farmers of Alberta government. Throughout the late 1920s, Prime Minister Mackenzie King courted Premier John Brownlee and his supporters by negotiating the transfer of Alberta's natural resources to the control of the provincial government.

Even after that transfer, though, waterpower within national parks would remain within the federal jurisdiction. Thus, the problem of water storage inside Rocky Mountains National Park became entangled in these wider negotiations, during which the King government showed a willingness to permit development of the Spray Lakes as part of the price of political support from Albertan MPs. The combined weight of the provincial and municipal governments, the Calgary Power Company, and its allies in the interior department's Water Power Branch eventually carried the day despite a determined rearguard action by Parks Commissioner J. B. Harkin and his staff. The Spray Lakes would be sacrificed to the electrical needs of southern Alberta and the political needs of the Mackenzie King government. In the end, some of the most ardent conservationists even became resigned to the loss of this battle, their only comfort being the hope that the surrender of the Spray Lakes might pave the way for a revised National Parks Act that would make it much easier to block such developments in future.

Following Charles Stewart's rejection of the Alberta government's application to control the use of the Spray Lakes as a power reservoir in the fall of 1925 on the grounds that the province was not then prepared to undertake the development itself, the political situation in Ottawa took a dramatic turn. In these new electoral circumstances, Mackenzie King became very eager to establish friendly relations with the government of Premier John Brownlee. In October 1925, King had called an election, asking the electorate to give him a clear majority. Instead, the voters turned in large numbers to the Conservative Party under Arthur Meighen, which recovered from the debacle of 1921 and captured 116 seats to become the largest party in the House of Commons. The 101 Liberals could remain in power only with the support of the 24 Progressives who had survived defeat in the election, and the 9 Alberta Progressives thus formed an important key to King's continued hold on office.[1]

Discussions with the Prairie Provinces over granting them control of their natural resources had been held in the early 1920s (when King also depended upon Progressive votes for his parliamentary majority). But these negotiations ultimately foundered upon the western premiers' insistence that their governments should not only receive the same powers as the other provinces but also continue to receive their subsidies in lieu of the resources. They wanted it both ways; the federal government at the time refused. Fearful of the opposition that such favouritism would generate in other provinces, the Liberals backed away from any agreement and the negotiations were allowed to lapse.[2]

WILDERNESS AND WATERPOWER

The election of 1925 transformed the situation. Early in 1926, Mackenzie King met with John Brownlee just before the opening of Parliament. The prime minister agreed to include in the Speech from the Throne a promise of the speedy transfer of Alberta's natural resources back to the provincial government. Now, however, a new snag arose: certain Liberal MPs from Quebec insisted that a guarantee of the continued existence of Catholic separate schools in Alberta should be repeated in the legislation ratifying the resource transfer. Nervous about creating Catholic-Protestant friction, Mackenzie King eventually persuaded the Alberta Progressive MPs to agree to postpone the transfer until the courts could rule on whether or not the separate school guarantees remained valid. While that was being done, however, the negotiations again lapsed.[3]

Failure to achieve agreement on the larger issue, however, increased the pressure on Charles Stewart, the federal minister from Alberta, to try and placate the provincial government by reaching some accommodation with the province over the development of the Spray Lakes. Keeping the nine Progressive MPs from the province happy was important because the Liberal minority government might find itself dependent upon their continued goodwill. In an effort to deflect the criticisms of the conservationists, Stewart introduced legislation that would require resources to be removed from the national park system before they could be developed commercially. Such boundary changes would require the passage of a private member's bill, thus shifting the focus of lobbying away from the minister of the interior to individual parliamentarians. But these amendments to the National Parks Act were not dealt with during the 1926 session of Parliament, so Stewart continued to be in the hot seat.

The Alberta government insisted that it should have control of the power potential of the Spray Lakes and hoped to exploit the situation in Ottawa to attain it.[4] Since the Calgary Power Company's federal charter of incorporation made it immune from expropriation by the province, control of the water stored at the Spray Lakes would be important if Alberta ever decided to establish a publicly owned electrical utility. In early March 1926, therefore, Premier Brownlee approached I. W. Killam, president of Calgary Power, offering to use his influence in Ottawa to secure approval

John Brownlee, premier of
Alberta (Glenbow Archives,
NA-1451-11).

of the company's development of the Spray Lakes, provided that Killam would agree to permit Alberta to take over the project in the future upon payment of the company's expenditure on the project. Killam refused, arguing that such an agreement would make it impossible to raise capital to finance the plan. As a counter offer, he indicated that he would accept an agreement that included the province's right to take over the company's properties at some later date at a price to be arbitrated.

Premier Brownlee, meanwhile, tabled a motion in the Alberta legislature calling upon Ottawa to grant the province the immediate authority to authorize the development of the Spray Lakes to meet the future power needs of southern Alberta. Admitting that such a project made no economic sense unless coordinated with the existing installations of Calgary Power lower down on the Bow River, Brownlee reiterated the demand that development rights be granted to the provincial government, not Calgary Power. Only with the power rights in hand could Alberta bargain effectively with the company and make the decision whether to grant them these rights or to establish a public enterprise. As soon as the resolution passed, Brownlee forwarded it to Charles Stewart and Mackenzie King, and also to one of the province's Progressive MPs, urging him and the other Alberta representatives to "press this matter as strongly as possible."[5]

Because Calgary Power was eager to see the Spray Lakes plan proceed (and because he knew that Stewart could only grant the rights to the actual developer), I. W. Killam offered to come up to the capital from Montreal to lobby other parliamentarians:

If you think it advisable for me to interview any members of the House for the purpose of educating them as to the importance of the Spray development proceeding on account of the power shortage in Calgary and Alberta, and as to the unreasonableness of further consideration of the scenery question ... I shall be glad to do so. It would require no great effort on my part to spend a day or two and discuss the matter with such members as might be helpful in the matter. I am personally on friendly terms with quite a number of members on both sides of the House, but nearly all of these are representatives of Quebec and the Eastern [i.e., Maritime] Provinces.[6]

Mayor George Webster of Calgary also weighed in, complaining to Stewart that "this matter has been dragging on now for some three years, and the situation in Calgary will soon become aggravated, so that it is very desirable ... that the decision be reached at the earliest possible moment." The Calgary Board of Trade followed this up with a lengthy complaint that the shortage of hydroelectricity in winter required the city to produce up to 12,000 hp annually of expensive thermal power. Since the provincial government did not seem ready to undertake the Spray Lakes development, Ottawa should license some private operator (read: Calgary Power) to get on with the job. The Board of Trade complained about how Ottawa was treating Alberta and briskly dismissed the notion that the reservoir would destroy the scenery of Rocky Mountains National Park as "sheer nonsense":

Instead of destroying the scenic beauty it will turn an unsightly valley denuded by fire of its forest into a beautiful lake. And if there are any who consider that the wheels of industry are a profanation of the face of nature, we would say that this site will be so small a part of the mighty area of mountain and canyon included in the park and so far removed from the line of travel, that none will see or hear them unless they make a special trip over a difficult trail to visit the site.

This mawkish sentiment did not prevent the Province of Ontario from developing the Niagara power site, and they had no outcry from the west that it was destroying its scenic beauty....

Alberta has no other source of waterpower than that found in the mountains from which to draw. Must this waterpower forever flow off to the prairies without turning a wheel, while the province stands awaiting the development of its industries?[7]

Calgary Power also conceived another means of putting pressure on the interior department to grant the company the rights. Managing Director G. A. Gaherty proposed that Ottawa give the Alberta Public Utility Commission responsibility for fixing its rates, ostensibly to help the company in negotiations with various southern Alberta municipalities over power supply contracts. Parks Commissioner Harkin angrily rejected this "most objectionable" suggestion as

... simply another manoeuvre to help land the Spray Lakes for Calgary Power. Mr Gaherty is the mouthpiece of the Calgary Power Company, and if his request were granted it would indicate that, the Minister having so assisted them in their negotiations with municipalities, favourably regards their application for Spray Lakes.

Moreover, the delegation of such an important regulatory task to a provincial body would be an important precedent, sure to be seized upon by the other two western provinces to undermine federal control of waterpower development.[8]

The renewal of pressure from the provincial government and from Calgary Power to develop the Spray Lakes set off another round of conflict within the interior department between the Parks Branch and the Water Power Branch in the spring of 1926. Branch director J. T. Johnston repeated his argument that the construction of reservoirs inside the national parks in southern Alberta was "*inevitable.*" In fact, he pointed out, the Parks Branch itself had constructed a power plant near Banff, adding that such installations could readily be made *"features of added beauty and interest."* In Johnston's view,

> … the question of power development in Park areas should not be approached from the basis that these two interests are mutually antagonistic. The actualities are quite the reverse. Constructive cooperation will not only preserve the aesthetic features essential to a successful Park development, but will also release to the surrounding districts the benefits accruing from an invaluable and inexhaustible natural resource, to which the district in question can undoubtedly lay substantial claim.[9]

Such claims provoked a sizzling reply from Parks Commissioner Harkin.[10] He dealt first with the history of the application. Calgary Power's two Bow River plants had never been able to generate more than 5,000 continuous hp (or less than one-sixth of their rated capacity) owing to low flow in winter. Efforts to correct this by damming Lake Minnewanka had failed to provide a remedy since only about 20 per cent of the additional flow reached Horseshoe and Kananaskis. Now, Calgary politicians were claiming that a power shortage existed when, in fact, peak loads had been falling since 1922 (despite rising consumption), so the existing city steam plant could meet winter requirements quite economically.

The empire builders in the Water Power Branch, argued Harkin, wanted to permit the damming of the Spray Lakes to create a development with an ultimate capacity of 200,000 hp, for which there was not even a market in southern Alberta. In any case, the availability of cheap power was no guarantee of industrial development; Medicine Hat could supply electricity at 60 per cent of Calgary's rates, but firms still preferred to locate closer to major markets. Yet the Water Power people were ready to proceed even before they had assembled adequate hydrographic data for the Spray basin, with the risk of repeating the same blunders made in developing the Bow. The parks commissioner harked back to a memorandum written four years earlier, in which Johnston himself had suggested that the most appropriate development sites probably lay in the headwaters of the Red

Deer, the Saskatchewan, and the Clearwater Rivers, and that other locations on the Athabasca and North Saskatchewan might be better future prospects than the Bow watershed. The Water Power Branch, he argued, had a fixation with hydraulic development that made it unwilling to give serious consideration to the proposition that thermal stations powered by coal or natural gas might be more economical than hydroelectric projects in southern Alberta.

Harkin reserved his most profound scorn for the argument that power developments need not be out of place in a park and might even add variety and interest to the landscape:

> Apparently, in Mr. Johnston's opinion, commercial developments would not affect the status of the park, and all natural resources in a park area might be developed. This is directly opposite to the whole purpose for which parks have been established. If we remove restrictions to commercial developments in our parks, they are no different to any other area.... The established attitude of the United States in regard to the sanctity of their national parks, and which is based on ripe experience, is sufficient rebuttal on [sic] the opinions advanced by Mr. Johnston.
>
> The memorandum further states that dams, power stations and similar structures can be made features of added beauty and interest to a park. This entirely overlooks the fact that tourists do not come to National Parks to see dams, penstocks and powerplants, nor would any park organization in any part of the world give publicity to any commercial development in their park areas, no matter how interesting it might be from a business standpoint. The hundreds of thousands of tourists who visit the National Parks on this continent come to see them because they are essentially in their natural state, and in doing so they record an appreciation of the governments who kept these areas intact for future generations.

Since the shortage of power in southern Alberta was illusory, the only purpose of the renewed pressure to develop the Spray Lakes was to render Calgary Power's Bow River plants more efficient (and hence, more profitable). That, in turn, would reinforce the company's monopoly in the region and enable it to force other municipalities to sign supply contracts on favourable terms. If demand for electricity failed to grow as expected, the provincial government might even be forced to step in and take over the project to save Calgary Power from financial difficulties. *"Obviously, then,"* concluded Harkin, *"there is no need for the Department to act on any application for power development in the parks while present conditions obtain."*

Thus, Charles Stewart remained faced with deeply divided counsel from his bureaucratic subordinates. Failure to grant the demands of the province and the company might imperil the minority government, yet a coalition of vengeful conservationists might pounce upon the Liberals at election time if he failed to protect the Spray Lakes from hydroelectric development. Despite a further visit to Ottawa to lobby by John Brownlee, the interior minister stuck to the position that he would not give the go-ahead for the Spray Lakes development until the provincial government had indicated whether or not it was prepared to undertake the project itself.[11] Despite this rebuff, the Alberta Progressives did not desert the Liberals in mid-June of 1926 when the Conservatives moved a motion of non-confidence in King's administration due to the failure to transfer Alberta's natural resources to Alberta. The Liberals survived in office by the slim margin of five votes. Within a fortnight, however, the government had gone down to defeat over a scandal in the Customs Department, and the Conservatives under Arthur Meighen took power after Governor General Lord Byng refused Mackenzie King a dissolution. When Meighen's government was, in turn, defeated, Parliament was dissolved on July 2, 1926, and a general election campaign got under way.[12]

The change of government seemed to offer a golden opportunity to Calgary Power to secure the right to develop the Spray Lakes, for the new minister of the interior was none other than R. B. Bennett, a former president of the company. Killam immediately got in touch with Premier

Brownlee to ask him to meet with Bennett in Alberta to see if they could come to some agreement to permit the project to go ahead at once. "So far as the Calgary Power Company is concerned," wired Killam to Edmonton, "I feel that any agreement or arrangements to meet the views of your government, which you and Bennett consider fair and reasonable to all concerned, would be acceptable to [the] power company."[13]

Owing to the press of the election, or perhaps from fear that any deal with the Calgary Power Company would be denounced far and wide as a conflict of interest, Bennett never found the time to take up the issue of the Spray Lakes. Unfortunately for the company, the Conservative campaign did not go well, and on September 14, 1926, the Liberals were returned to power with a clear majority. By the end of the month, Charles Stewart was back in office as minister of the interior. This time, however, with a majority in the House, the impetus for a speedy settlement with Alberta on the Spray Lakes faded.

Nevertheless, concern about a looming power shortage in southern Alberta meant that the issue would not go away. Late in the fall of 1926, a group of Calgary businessmen and politicians met with Premier Brownlee and pressed him to resume negotiations with the federal government. The premier tried to shift the blame for delay onto Ottawa, citing the refusal to award the licence to Alberta . The Calgarians were unsympathetic: either the province should undertake development itself immediately, they told Brownlee, or it should stand aside and let Calgary Power go ahead with its plans, leaving it to the Public Utilities Commission to regulate rates.[14]

This pressure was sufficient to persuade Brownlee to reopen negotiations with Ottawa. He wrote to Stewart suggesting that a conference of all interested parties be held in Calgary as soon as possible. Getting wind of this idea, the Canadian National Parks Association rushed into print a circular headed, "*Important! Attention!* A Projected Raid on the National Parks of Canada," and urged all members to write to Stewart and protest any revival of the Spray Lakes scheme. Letters began to flood in at once. The Canadian National Parks Association demanded that it be represented at any conference, but on no account, said W. J. Selby Walker, should the meeting be held in Calgary, where the press was full of "insidious propaganda" for the power company and ignored the millions of feet of natural gas fuel being wasted annually. He claimed that support for the Spray Lakes scheme was being aroused among local businessmen by phony comparisons with the level of industrial development in Winnipeg and Vancouver, which supposedly depended upon cheap hydroelectricity. Walker appealed to Stewart to defend the national park system against provincial efforts to dismantle it for commercial purposes.[15]

Interior department officials were equally unenthusiastic about any meeting in western Canada, which they believed would only embarrass their minister in front of his fellow Albertans by forcing him to take a public stand on the issue. Stewart evidently agreed with this advice, for he quickly telegraphed Brownlee to say that he had no plans to visit Calgary even after the parliamentary session ended. Still, the pressure of public opinion in Alberta was so strong that it soon became clear that some sort of meeting would have to be convened early in the New Year to provide at least the illusion of activity.[16]

Officials of the Parks Branch did their best to stiffen their minister's resolve to resist the demands to develop the Spray Lakes. Parks Commissioner Harkin repeated his arguments that during the brief periods in winter when hydroelectric supplies fell short of demand, the city's power needs could be efficiently supplemented by the 14,000 hp civic steam plant. Thermal generating capacity could easily be expanded, using coal or natural gas presently being flared off in Turner Valley, sufficient to produce 30,000 hp annually. Spending about $4 million to produce 20,000 hp using water from the Spray Lakes would be a much more expensive means of meeting the shortfall of about 7,500 hp.[17] In addition, Harkin noted that federal waterpower regulations provided that Ottawa should fix power rates so as to provide a fair return on investment. "If eventually the scheme proved a failure, as I believe it would ... then the Department would undoubtedly find itself facing demands for compensation from investors."[18]

On January 11, 1927, Premier Brownlee travelled to Ottawa to meet with Stewart and his deputy minister, W. W. Cory, accompanied by an Alberta MP and two members of the provincial legislature, one a former

CHARLES STEWART, MINISTER OF THE INTERIOR (LAC, PA 041394).

mayor of Calgary. The Calgary Power Company was represented by its president, I. W. Killam, and managing director, G. A. Gaherty. Familiar ground was trod over yet again, with former Calgary mayor George Webster expatiating upon the city's need for additional power. Although Brownlee's officials had recently advised him that the interior department had no authority to grant a licence to anyone other than an actual power developer,[19] the premier refused to commit his government to undertaking the work but continued to demand that Ottawa delegate this authority to the province. Company officials declared themselves ready to start work at the Spray Lakes as soon as the necessary licence was issued and to accept rate regulation by the Alberta Public Utilities Commission.

Charles Stewart's contribution must have dismayed the Parks Branch officials. Having heard the others out, the minister declared that he had no objection to the development of reservoirs inside parks and at the Spray Lakes in particular. In an effort to stem criticism from conservationists, Stewart reminded them that he had already announced his intention to

WILDERNESS AND WATERPOWER

amend the National Parks Act to require a private member's bill to approve the removal of any lands from the park system for commercial development. He declared that he would bring in such amendments at the next session of Parliament and pass them before granting permission for any development in Rocky Mountains National Park.[20]

Stewart's commitment marked an important stage in the debate over the future of the Spray Lakes. If they were to be developed as storage reservoirs for a hydroelectric project, they would first have to be removed from Rocky Mountains National Park by an act of Parliament. Both sides in the debate continued cranking out propaganda as they awaited passage of Stewart's promised legislation. The National Council of Women expressed the view that permitting development of the Spray Lakes

> … would constitute a violation of the primary purpose for which National Parks were created, namely the complete conservation of a few places of outstanding scenic beauty for the use and enjoyment of the people of Canada for all time.… [T]he invasion of such areas by private interests for industrial purposes will involve the virtual destruction of their original character, with an immense loss to Canada from the economic, scientific and aesthetic points of view. And that one such application granted will constitute a precedent which will open the way to further invasions of a similar kind.

The Canadian National Parks Association produced another circular on the Spray Lakes, urging members to lobby their MPs to oppose any development if the matter was raised in Parliament.[21]

A new organization called the Alberta Power Research Association now entered into the debate. Composed of Calgary businessmen and professionals, it issued a series of printed bulletins strongly critical of the Calgary Power Company and its expensive and unsatisfactory hydroelectric developments on the Bow River. The association argued for the construction of new thermal stations using either coal or natural gas to meet future needs.[22] Charles Stewart particularly welcomed this intervention from his home province, which helped to deflect provincial criticism that he was blocking action by the Alberta government: "I am thoroughly disgusted with their endeavour always to lay the blame on the doorstep of the federal authorities," he wrote to the chairman of the Alberta Power Research Association. He promised that he would press ahead with his proposed legislation, which would "at any rate settle the policy with respect to commercial interests within the National Parks."[23]

Proponents of the development were equally active. When Parliament reconvened in early 1927, H. B. Adshead, MP for Calgary East, introduced a motion to approve the Spray Lakes development. Adshead argued that with a 1,300-foot working head, a plant there could produce 40,000 continuous hp of electricity annually, while at the same time enhancing the flow of the lower Bow so as to permit the existing plants to turn out an additional 60,000 hp. Such a large block of cheap power, equal to 200,000 hp annually for commercial purposes, would not only permit rapid industrial development but also make a transmission line to Edmonton commercially feasible as the first step toward a province-wide grid. As its contribution to this debate, Calgary city council issued a brief pamphlet entitled *Spray Lakes, the Need and ... the Answer*, designed to convince members of Parliament by reiterating the familiar arguments.[24]

The tabling of this motion reignited heated debate inside the interior department between the Water Power Branch and the Parks Branch. Proponents of the development, such as J. T. Johnston, repeated the claim that storing water at the Spray Lakes was no different from creating a park around a city reservoir. Parks officials repeated all the familiar conservationist criticisms: the empty reservoir would be surrounded by unsightly mudflats all summer long, the fish spawn would be destroyed, and the project would set a terrible precedent.[25]

Commissioner Harkin again worked himself into a high dudgeon toward those bureaucrats who disagreed with him. He complained that Johnston viewed the problem purely from the parochial point of view of developing the maximum amount of power rather than regarding the real interest of Calgarians and other Albertans in park preservation. He grumbled that a memorandum by Johnston was

... really an academic discussion of the subject. Now academic treatises are interesting but out of place in a situation like the present one.... I hold that when a proposition like the Spray is approved by a Government Branch, that Branch should first show that there is a need to be served by the scheme, and then that the particular scheme meets that need better than any other.

Only Calgary among the municipalities of Alberta was keen on the scheme, and the power shortage there could easily be met by thermal power. "I am at a loss to understand," Harkin fumed, "why the Water Power Branch recommends the invasion of a National Park under such circumstances." Harkin seems to have composed such memoranda mainly for psychic satisfaction rather than to influence policy since they are marked "Not Sent." Meanwhile, he relied upon the conservationist lobby to remind the higher-ups of the political dangers posed by the Spray development.[26]

Premier Brownlee wrote to the minister of the interior to complain that his recently introduced bill requiring an act of Parliament to alienate natural resources inside national parks was unfair to Alberta, representatives of which had been discussing the development of the Spray Lakes and the coal reserves inside Rocky Mountains National Park with Ottawa for some time past. Under the abortive agreement of January 1926 between the province and the federal government, he pointed out, control of national parks was to continue to rest with Ottawa, but all mineral resources even inside parklands were to pass into Edmonton's jurisdiction although the federal government would still have the right to regulate their development.

However, Brownlee seems to have realized that the best way for Alberta to gain control of the Spray Lakes development was to accept Stewart's idea of redrawing the park boundaries in order to permit commercial development. In view of the amount of parkland in Alberta, Brownlee argued that a resurvey of boundaries was the best way to solve such problems. The idea appealed to both men, and surveyor R. W. Cautley was quietly handed the task of reviewing the boundaries of Rocky Mountains National Park to delineate the commercially valuable resources that might be cut out from it.[27]

By the spring of 1927, the Parks Branch and its allies in the conservation lobby, which had come into existence in the first place to fight for the preservation of the Spray Lakes, seemed to have lost their lengthy battle. Although this was not made public, Charles Stewart had made up his mind by the spring of 1927 to try and deflect the criticisms of the conservationists by removing the area from the park system before his bill requiring a parliamentary vote on such boundary alterations became law. That would leave it to the provincial government to decide on whether this development was required to meet the power needs of Calgary.[28] When the activists recognized their defeat in the struggle to preserve the Spray Lakes as wilderness, some of the long-standing members of the Canadian National Parks Association became resigned to the redrawing of the park boundaries. W. J. Selby Walker, the executive secretary of the association, advised Charles Stewart in the fall of 1927 that I. W. Killam of Calgary Power had been in Alberta predicting an early settlement of the question. "This Spray Lakes delay," Walker declared, "has been the first check the group of eastern financiers have had in a most successful career of manipulating everything and everybody for their own financial gain." Walker sought a promise that Stewart would drive a hard bargain so that any resources would only be turned over to the provincial government in exchange for a guarantee of complete control by Ottawa over all territory left in the park system. Stewart took note of Walker's "suggestion that the sacrifice of the Spray Lakes may be necessary to ensure the sanctity of the balance of the Parks," but fended him off by urging him to await surveyor Cautley's formal report.[29]

Once this was received, Premier Brownlee travelled to Ottawa for further discussions in January 1928. The prospects for a quick settlement appeared promising, but a difference of opinion soon developed. Stewart offered to redraw the boundaries of Rocky Mountains National Park so as to exclude the Spray Lakes,[30] but only on the condition, as the Canadian National Parks Association wished, that the province renounce all future claims to any minerals or other natural resources left inside the park system. In addition, he insisted that Alberta formally agree that the water in the Spray reservoir should be diverted directly into the Bow valley through a tunnel rather than being allowed to flow down the Spray River, which joined the Bow right at the Banff Springs Hotel, because of possible damage to the beauty of that area.

Brownlee protested that the first of these conditions was a departure from the terms of the 1926 agreement, by which all mineral reserves were to have become provincial property. What, he asked, if at some future date metals were found on land inside a park, metals so precious that Ottawa decided to permit their exploitation? Was it fair that Alberta should derive no economic benefit from such a development? As to the second point, the premier contended that the condition was unnecessary since the shortage of power in Calgary was so acute that a tunnel to link the Spray reservoir with the Bow River would have to be constructed immediately. But Stewart refused to redraw the boundaries without a formal commitment from the provincial government on these issues.[31]

With the power shortage in Calgary growing more acute, Brownlee once again renewed Alberta's application to dam the Spray Lakes, even travelling to Ottawa again to see Charles Stewart in mid-April 1928. The premier refused, however, to commit his government to an immediate start on the reservoir project. In June, Stewart told the House of Commons that if a reservoir was not going to be built, he wanted the Spray Lakes to be retained inside the national park system.[32] Once more, however, political considerations forced the minister to be more accommodating to Alberta's demands. Preparing for the next general election, Mackenzie King turned his hand to strengthening the feeble Liberal party in the three Prairie Provinces. He hoped, of course, to capture the farmers' movements that had originally undermined Liberal dominance in the region, and he seemed to be succeeding in Manitoba. In the fall of 1928, King travelled to western Canada to meet with each of the provincial premiers.

Charles Stewart, the Alberta minister in the federal cabinet, had always preferred to fight the United Farmers of Alberta, but the Liberal party remained weak and divided. By 1928, King was hoping to persuade John Brownlee to join his cabinet in place of Stewart as part of his strategy to revive western Liberalism, so the prime minister was quite ready to make a generous settlement on the return of natural resources to provincial control in order to woo Brownlee. King now offered to return the resources but to continue the subsidies in lieu of them in perpetuity and to increase those grants as the population increased. Brownlee readily agreed to these terms although he hesitated at accepting King's offer to enter the federal government. A formal conference of the western leaders in December 1928 approved this agreement, and the return of the resources was formally announced in the spring of 1929.[33]

That settlement, however, still left the question of authorizing the use of the Spray Lakes as a storage reservoir in federal hands so long as they lay inside a national park. R. B. Bennett raised the matter once more in the House of Commons in the spring of 1929, complaining that the refusal of the Parks Branch to license the project was "a ridiculous position taken in relation to a dam away up in the mountains in connection with the Spray Lakes. The minister himself felt the position was little short of ridiculous." The signing of the resource agreement with Alberta meant that now development on lands outside the park system would be a provincial responsibility. Evidently tiring of the criticisms of his policy, Charles Stewart reversed the position he had taken a year earlier that the Spray Lakes would remain as part of the national park unless the dam were actually to be built. The interior minister now told Parliament that the Spray Lakes would definitely be placed outside the park system when the boundaries were redrawn.[34] Stewart had obviously concluded that the only way to dampen the controversy was to remove the lands that might ultimately be required for hydraulic storage out of the park system once and for all "in order to protect the parks from private exploitation in future."

The interior department went to work drafting a new National Parks Act. As far back as 1922, Harkin had campaigned for new, comprehensive legislation. In 1923, he actually succeeded in having a bill introduced for first reading in the House of Commons, but its strict prohibitions against development aroused the ire and opposition of the bureaucrats in other branches within the Department of the Interior who had not, apparently, been consulted. The government did not proceed with further readings.

Minister Stewart, having been burned once, refused to reintroduce the legislation, especially with the contentious Spray Lakes issue still unresolved. Interestingly enough, Harkin had early on privately concluded that in order to maintain what he called the "inviolability" of the parks against commercial development, he would have to concede that the parks would have to be smaller with potentially developable areas removed.[35] When the National Parks Act was finally presented in Parliament in 1930, it cut out of Rocky Mountains National Park 630 square miles in the Spray watershed, along with 77 square miles at the headwaters of the Ghost River, 291 square miles at the head of the Red Deer, and 377 square miles on the Clearwater. The granting of commercial development rights for any other land within a national park would, as Stewart had pledged, require the passage of a private member's bill. Harkin had won the battle for "sanctity" but, as he had expected, at the cost of major territorial reductions. While regretful at losing the battle for the Spray Lakes, the Canadian National Parks Association supported this proposal, calculating that conservationists would be able to exercise greater influence on parliamentarians in this situation. The new National Parks Act was finally passed in May 1930, dividing Rocky Mountains National Park into four new units – Banff, Jasper, Yoho, and Glacier – and removing from the park system commercially valuable natural resources.[36]

The conservation movement that had been called into existence by the threat to the Spray Lakes in the early 1920s thus proved unable to ensure their preservation as wilderness. The argument that hydroelectric development should not take place within national parks, a point of view that seemed to gain wide public acceptance, when forced through the sausage machine of federal politics in the late 1920s, led to the remarkable conclusion that such places should not be within national parks in the first place. After lengthy negotiations between the Province of Alberta and the federal government, it was finally agreed that these lands should be removed from what had become Banff National Park because of their potential commercial value as a hydroelectric storage reservoir. The Canadian National Parks Association and its allies such as the Alpine Club of Canada could draw some comfort from the fact that in future no further lands

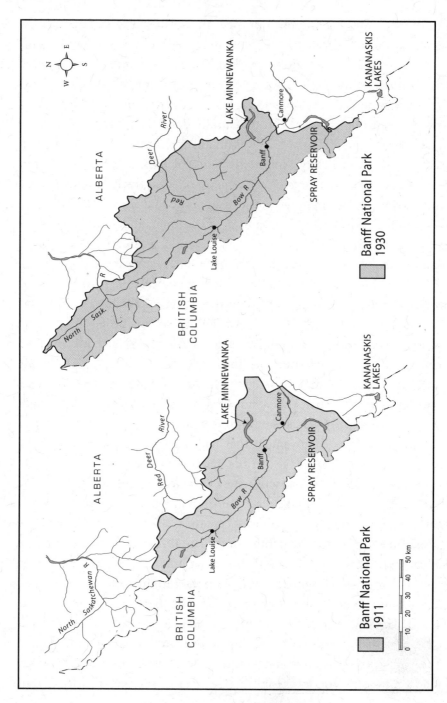

BANFF NATIONAL PARK BOUNDARIES, 1911 AND 1930.

WILDERNESS AND WATERPOWER

would be withdrawn from the parks in this way without parliamentary approval. Nonetheless, the argument that these lakes were more valuable as part of a campaign to "sell scenery" to tourists did not prove persuasive enough in the face of the insistence of the provincial government, the City of Calgary, and the Calgary Power Company that a reservoir was essential to meet the power needs of southern Alberta.

Had the political situation been different, Charles Stewart and his officials in the Parks Branch of the Department of the Interior might have been able to block the boundary change, but with the Liberal Party in need of support from Alberta, Mackenzie King regarded the resource question as no more than a useful bargaining counter. By 1930, the decision to develop the Spray Lakes as a storage reservoir finally seemed to have been made once and for all.

CHAPTER 7

Minnewanka Redux

History takes unexpected turns. It never seems to proceed in linear fashion. With the transfer of natural resources to the Province of Alberta and the carving of the Spray Lakes out of Banff National Park in 1930, one might reasonably expect that having been long postponed, the much-needed hydroelectric project would immediately go forward. Not so. The fateful date hints at only part of the story.

While Albertans had waited during most of the 1920s for politicians in Ottawa to make up their minds about the Spray Lakes, Ottawa had waited for the political leaders of Alberta to decide whether or not the province would go into the electricity business. The decision to develop the waterpower of the Spray Lakes now lay entirely in the hands of the Alberta government. Would it finally seize this opportunity to create its own public utility to serve the entire province? Or would the task be left to the Calgary Power Company?

Ironically, however, by the time the battle to open up the Spray Lakes to hydroelectric utilization had been won, the Calgary Power Company had lost interest in the undertaking. Even before the new National Parks Act had become law, the company had revived a familiar theme: the need to raise the dam at Lake Minnewanka higher so as to store more water. That proposal, of course, was even more of an anathema to the Parks Branch and their allies in the wilderness preservation movement than the plans for the Spray Lakes because it involved extensive construction within the now "sacrosanct" park itself. The election of a Conservative government, headed by R. B. Bennett, in 1930 led many to anticipate that the company's request would be speedily granted, and Calgary Power certainly lobbied strenuously. Old combatants regirded for a fight, but once again, fickle fate intervened.

From 1922 on, politicians, bureaucrats, and private interests alike had assumed that if the generating capacity of the hydroelectric plants on the Bow River were to be expanded, the best means would be to dam the Spray Lakes. The first doubts were cast upon that assumption during discussions in Ottawa about the removal of the lakes from the national park. A question arose as to how much water would continue to flow down the Spray River and into the Bow just outside the Banff townsite once the dam had been erected at the outflow of the Spray Lakes. This was an important question, because the Spray ran through the golf course that the CPR had constructed just below the Banff Springs Hotel. As one CPR official later wrote to the minister of the interior, "The company has spent many millions of dollars in our hotel, and your department has gone to great lengths to retain the natural beauty features in the district."[1] Neither the hotelmen nor the Parks Branch bureaucrats would countenance the flow of the Spray being cut off altogether, leaving an almost dry riverbed for the tourists and golfers to look at.

At a meeting in Charles Stewart's office in April 1928, the minister informed Calgary Power officials that if they were permitted to dam the Spray Lakes, they would have to release five hundred cubic feet of water per second (cfs) into the river to maintain a flow roughly equal to normal September levels.[2] Managing director G. A. Gaherty replied that to release that amount of water was "utterly out of the question," since it would use up so much water that it would render the storage capacity of the reservoir uneconomical for power purposes. Apparently Gaherty, who had originally devised the Spray Lakes plan, had simply assumed that the company would be permitted to cut off the Spray River altogether and pass all the water in its reservoir through a tunnel into the Bow valley far downstream at Canmore. His solicitor observed that if so much water had to be released, Calgary Power would have no interest in the development. To the annoyance of Parks Commissioner J. B. Harkin, one of the engineers from the Water Power Branch concurred, arguing "that the project could not afford to have any water released from storage for scenic purposes."[3]

Wrangling continued over this issue for some weeks. The mayor of Calgary, donning the mantle of hydrographic engineer, gave his opinion that between 150 and 200 cfs flowing down the Spray River in the summer would be quite sufficient to preserve its natural beauty. The Parks Branch pointed out that a flow of 500 cfs would require just 6.7 per cent of all the water to be stored in the proposed Spray Lakes reservoir. If the project was being planned with such a slender margin of error, then it ought not to be approved. The minister was evidently prepared to accept a flow as low as 350 cfs in the Spray River, but the company would agree to release no more than 200 cfs.[4]

Negotiations between the province and the federal government over the removal of the Spray Lakes from Rocky Mountains National Park continued during the next two years until Stewart's bill was finally passed in the spring of 1930. Ironically, however, Calgary Power seems to have been sincere in its refusal to even consider damming the Spray Lakes if it was required to release as much as 500 cfs over the dam. The knowledge that the CPR was on the side of the Parks Branch in this battle must have had its effects, too. The railway company was a much tougher and more potent antagonist that the mountain climbers and bird watchers in the Canadian National Parks Association.

Moreover, Calgary Power had an alternative plan to meet its immediate future requirements. Outside the eastern boundary of Rocky Mountains National Park, the Ghost River flowed into the Bow River from the northwest near Radnor, Alberta, just downstream from the company's existing plant at Horseshoe Falls. Calgary Power had acquired rights to this Radnor site at its founding in the deal with Alberta Portland Cement. Now, some twenty years later, company engineers calculated that a development at Ghost Falls could turn out 36,000 hp annually with the possibility of expansion to 54,000 hp if required.

A new source of power was urgently needed by Calgary Power since the contract with the city was due to expire in the spring of 1928 and demand for electricity was rising rapidly. Premier Brownlee was prepared

POSTCARD IMAGE OF THE SPRAY RIVER RUNNING THROUGH THE BANFF GOLF COURSE.

to give his support to the Ghost development. At that very meeting in Charles Stewart's office in April 1928 where the Spray project was discussed, Gaherty asked for the necessary federal licences to develop the Ghost site. Stewart quickly agreed, and within a few weeks, the city and the company had reached an agreement extending to 1940: the company would proceed with the new hydroelectric project and the municipal steam plant would be leased to the company for $75,000 per year to meet winter peak loads.[5]

The extension of its contract with the city greatly strengthened the financial position of Calgary Power and ensured that it would be able to raise the money required to construct its new plant. The board of directors had voted for the first regular dividend ever paid by the company in the last quarter of 1927, and thereafter, the shareholders received a regular 5 per cent per annum. In the fall of 1928, the holders of the twenty thousand shares of common stock were also given the right to subscribe at $100 each for five thousand shares from the treasury in the ratio of one new share

GHOST RIVER DAM NEARING COMPLETION (GLENBOW ARCHIVES, NA-4477-12).

for every four held. In order to raise the $7 million required to build the Ghost plant, the shareholders approved the issue of fifty thousand new $100 preference shares and twenty thousand additional common shares. G. A. Gaherty now replaced I. W. Killam as president of the company, although Killam's Royal Securities Corporation remained in firm control through the ownership of most of the common shares.[6]

Even though the Calgary Power Company had lost interest in the Spray project for the time being, Stewart remained under pressure from Albertans to act. In the summer of 1928, the mayor of Calgary complained to him that the Ghost plant would only be sufficient to meet projected needs for about five more years, after which more cheap hydroelectricity would be needed to promote industrial development. The Calgary Board of Trade echoed these sentiments:

Unless arrangements are made for the development of electrical energy sufficient to take care of the future needs of this city and province, we shall be badly handicapped and our progress and prosperity severely retarded.

We deeply resent the propaganda which is seeking to make it appear that the use of the Spray Lakes will destroy the beauty or use of the park as a playground or tourist centre when as a matter of fact it would improve it.[7]

By the summer of 1928, Premier John Brownlee was equally eager that the interior department should grant the development rights at the Spray Lakes to his government immediately, even before a new National Parks Act was passed. The reason for Brownlee's impatience lay in a shift in Alberta politics. Prior to 1928, the issue of hydroelectric development had been an issue of little concern except in Calgary. Edmonton was already served by its own city-owned thermal station, and the effort in 1925 to interest other municipalities in financing a provincial grid based on Bow valley power had elicited no enthusiasm. Now, however, the issue of rural electrification was taken up by the grassroots members of the United Farmers of Alberta (UFA), and the Brownlee government was suddenly forced to pay attention to the idea. In January 1928, the UFA convention passed a resolution favouring the immediate development of the Spray Lakes under joint federal-provincial control.[8] Articles and editorials on the benefits of electrification began to appear regularly in *The U.F.A.*, calling for the establishment of a provincial electrical utility modelled on Ontario Hydro. For instance, the pseudonymous Lee Vincent warned against handing over precious resources to private companies:

We have seen our farm cooperatives wrest control of our marketing system from the domination of powerful and strongly entrenched private interests. We have secured ourselves against the inroads of a telephone monopoly; why should we rest on our oars and let power trusts lead us into voluntary captivity? In a dozen years electricity will be a dominating factor in the life of our Province. If we wait until then to assert our rights it will probably be too late or too expensive to accomplish what may readily be done now.[9]

The Brownlee government could not afford to ignore this shift in opinion among its rural constituents. R. P. Baxter, the deputy minister in charge of Alberta Government Telephones, was consulted about the cost of setting up a provincial electrical utility. The costs would be substantial, he reported: about $5 million would be needed to buy out Calgary Power and another $4.5 million to build the storage works at the Spray Lakes needed to provide enough capacity to serve a provincial grid. "It appears from the information that we have now that the Government could not sell power any cheaper than the present rates, at least, for the first six or seven years." Despite this, Baxter pointed out the virtues of nationalization:

> We are interested because of the fact that the power business in this province links up very closely with the telephone business. We have an organization over the province built up and now giving telephone service; much of this organization could be used in the power business. The same commercial office in every exchange could serve for the two lines of business. Our construction organization could easily be extended to take in all of the work in connection with power lines throughout the country. Our accounting organization could very easily be made to take care of the accounting work.

What was needed at once was further investigation: "If you wait for ten years, regardless of the contract that you make with the power company, there is [sic] going to be all kinds of complications as well as duplication."

Baxter was soon sent east to carry out a discreet investigation of public electrical systems in Manitoba and Ontario.[10] On his return, he reported that he had met with I. W. Killam and G. A. Gaherty to sound them out about the possibility of a takeover of Calgary Power as a first step. Killam insisted that the company had no wish to sell out, having recently been offered $300 per share, although he claimed that the difficulties in securing adequate water storage from the federal government had so far made it impossible to earn a fair return on its investment. In light of this, Killam argued that Calgary Power had "a strong moral claim to the support and sympathy of the province in carrying on the undertaking throughout the whole province." Nevertheless, he promised that if the provincial government was determined to nationalize the company, the board would be prepared to sell at a price to be fixed by arbitration, though he made clear his strong opposition to public ownership.[11]

Despite the predictable coolness on the part of the private company,[12] the UFA government became increasingly attracted to the idea of a provincial electrical utility. In the summer of 1929, Brownlee approached the chair of the Ontario Hydro-Electric Power Commission to ask for assistance.[13] Eventually, A. G. Christie, a Canadian professor of engineering at the Johns Hopkins University, was commissioned by the Alberta government to study the situation. Christie's report, delivered a few months later, carefully set forth the pros and cons of private versus public enterprise. Christie estimated that the cost of acquiring the two private utilities (Calgary Power and Midwest Utilities, which had recently established itself in the southeastern part of the province) plus the civic steam plant in Edmonton would total about $18 million and that another $7 million would be required to construct new transmission lines to connect them. He admitted that "there can be no hope of immediate reductions in power costs through government control, and that the benefits of such a situation will only accrue after several years and when the system has been extended and enlarged." Nevertheless, he predicted that if the two companies were not purchased, they would soon merge, and that their rates would likely rise in future. While leaving the choice up to the government, Christie clearly favoured nationalization.

Ontario consulting engineer H. G. Acres, who had been retained by the City of Calgary, heartily endorsed Christie's conclusions and advised one of Brownlee's ministers that

> ... it was simply a question of whether or not we had a vision of growth and development in the province or not. If we were convinced that development was going to take place, and from everything he could see that growth was going to take place, then in his opinion there would be no question that we should take

hold of it. He said apart from that one consideration, it was simply a matter of courage.[14]

Certainly, the idea of a public power system was attractive to many within the UFA,[15] but the fact remained that with its federal charter, Calgary Power was immune from expropriation by the Alberta government.[16] The company would have to be bought out, and that meant paying a hefty premium to I. W. Killam. The provincial government hesitated, and once the depression struck, it rapidly lost interest in the idea of a provincial electricity distribution system.

Ironically, however, the economic crisis that began in 1929 increased rather than decreased the threat from hydroelectric development to the integrity of the national park system in Alberta. Calgary Power now had three hydroelectric stations on the Bow, all of them suffering from the same recurring problem: low winter streamflow and therefore reduced operating efficiency. Although the decision had been made to cut the Spray Lakes out of Banff National Park, Calgary Power, anticipating future load growth, now determined to overturn the decision made in 1922 to forbid the raising of the dam at Lake Minnewanka, since raising the dam would offer the chance to create a large block of power at a small capital cost: increased storage at Minnewanka would immediately return dividends three times over. Events soon played into the company's hands. With unemployment rising in Calgary, a group of concerned citizens gathered in December 1929 to consider remedies, and Calgary Power's general manager seized the opportunity to announce that the construction of a thirty-foot dam, sixteen hundred feet long, could provide four hundred jobs. Immediately, civic officials began to pressure the interior department to approve the project.[17]

This infuriated Parks Branch officials, who had anticipated that the new National Parks Act, which would come into force in a few months, had finally put a stop to such commercial developments. Commissioner J. B. Harkin complained, "Under the circumstances it seems extraordinary that the demand for Minnewanka should be so suddenly sprung. One cannot help feeling that the real purpose is to challenge the inviolability of the National Parks." The company's aim, he wrote, was either to open the way for the use of Lake Louise or any other part of the national parks for hydraulic storage or to lock up all the power rights in the southern Rockies to exclude all competition and aid in the creation of "a huge power trust." Killam and Gaherty were simply trying to use the unemployment situation in Calgary "to stampede the department into a sudden change of policy," even though it was clear that four hundred men would not be required to clear the brush from the shoreline of Lake Minnewanka efficiently. "[S]omeone has conceived the idea that instead of having the Minnewanka case considered on its merits, a decision should be forced on emotional grounds based on unemployment," Harkin concluded.[18]

Initially, the minister of the interior accepted this point of view. Charles Stewart reminded Calgarians that the power company could start work on the Spray project as soon as they got permission from the provincial government. But the Trades and Labour Council and the Central Council of Unemployed kept the pressure on the municipal politicians in an unusual alliance with the Board of Trade.[19] All the familiar arguments for and against raising the level of Lake Minnewanka were trotted out once more. Commissioner Harkin spoke of the "ghastly damage" to the scenery created even by the existing dam, while the secretary of the Board of Trade pointed out that Loch Katrine in Scotland, "one of the most famous beauty spots in the world," supplied Glasgow's water, and the Swiss Alps were full of hydroelectric reservoirs.[20]

Stewart remained unmoved: the redrawing of the park boundaries, which Parliament was about to approve, had settled the matter once and for all. He did, however, rein in the Parks Branch from publicly attacking the Minnewanka plan and creating public controversy. Behind the scenes, however, Harkin continued to fulminate against Calgary Power and its claim that it only sought more water from Lake Minnewanka to make its Bow River plants more efficient in winter. Nonsense, said the commissioner. "I submit this stand is taken solely as a first step, and that the only real purpose in mind is the establishment of a commercial generating plant in the Park. In plain English, they are not being frank." Harkin believed that the company was trying to get permission to raise the Minnewanka dam before the new National Parks Act became law, since it would require parliamentary approval of any future development. Once the new legislation came into force in May 1930, he felt relieved that there was "now no immediate danger" from the proposed scheme.[21]

His confidence was shaken within a couple of weeks, however, when, on the eve of a general election, Stewart announced that after consultations with local Liberals, he was now "prepared to recommend to the government that Lake Minnewanka be considered outside the boundaries of Banff National Park in order to permit development of this source of water power for storage purposes." The Conservative victory in the election made Calgarian R. B. Bennett prime minister, which the mayor and the local Board of Trade hoped would ensure speedy passage of a bill to permit raising the dam at Lake Minnewanka as an unemployment relief scheme. The Canadian National Parks Association, meanwhile, did its utmost to mobilize its members to resist "this contemplated grab of part of a park area which belongs equally to all Canadians."[22]

The Conservative election victory threw matters into flux. Within the Interior Department, the bureaucrats struggled to gain the confidence of their new Conservative masters and to demonstrate to the new interior minister, Thomas G. Murphy, how well organized the conservationist lobby was. Deputy Minister W. W. Cory suggested that the prime minister should make no commitments before carefully studying the issue. Sensing an opportunity unlikely to be repeated, Calgary Power also turned on the pressure to obtain parliamentary approval to use Lake Minnewanka as a power reservoir. The company now proposed to raise the dam by fifty-five feet and to increase the amount of water flowing into the lake by diverting the headwaters of the Ghost River into it. This water would be taken by a canal to the Bow River at Anthracite where 25,000 hp would be generated with a 310-foot head. The same flow could then be utilized at each of the other Calgary Power plants lower down on the Bow. The company even suggested that the federal government start the work itself as an unemployment relief project and turn it over to the company once the necessary enabling legislation had been passed.[23]

Parks Commissioner Harkin sensed that the change of government had placed him in a weaker position. The prime minister was a former president of the power company and was known to be sympathetic to its plans. J. T. Johnston of the Water Power Branch of the Department of the Interior remained a strong proponent of the use of Lake Minnewanka as a reservoir; it was Johnston, in fact, who had conceived the scheme of diverting the Ghost River into the lake. Local organizations in Calgary – and, surprisingly, even in Banff – expressed embarrassingly strong support for the project. A plebiscite held in Banff, for example, indicated that local residents favoured not a thirty-foot but a fifty- to sixty-foot increase![24] Harkin, therefore, consented to exploratory work being commenced. The only comfort he could draw was that the headwaters of the Ghost River had also been removed from the national park by the 1930 act, so even if the federal government approved the plan, Alberta's consent would also be required before any actual work could commence.[25]

Despite the worsening economic depression, the Calgary Power Company kept the pressure on the government. Gaherty personally lobbied the new minister, T. G. Murphy, by calling him and submitting a report from T. H. Hogg of Ontario Hydro endorsing the project. While Hogg admitted that Lake Minnewanka might not refill completely during years of low precipitation, he argued that careful clearing of the shorelines, as was done in Switzerland, would ensure that the scenic effects remained undamaged. Johnston, the director of the Water Power Branch, continued to support the idea of a new development supplied with water from Lake Minnewanka: "The Cascade project possesses power potentialities in relation to the company's present power system which make it of outstanding value as a source of power supply, quite out of proportion to its value taken simply and solely as an independent power project." The idea that the provincial government should be given control of all potential hydroelectric sites as the basis for a public power system was pooh-poohed by Johnston because it would fragment control over the park system.[26] Minister Murphy quickly referred the company's application to the prime minister, hoping for advice on how to deal with it. The matter had to be handled carefully: any appearance of favouritism toward Calgary Power was certain to create an outcry against the government.

The Alberta legislature entered the fray by passing a Labour Party resolution on March 5, 1931, calling for the transfer of water power resources within the Alberta national parks to the provincial government. Development would then depend upon the approval of both levels of government. This resolution created legal complications for the federal government since it pitted the terms of the Dominion Water Powers Act against those of the National Parks Act.[27]

But as the Depression worsened and the demand for power stopped growing, the need to resolve this conflict was soon rendered academic. The economic crisis of the 1930s blocked further development of water-power inside the national parks of Alberta more effectively than all the lobbying of the 1920s had done. Although the Spray Lakes had been cut out of the park so that development could proceed, the project was too big and too costly for Calgary Power to undertake in 1930 after having invested heavily in the Ghost/Radnor project. Instead, the company once more trained its guns on Lake Minnewanka and seemed on the verge of success. But a collapse in the demand for power and the crisis in the financial markets rendered any expansion of generating capacity uneconomical for the time being. Besides, with the Ghost hydroelectric plant coming on stream, Calgary Power, now experiencing surplus capacity, simply allowed its renewed application to control Lake Minnewanka to lapse. Lake Minnewanka and the parks lobby could rest for the remainder of the decade.

CHAPTER 8

War Measures

The economic crisis of the 1930s effectively ended debate over the expansion of the hydroelectric generating capacity of the Calgary Power Company. The idea of erecting a new dam at Lake Minnewanka, even as an unemployment relief project, evaporated once it became clear that there was no market for the power. Throughout the 1930s, Calgary Power had excess capacity; it produced more than enough electricity from its three Bow River plants to meet the needs of Calgary at the city's much reduced rate of growth for the foreseeable future.

In 1940, however, the situation changed dramatically as the Canadian economy geared up for war. That summer, the company renewed its application to raise the dam at Lake Minnewanka, claiming that this was the cheapest and speediest means of producing additional power needed for the war effort. Although the bureaucrats responsible for the national park system fought against this proposal, they waged an uphill struggle. The urgent needs of war subdued the public pressure from wilderness preservationists, which had helped to protect Lake Minnewanka in the 1920s. Moreover, the power company had acquired a potent ally within the federal government in the minister of munitions and supply, C. D. Howe. He and his advisors were convinced that in this emergency, Calgary Power should be granted permission for development inside Banff National Park. In the end, those officials who opposed the plan could do little more than try to compel the company to design and landscape its new construction so as to make it as unobtrusive as possible.

Despite the economic collapse of the 1930s, it was clear that the issue of power development in the national parks would arise once again when recovery was well underway. In early 1939, G. A. Gaherty of Calgary Power, in communication with the Engineering Institute of Canada, predicted that the issue of reservoirs inside the park would recur and expressed his hope that this time the debate would be conducted on different terms: "The situation will be further complicated if the National Park officials continue their uncompromising opposition on sentimental grounds to any further storage development within the parks.... It is to be hoped that by the time this question becomes acute machinery will have been set up to deal with it on broad national lines."[1] But the matter did not actually come to a head until the summer of 1940, when Canada and Great Britain faced the most acute crisis of the war against Germany.

In late August, the Department of Munitions asked Calgary Power to supply up to 26,000 hp of electricity per year to a new plant established in Calgary. The Alberta Nitrogen Company needed this additional power to produce anhydrous ammonia from natural gas for the munitions indus-try.[2] The power company seized the opportunity to immediately revive its long-standing request for permission to build a sixty-foot dam at the outlet of Lake Minnewanka, inside Banff National Park, to store the additional water required to produce this electricity. The long-suspended debate over waterpower development within national parks swiftly resumed.

During the 1930s, the bureaucracy responsible for administering the park system had undergone changes. In 1936, the Department of the Interior had been abolished and replaced by the Ministry of Mines and Resources.[3] R. A. Gibson was now director of the Lands, Parks, and Forests Branch in place of Parks Commissioner J. B. Harkin, while J. M. Wardle held the post once occupied by J. T. Johnston as head of the Surveys and Engineering Branch, under which fell the Water Power Bureau. Both Gibson and Wardle, of course, were long-serving departmental veterans who had been through all the battles of the 1920s over Lake Minnewanka and the Spray Lakes. W. W. Cory had retired as deputy minister to be replaced by Charles Camsell; the minister of mines and resources since the Liberals had returned to power in 1935 was Manitoban T. A. Crerar, who would hold the portfolio until 1945.

Gibson and Wardle were, therefore, thoroughly familiar with the background of this issue when it surfaced again, but it was clear from the outset that the wartime emergency had greatly altered the situation. The first approach to the Department of Mines and Resources in August 1940 came not from company officials but from the power controller of C. D. Howe's Department of Munitions and Supply, who had been appointed under the War Measures Act to allocate energy supplies among strategic-ally important consumers. And the power controller was Montreal lawyer H. J. Symington, a dollar-a-year man who was also a member of the board of directors of Calgary Power. Obviously, the company now had friends in very high places, and the battle to preserve the scenery around Lake Minnewanka would be an uphill one.

Discussions between company and departmental officials, hastily con-vened in September 1940, made it clear that Calgary Power had firmly set its sights upon obtaining approval to raise the dam at Lake Minnewanka by sixty feet, which would flood nineteen hundred additional acres around its shores. Not only could the 150,000 acre-feet of water from this reservoir be used at the three existing plants lower down on the Bow River, but the company intended to commence construction of a 23,000 hp plant at Cascade to utilize the three-hundred-foot drop from the canal out of Lake Minnewanka to the bed of the Bow. It was believed that this new project could be completed in as little as eight to twelve months, in time to cover an anticipated shortfall in power supplies of 5,000 hp during the winter of 1941–42, when the Alberta Nitrogen Company plant would reached full production. Asked by a departmental engineer

> … whether or not the company were using the war as a lever
> to obtain increased pondage at Lake Minnewanka, the rights
> for which they were not able to obtain on previous application,
> Mr. Gaherty acknowledged that, in a sense they were using such
> leverage.[4]

And it quickly became clear that Calgary Power proposed to exploit this leverage for all it was worth. The Parks Branch asked why the company did not develop the storage capacity of the Spray Lakes, which it had fought so hard to secure in the 1920s and which had lain outside the national parks since 1930. The company replied that it would require three years and many thousands of dollars to drill the two-mile tunnel to conduct the water to the rim of the Bow valley above Canmore. Moreover, once the dam site at the head of the Spray River was unwatered, unanticipated problems might be encountered that would set the whole project back further.[5]

What about a development on the upper Kananaskis River, which flowed into the Bow further east near the company's original power plant? That, officials of the Lands, Parks, and Forests Branch (hereafter Parks Branch) were told, would require the construction of up to twenty-five miles of access roads to reach the site and would take at least two years to bring into production.[6]

Well, then, what about a thermal station, asked the Parks Branch people? Natural gas supplies from Turner Valley were too uncertain to be depended upon, replied Gaherty. Then why not a coal-fired plant either near the mines at Drumheller or in Calgary itself? Construction could begin on the foundations at once, and power could be ready sooner than from any hydroelectric project. Perhaps in normal circumstances that was true, answered company officials, but in wartime, it would be difficult to secure the necessary steam equipment from British manufacturers, and they preferred not to buy in the United States.[7]

Although Parks Branch staff remained as opposed as ever to the company's plans, from the first, this opposition was mixed with an uneasy sense that the battle for Lake Minnewanka might already be lost. P. J. Jennings, the superintendent of Banff National Park, noted that the height of the proposed dam meant that the natural shoreline of Lake Minnewanka would be completely drowned and the artificiality of the water levels plainly evident. In summer, large, unsightly mudflats would always be visible. "A great deal of public criticism will inevitably result, should the company be granted the right to increase the storage at this point," the superintendent continued glumly, "and it is therefore as well to prepare to meet this type of opposition and present arguments in rebuttal." The national emergency could not, after all, be ignored, and there were examples in countries like Switzerland of joint recreational and commercial use of reservoirs.[8]

Another official, J. H. Byrne, observed that asking to dam Lake Minnewanka rather than the Spray Lakes seemed particularly offensive in light of the alteration of the park boundary in 1930 despite the "strong opposition" of preservationist groups. That boundary revision represented "a great concession to those seeking the power rights in that area" but had appeared necessary in the "general public interest and in the opinion of recognized power authorities." Now Calgary Power wanted to build a new plant and store more water at Lake Minnewanka, leaving the company, when the war ended, with "a gilt-edged bargain" in the form of its increased generating capacity. "Under ordinary circumstance and normal conditions the above drastic action could hardly be accepted by the Parks Bureau without vigorous protests and opposition," wrote Byrne, adding pessimistically, "but as matters stand at present this might be futile and unavailing."[9]

The Engineering Branch, while considering the project technically feasible, was initially sympathetic to the objections raised by their bureaucratic counterparts in Parks. Although the Spray Lakes project might take longer to build, the Minnewanka reservoir was unlikely to be filled in less than two years, and the most significant constraint on increased power production was likely to be the acquisition and installation of new generating equipment. Branch chief J. M. Wardle admitted that "once the Lake Minnewanka project is well under way the scenic value of that area is irretrievably lost."[10]

Calgary Power's proposal seemed to acquire almost irresistible momentum. When the acting deputy minister and his aides met with Gaherty and other company officials in early October, the latter were told that alternative schemes would have to be considered and proven less satisfactory. But almost at once, noted the director of the Parks Branch gloomily, discussion then turned to the practical requirements of dam construction at Lake Minnewanka such as housing for the workers and realignment of roads, as though the decision to go ahead was a foregone conclusion.[11]

Still, the bureaucrats did their best to compel Calgary Power to give serious consideration to a thermal power plant. Gaherty insisted that neither American nor British suppliers could supply the steam-generating equipment needed in the required time. Yet enquiries at the British High Commission in Ottawa revealed that the current delivery time guaranteed by British engineering firms was running around sixty-six weeks, and that this might be reduced for war orders. The company, however, was adamant that it could secure no promise of deliveries before the spring of 1942 and that, in any event, the submarine warfare in the North Atlantic made this too risky. American factories were working flat out to supply propulsion systems for the US Navy. Furthermore, while any foreign purchases would consume scarce foreign exchange reserves, hydroelectric turbines and generators were being manufactured in Canada and could be delivered by July 1941.[12]

Meanwhile, the Division of Fuels of the Department of Mines and Resources received the idea of a coal-fired plant enthusiastically. A 26,000 hp station near an efficient mine would entail a capital cost of only $125 per hp versus $200 per hp for hydroelectricity. Not only that, but the consumption of 150,000 tons of coal per year would be an important boost to the depressed mining industry in western Canada. The deputy minister advised Gaherty that he should seriously consider this, since only a "very strong case" could justify the alienation of resources inside a national park for commercial purposes, and a thermal plant could be brought into production in about the same period of time as a hydraulic development.[13]

In truth, however, the company had little interest in considering such a plan. Gaherty, a hydro engineer by training, was unwilling to give serious consideration to a thermal development. "[L]ooking to the future," he wrote to the head of the Parks Branch, "the Power Company would hesitate to invest its money in a steam plant on account of the higher cost of generation as compared with water power." Provided that the British government would give some assistance in meeting the borrowing costs on the capital in the event of a postwar depression, Calgary Power was prepared to arrange the financing of the hydroelectric project itself. Gaherty was convinced that if the dam were completed in time to catch the spring runoff in 1941, the new plant could be in production by the autumn when the nitrogen plant would require the power: "[I]n this emergency every minute counts and it is unsound to run unnecessary risks. The Cascade project is simple and quick to construct and involves the minimum hazards. It alone offers reasonable assurance of being completed in time."[14]

Faced with the company's implacable determination, the Parks Branch insisted that the power controller from Munitions and Supply examine all other options and make a finding that it was "absolutely necessary to invade the National Parks."[15] This placed H. J. Symington, a director of Calgary Power, in an embarrassing position as the power controller of Munitions and Supply, and he referred the matter to R.A.C. Henry in that department. After consultations with Henry, Charles Camsell, the deputy minister of mines and resources, wrote to Gaherty to tell him that the government was not convinced of the superiority of the hydroelectric option over a thermal station.[16]

The company quickly exerted its influence. Less than two weeks later, Gaherty attended a meeting with the deputy minister to explain his refusal to consider other alternatives. To avoid the conflict of interest in having Symington certify that the Minnewanka project was necessary for the war effort, Calgary Power had persuaded the minister himself, C. D. Howe, to write directly to T. A. Crerar, the minister of mines and resources. Howe put the matter as though the decision to dam Lake Minnewanka was a foregone conclusion. He simply explained the power requirements of the new munitions plant and concluded, "Having in mind the urgency of the situation I would appreciate the favour if you would expedite the granting of the licence to the Calgary Power Company to the fullest possible extent."[17]

Dissatisfied with the tenor of their meeting with Gaherty, the officials of the Department of Mines and Resources refused to give way. R. A. Gibson, the director of the Parks Branch, particularly resented the fact that Howe had written his letter without seeing any studies on the economics of a thermal station. "It is quite evident that the Calgary Power Company is endeavouring to force the government into an immediate decision," wrote Gibson.[18]

In a firm reply to Howe, Crerar set forth the reasons for opposing Calgary Power's plans. Despite being asked, that company had made no serious effort to investigate a steam plant as an alternative. The company had in hand enough power for the initial needs of the Alberta Nitrogen Company, and the additional power was required only as reserve in case of emergencies. Although little water would be available until 1942, Calgary Power had made no serious attempt to see if steam equipment could be put into operation before that. Crerar bluntly observed,

> It would seem that the conclusions the company have reached have been influenced by the fact that the Lake Minnewanka storage will be of very great value in the postwar years to their existing hydro plants, which now need more storage, and when once secured would avoid or at least postpone the more costly development at Spray Lakes.[19]

Sensing, however, that Calgary Power was gaining the upper hand, Gibson and his Parks Branch staff mounted another round of internal lobbying in which they rehearsed the kind of arguments that, in 1922, had led to the refusal to permit a dam at Lake Minnewanka:

> Its unique beauty lies in the wonderful blue of its waters, surrounded by mountains clad on the lower slopes with Douglas fir, Lodgepole pine, spruce and poplar. It is one of the most popular places for fishing in the National Parks.

Located just six miles from the town of Banff, the drive to the lake had become a popular attraction for sightseers. Since 1930, when the commissioner of parks had estimated its capital value to the tourist trade at $10 million, the number of visitors to Minnewanka had increased by 40 per cent. Hydrographic records indicated that the basin behind the new dam could not possibly be filled during the summer months:

The result would be the exposure of a large acreage of unsightly mudflats and banks, in spite of every attention that could possibly be given during construction for the clearing up of brush and debris in the area to be flooded. These areas would not only be a breeding ground for increasing hordes of insect pests, but would undoubtedly give off the offensive odour of decaying vegetation during the hot weather.

Failure to adhere to long-standing parks policy of prohibiting commercial development, the Minnewanka scheme would place at risk the $14 million already invested in the development of the national parks in Alberta as a tourist attraction:

In this connection it should not be overlooked that American parks, which are our main competitors for travellers, have resisted hydroelectric developments, mining operations and lumbering and pulpwood operations in National Parks. These American parks have hard-surfaced, wide, highways and are favoured by American booking agents.... Against all these complications and difficult features, we urge as our first drawing card "unspoiled scenery."

What Calgary Power was really attempting to do, Parks Branch officials argued, was to improve its efficiency and profitability:

The application of the company, while specifically based on a war requirement, is primarily designed to strengthen the power structure of the company for its ordinary business. The company admits that its practice has been to draw down the present Lake Minnewanka storage as quickly as possible in order to increase the water available for its plants on the Bow River.[20]

Moreover, the National Parks Act of 1930 was quite clear: any area that was to be used for commercial development should be excluded from the park system.

> If Lake Minnewanka is to be looked upon as a commercial asset it really belongs to the province, and the province should be left free to deal with the company so that maximum benefits may accrue to power users and that other provincial interests may be served.

If the dam were to be built, the whole area around the lake probably ought to be withdrawn from Banff National Park, and the authority to approve the development left in the hands of the Alberta government.[21] Even in a wartime emergency, the Parks Branch people drew their line in the sand.

The defenders of Lake Minnewanka against power development plans were hampered, however, by the lack of a strongly organized preservationist lobby in 1940. Unlike the 1920s, when the fight over Lake Minnewanka had created a big public outcry and the proposal to dam the Spray Lakes had brought the Canadian National Parks Association (CNPA) into being, there was little public protest this time around. W. J. Selby Walker of Calgary, a long-time campaigner for wilderness preservation, did write with characteristic brio to the Parks Branch on behalf of the CNPA as soon as the plan was aired:

> This has all the earmarks of another attempt by the U.S. Power Trust to open all park water for power, to be followed by the miners and the lumbermen and the complete destruction of our National Park system, as was attempted some years ago at the Spray Lakes, which were essential to the welfare of the world to be developed immediately but when taken out of the Park and made available for the last 12 years seem to have lost all their vaunted utility.[22]

But the decade of the Depression had evidently taken its toll upon the vigour of the CNPA and its members. Although Walker still claimed to be executive secretary of the association, he did not orchestrate a lobbying

1941 DAM AT LAKE MINNEWANKA (AUTHOR PHOTO).

campaign of the sort that had succeeded in the past. Obviously, the fact that the development of additional power was justified as part of the war effort would have made any such campaign more difficult. In this emergency, many people were willing to give the company the benefit of the doubt. Walker complained that there was plenty of energy from natural gas simply going to waste in Turner Valley: "Suicidal exploitation of our natural resources will not help the next generation to retire our bond issues." But, he added, "the possibility of having the project constructed as a war measure at public expense and becoming available as salvage after the war is less patriotic than alluring to St. James St. [the financial centre of Montreal]." All he could suggest was that the lands around Lake Minnewanka, including the Banff townsite, be removed from the national park if they were to be developed commercially, as had been done with the Spray Lakes. This idea had already been carefully considered and rejected. The superintendent of Banff National Park advised that there was no suitable natural boundary line. He was particularly opposed to cutting the town of Banff out of the park, since it was "a pathetic little hamlet" that could not even afford to fund its school system without a sizable annual subvention from the CPR.[23]

The only other public opposition seems to have come from the Alberta Fish and Game Association, whose vice president complained that Calgary Power had deliberately taken on the contract with the Alberta Nitrogen Company as a means of justifying the new development: "It is, however, a cleverly contrived scheme to wangle something that the Power Company knows that they would otherwise never get." But the director of the Parks Branch could only reply that if the application was justified by a genuine war emergency, then it would be up to Parliament to decide whether or not to grant it.[24]

Balanced against these feeble pressures was the support of the Town of Banff's Advisory Council, which in the past, had often taken an ambivalent position on power development in the park, the dependence on tourism being balanced by the desire for more industrial and commercial growth. The superintendent of Banff National Park reported that many local residents now favoured the plan: "The local working men are, of course, in favour of the project chiefly because of the possibility of work and wages for another year at least – a very short-sighted and extremely selfish view." The council advised all Alberta MPs to support the damming of Lake Minnewanka since the availability of low-cost power would be a strong inducement to industry to locate in the region once the war was over.[25]

With that kind of support, Calgary Power began to act as though a decision in its favour was a foregone conclusion. The director of the Parks Branch complained about the company's attitude:

> The actions of Calgary Power Company's field organization since the negotiations were commenced a few weeks ago no doubt indicate the degree of consideration that the National Parks administration may expect from the company. Even with the knowledge that the chief officials of the company are at Ottawa lobbying for a concession, which, if granted, will be extremely valuable to the company, the field staff ignore the Park

Superintendent, notwithstanding the fact that they are well aware that the Superintendent is in full charge of the park and must answer for whatever goes on inside the park boundaries.

This attitude was made plain when the company simply added to its application a proposal to divert Carrot Creek into Lake Minnewanka to increase its storage capacity without even consulting the Parks Branch.[26]

The redoubtable C. D. Howe remained unwavering in his support of the project. When Alberta MPs complained that not enough new industries had been located in the province, the minister told them that war factories could not be located in Calgary at present owing to the shortage of electrical energy. "We want all the power that Alberta can produce now, and we can use the whole lot and more, if we can get it," said the minister. Faced with this implacable resolve, Crerar gave way and advised Howe on November 30 that in view of the ammonia plant's power needs, Calgary Power's application would be granted.[27] The long struggle to prevent Lake Minnewanka from becoming a much larger hydroelectric reservoir ended in the flux of wartime.

Up popped a new obstacle. How could such works be constructed inside a national park from a legal perspective? The Justice Department believed that the National Parks Act would have to be amended because the cabinet's powers under the War Measures Act were not broad enough to permit activities specifically forbidden by an act of Parliament. For Howe, this was not good enough. There was no time to lay the matter before Parliament. The power company wanted work on the dam to be far enough advanced in the spring of 1941 to capture the runoff, which required an immediate start.[28]

Eventually, the Justice Department was persuaded to agree that since the work was required for war purposes, the cabinet could issue an order-in-council granting temporary approval for the project. However, both the federal and provincial legislative bodies would have to approve the project with the necessary legislation at a later date. Premier William Aberhart quickly announced his support. He made no reference to the province's previous efforts to gain control of any water storage in the Bow watershed, noting, "This province is anxious for development of power to aid industrializing our province and to do our utmost in contributing to the war effort." Within a fortnight, the necessary order-in-council was passed.[29]

Only the granting of an interim licence to the company remained before the work could begin at Lake Minnewanka. This proved more time consuming and contentious than anticipated because the Parks Branch insisted that an independent landscape architect should supervise design work to ensure that the installations inside the park should be as unobtrusive as possible. Initially, Calgary Power authorities seemed quite agreeable to the idea, but they soon began to resist, arguing that because the power produced at Cascade was to be sold to Alberta Nitrogen at less than cost, the utmost economy would have to be practiced in construction. The company wanted its consulting engineer, T. H. Hogg from Ontario Hydro, to have the final say on all design questions.[30]

Hogg, however, made it clear that he would resist any substantial spending on landscaping. Eventually, the company reluctantly agreed to retain landscape gardener Stanley Thompson and to carry out any design changes that he considered necessary. With that question settled, the job of clearing the brush and timber from the hillside around the lake finally got under way in February 1941, the contract having been awarded to members of the Nakoda Indian band who lived nearby.[31]

With construction under way and the process of drawing up formal agreements between the two levels of governments slowly proceeding, Mines and Resources Minister Crerar finally made a public announcement of the plan to amend the National Parks Act to legalize the power development within Banff National Park in April 1941. Anticipating criticism, he admitted that the development represented "a drastic departure from the policy established for many years." He pointed out, however, that Calgary Power had been using Lake Minnewanka to store water since 1912 and that there appeared to be no other means of procuring the power required for the war effort.[32]

That argument, needless to say, did not placate Selby Walker of the Canadian National Parks Association. He had already complained to

J. Selby Walker on a hike in the mountains (Glenbow Archives, NA-5566-4).

the minister about this short-sighted policy, contending that American park administration was far more enlightened. In correspondence with another Parks Branch official, Walker claimed that the association was drawing growing support

> from an increasing number of influential people ... who are ... beginning to realize that your department has too long been deprived of that influence, to which its importance both as a producer of revenue and development of high standard of national health entitle it.[33]

Walker continued to fuss and fume. After listening to an engineer from Calgary Power describe the planned project to the Calgary Canadian

Club, he complained that the company seemed intent upon actually drawing attention to their works:

> Their power plant will not only be plainly visible from the road, but the motoring public will be encouraged to take a good look at the project because a road is to be constructed leaving the highway near the power plant and running beside their hydro pipe and across the top of the dam to connect with the one-time Minnewanka highway.... [I]n fact, the whole project is to be a joy forever to the Park visitors, and a blessing to the shareholders of the Calgary Power Company and built by about three million of the ten million appropriation.... How long must this suicidal exploitation of the natural resources of western Canada for the benefit of the eastern capitalist and the votes of the eastern majority be carried on?[34]

But the fact that Walker alone bothered to register a formal protest suggests that public opinion was little aroused about this issue in 1941.

Near the end of the parliamentary session in June 1941, Crerar introduced the legislation necessary to amend the agreement to transfer the natural resources of Alberta so as to permit the Minnewanka development. Crerar set forth the background and argued that the government would not have agreed to the application except for the national emergency:

> We are in a desperate war. We do not know how many dreary, heavy months lie ahead. We do know this, if we are to succeed the ... munitions must be supplied. The government felt that under the circumstances this plant should be brought into operation at the earliest possible day, and the importance ... is the justification for a departure from what has been the policy of all governments in this country for the last twenty years. It does not establish any precedent, because it is definitely tied up to war needs.[35]

Parliamentarians were quite prepared to let the bill go through with no serious challenge, with the exception of Toronto Conservative T. L. Church, who launched into a ringing tirade against I. W. Killam and his financial associates for using the wartime emergency for personal gain:

> We know these people in Ontario; we have learned about their methods and how they go about getting things through this parliament, as they have for nearly thirty years in the past. Some of the millionaires who are at the head of the super power trust centred in Montreal know no politics; ... they are millionaires first, last and all the time, grabbing the public domain.[36]

But no MPs supported Church, and the measure was speedily passed into law.[37]

All that now remained was for the Parks Branch to see that Calgary Power carried out its commitment to landscape the development as agreed upon to minimize its visibility. That did not prove easy. In the fall of 1941, Parks Branch employee James Smart, in correspondence with his superior, Roy Gibson, predicted: "I believe we are bound to have a lot of trouble in connection with getting the Calgary Power Company to undertake the landscape work they have promised, and it is liable to drag along for a number of years." At a meeting in the deputy minister's office with Gaherty and Hogg, the consulting engineer claimed that no equipment could be spared from the construction project for landscaping, and Gaherty tried to retreat from an earlier promise to build a loop road around Lake Minnewanka.[38]

Despite the efforts of departmental officials, the company continued to evade their obligations. In the spring of 1942, with the Cascade power plant almost ready to come into production, the Parks Branch stepped up the pressure, but in spite of another meeting with Gaherty, the work was left undone, reportedly because I. W. Killam considered it too expensive.[39] At a further meeting that autumn, Gaherty finally offered to pay $35,000 toward the cost of landscaping but failed to produce a final agreement.[40]

CASCADE POWER PLANT (AUTHOR PHOTO).

Smart's prediction proved correct and the matter remained unsettled for years.

What particularly irritated these officials was that Calgary Power installed a powerful pump behind the dam at Lake Minnewanka so that even while the reservoir was filling, they were drawing it down below the levels previously permitted in order to supply water to their other Bow River plants. At the same time, Gaherty tried to persuade Ottawa to replace the interim development licence with a final one, which would make it all the more difficult to exert control over the company. The new Cascade plant even operated during the summer of 1943, leaving mudflats twenty feet wide around the lakeshore, although it had always been assumed that the reservoir would be left to fill up during the tourist season.[41]

In the spring of 1944, the company asked permission to draw down the level in Lake Minnewanka even farther than usual, claiming that it had faced an unprecedented demand for power in the fall of 1943 owing to a coal shortage in Edmonton, which had forced the company to ship power north. In addition, the ammonia plant was operating at full blast and the lateness of the spring breakup was diminishing the flow out of the mountains into the Bow. When the Department of Mines and Resources investigated these claims, it discovered that a special allotment of coal had been granted to the company to produce power for Edmonton. Finding, however, that it was cheaper to produce hydroelectricity, Calgary Power had simply used more water than usual. Eventually, the department was forced to agree to allow the exceptional drawdown, although the onset of the spring thaw rendered this unnecessary in the end.[42]

Faced with the intransigence and aggressiveness of the Calgary Power Company, the Parks Branch retreated to trying to reduce the visual impact of the Cascade power plant and, in particular, of the tall, watertower-like surge tank – a shock absorber against water hammer effects in the penstocks – standing on the rim of the Bow valley where the feeder pipes plunged down the hill. The result was an unintentional comic interlude.

Canadian officials approached the British High Commission in the spring of 1942. Was it correct, asked Parks Branch employee James Smart, that a camouflage expert named Professor Webster was visiting Canada? Would he have time to consult about some camouflage? This was, he clarified,

> ... not in connection with war purposes, but more or less to blend in a piece of construction which has been imposed on the landscape of our mountain country in Banff National Park, and it has been considered that through the means of camouflage we may be able to render this piece of construction less conspicuous.[43]

After some confusion, it turned out that the expert was not Professor Webster but a landscape artist named Mr. Ironside. After looking at photographs of the site, Ironside suggested that the plan to paint the surge tank grey was probably a mistake. England was full of gasometers and water towers painted grey, which only made them ugly and conspicuous. The artist suggested that it would be better to paint the tank white.

Admittedly, this would not make it inconspicuous, but it would be more pleasant to look at.[44]

Rejecting this rather implausible advice, the Parks Branch continued to worry about how to improve the appearance of the surge tank. By the fall of 1942, Smart was wondering if it would be a good idea to coat it in "haze" or "mist" paint, which the National Research Council had developed for camouflaging ships at sea, on the grounds that the tank was seen from the highway silhouetted against the sky like a ship's superstructure. When the National Research Council was unable to make a supply of the new paint available, it was decided to use "invisible grey" paint, perhaps with a little blue added to help blend into the mountain sky.[45]

As it turned out, woodpeckers had the last ironic word in the long-running anxiety about shielding hydroelectric installations from visitors to Banff National Park. The penstocks at the Cascade plant had been surrounded in wood cladding. Not only did this protect them from frost damage on the exterior, but the wood blended well into the landscape. When new penstocks were constructed in the postwar era, they too were framed in wood, along with the towering surge tank, which loomed on the banks of the Bow just inside the eastern gate of the park. Not only did this cladding soothe the bureaucrats, but, unexpectedly, it especially pleased the birds. Woodpeckers eventually discovered these wood-clad structures, and for whatever reason – insect infestations, or perhaps the resounding noise they gave off when hammered – they tore the wooden siding to shreds. When the dilapidated cladding had to be removed, parks bureaucrats resigned themselves to the naked aluminum-painted metallic structures that remain to this day.[46]

These cosmetic efforts on the surge tank could not conceal the fact that raising the dam at Lake Minnewanka produced all of the unfortunate results that the Parks Branch had long predicted. As forecast, Calgary Power continued to drag its feet about paying the cost of landscaping; it took until 1947 to extract the final $35,000 owing.[47] The major problem, though, was the extent of the mudflats around the shores of the lake during tourist season. Calgary Power's interim licence did not contain any precise commitments about summertime water levels at Lake Minnewanka. When the dam was raised, the company had promised to allow the lake to fill up quickly in the spring except in emergencies, but in 1946, the bureaucrats were still complaining that for the past two years, the water had been as much as fifteen feet below the promised level on July 1.[48]

The only lever that the Parks Branch possessed was that no final licence for the dam had been issued. By 1947, Calgary Power was eager to have this settled since they were planning a new issue of debentures and feared that lack of the licence would reduce their price. Eventually, they persuaded Minister of Mines and Resources J. A. Mackinnon to intervene and order the bureaucrats to issue the licence.[49] Still, company negotiators refused to commit themselves firmly to ensuring that the water at Lake Minnewanka was at any particular level in the summer months, pleading the growing demand for electric power. In the end, the minister was given the formal authority to regulate water levels at the lake although no levels were specified. However, the company was given an incentive – a sliding scale of rental payments – to keep them high in the summer. That settled, the final licence converting Lake Minnewanka into a power reservoir was issued in May 1947.[50]

The experience of the Department of Mines and Resources in dealing with Calgary Power, once the dam at Lake Minnewanka had been raised and the Cascade power plant built, only seemed to confirm what national parks administrators had been arguing since the 1920s: hydroelectric reservoirs had no place inside the park system. Had it been practically possible, the lake would have been cut out of Banff National Park as the Spray Lakes had been in 1930, but that did not seem easy to do.

So that is how, as a war measure, an elegant rectangular building housing hydroelectric-generating equipment came to be planted prominently beside the highway and still greets visitors today on the eastern approaches to Banff National Park. So too, as a war measure, a huge earthen berm and regulating headworks raised the level of Lake Minnewanka sixty feet, drowning the former dam and the park's own hydroelectric facility in the process.[51] The wartime emergency made it impossible to resist the company's demands for additional capacity to supply power to the ammonia plant, particularly in view of Calgary Power's strong political connections to C. D. Howe's Department of Munitions and Supply. The public outcry that had stopped the Minnewanka dam in the 1920s was muted in 1940 by the experience of depression and war. The company emerged victorious. And as a signal of triumph, a solitary surge tank rose like a gleaming technological obelisk in plain view on a bench beside the highway.

CHAPTER 9

Public Power

For fifteen years, an important question of public policy lay dormant. Would Alberta embark upon a program of public ownership electrification? First the Great Depression and then the Second World War intervened to prevent the question from even being posed. The issue had been raised, as we have seen, at the end of the 1920s, when for a moment it seemed as if Alberta was poised to follow Ontario's example. But the onset of the Depression meant that the province could scarcely meet its existing obligations, much less contemplate borrowing the millions of dollars necessary to buy out the private electric companies. Some of the rights to control natural resources so eagerly sought by the provincial government were even turned back temporarily to federal jurisdiction. A world war created other, higher priorities and temporarily commandeered provincial fiscal room to prosecute the war effort. But once the war was over and, especially, as a new era of economic growth and prosperity began to bloom, the time had surely come to pose this question once again.

The transition from a rural and agricultural province to an urban and industrial one created new political pressures. The province's Social Credit government – which had swept into power, led by William Aberhart, during the depths of the Depression in 1935 – had to adjust to the changing times if it were to retain office. When Aberhart died in 1943, he was succeeded as party leader and premier by his young associate, Ernest C. Manning. It thus fell to Manning, an immensely shrewd politician, to preside over the transformation of Social Credit from a populist, rural protest movement into a pragmatic, conservative party that emphasized conservatism and efficiency in government. One of the issues with which Manning had to grapple was the campaign for a publicly owned electrical system like that in Ontario or Manitoba. That demand came primarily from the traditional sources of Social Credit strength on the rural roads and in small towns, where an agitation for rapid rural electrification arose during the late 1940s. Many farmers, accustomed to the co-operative traditions of western Canadian agriculture and to the province's government-owned telephone system, looked to the Government of Alberta to take up the task of supplying them with low-cost power.

Manning, however, recognized that his new-found friends in the oil industry, many of whom came from the United States, would not be enthusiastic about actions by a provincial government that smacked of "socialism." The premier decided, in fact, that the way to stay in power was to redefine Social Credit as a vital weapon in the fight against the menace of the Left, embodied in the Co-operative Commonwealth Federation (which had won power in Saskatchewan in 1944). In the context of the Cold War struggle against communism, this political manoeuvre proved popular with Albertans, who continued to re-elect Manning with overwhelming majorities until the end of the 1960s.[1]

The growing anti-socialism of Social Credit made it more difficult for the provincial government to support the creation of a public electrical system, despite the fact that the strongest pressure for it came from some of the movement's long-standing supporters. The debate over public power in Alberta, which ultimately ended with a victory for the supporters of private ownership, naturally affected the development of the private utilities, in particular Calgary Power. As long as the issue hung in the balance, the company showed little enthusiasm for new capital projects to enhance generating capacity, despite the steady growth of demand. Only after it became clear that the provincial government was ready to allow the private utilities to operate within a regulatory environment did Calgary Power begin to press for more water storage. Thus, the time required to resolve the issue of public versus private power in Alberta removed the pressure for more construction inside Banff National Park for several years.

At the end of the Second World War, no more than eighteen hundred of the fifty-five thousand farms in Alberta, slightly over 3 per cent, had electrical service.[2] The Social Credit government, with its rural and small town base, was naturally particularly sensitive on this issue. Near the end of 1944, the province established the Alberta Power Commission to survey the power requirements of the province and to study the equalization of rates charged to various classes of consumers. Auditors were appointed to value the assets of the Calgary Power Company and its smaller counterpart, Canadian Utilities (formerly Mid-West Utilities), which served the southeastern part of the province, in case their expropriation or purchase was contemplated. The northern portions of the province, as noted earlier, were served by lines running out from the municipally owned steam-generating plant in Edmonton. The Alberta Power Commission quickly concluded that a comprehensive review of the electricity situation could not proceed until the provincial government had made the formal decision to take control of the electricity industry completely, to build a public distribution system to distribute privately generated power, or to leave the industry entirely in private hands.[3]

The cabinet considered the issue during the next year or so. A good many Albertans proved dubious about the idea of creating a large public enterprise modelled upon Ontario Hydro or the Manitoba Power Commission. The chairman of the Electrification Committee of Ponoka, Alberta, for instance, pressed the Social Credit government to allow the Calgary Power Company to proceed with the task of wiring the rural areas and small towns. A study by the staff of the Department of Economic Affairs in the spring of 1946 concluded that pressure for the acquisition of electrical systems by governments might be peaking at the very moment when private interests were actually eager to unload their high-cost conventional generating stations and replace them with much cheaper nuclear power plants.[4]

By the summer of 1946, Premier E. C. Manning's cabinet, having concluded that the existing private utilities should undertake rural electrification, began pressing the two companies for precise targets.[5] When

ERNEST MANNING, PREMIER OF
ALBERTA (GLENBOW ARCHIVES, NA-
2922-14).

the private utilities stalled, unhappy about committing themselves to this high-cost, low-volume segment of the electricity market, Manning ordered the Alberta Power Commission to draw up a plan.

The commission, in turn, recruited Herbert Cottingham, the former chairman of the Manitoba Power Commission, to undertake a study. In February 1947, he strongly advised against any scheme by the province to undertake rural electrification apart from the existing distribution system: "Farm electrification is the most costly service in the West," he warned, "and can only be economically performed in conjunction with general service to cities, towns and villages." Cottingham, not surprisingly, was a fervent public ownership man:

> The acquisition of the utilities is the best solution of the farm electrification extensions and is in the interest of urban, rural and farm population. If this is done the Government of Alberta will duplicate the phenomenal success achieved by other provinces.

He was convinced that the result would be electricity supply at lower rates than at present charged by Calgary Power and Canadian Utilities.[6]

Doubtless aware of the tenor of Cottingham's report, Calgary Power became sufficiently concerned about the possibility of a government takeover that it reorganized its corporate structure in the spring of 1947. During the 1930s, I. W. Killam and his associates had used the Montreal holding company to acquire, in addition to its Alberta assets, 85 per cent of the capital stock of the Ottawa Valley Power Company. The company now applied to the federal minister of mines and resources to divide its properties into two legally separate elements. Calgary Power Limited, with a head office in Calgary, would operate all the Alberta utilities while the Montreal holding company (called Calgary Power Company Limited) would control the entire undertaking. This division would presumably have made a severance easier in the event of a takeover. The federal authorities raised no objections to this restructuring.[7]

Killam and his friends need not have worried so much. Cottingham's advice was not well received. After a final flirtation with the orthodox doctrines of Social Credit around the end of the Second World War, Premier Manning had quickly adopted conventional economic policies that emphasized fiscal prudence and resisted an expanded role for government in most sectors. Socialism was now the main enemy of the Social Credit movement, opening an Albertan salient in the Cold War battle against communism.[8] Taking its cues from its political masters in the spring of 1947, the Alberta Power Commission ignored Cottingham's views and proposed that the private utilities should undertake a ten-year program to make power available to three-fifths of all farms in the province, all those that were not too remote or not likely to be only marginal users of electricity. If 70 per cent of those 33,000 farms were to be hooked up, then 21,300 connections would have to be made, nearly 80 per cent of them by Calgary Power. The targets recommended were two thousand farms each in 1948 and 1949, followed by twenty-five hundred connections yearly over the succeeding seven years.[9]

In July 1947, Premier Manning wrote to the presidents of Calgary Power and Canadian Utilities asking that they commit themselves to undertake this proposed program. To make the service attractive to farmers, the basic rural electricity rate would be limited to a base rate of four dollars per month for up to twenty kilowatt hours of current. Manning hoped to induce the companies to co-operate by offering them a subsidy equal to half the amount that they paid in federal corporate income taxes, a sum estimated at about $217,500 annually, which was rebated to the province by Ottawa under the tax-sharing agreements. This rebate, as he reminded the utility men, the provincial government stood to lose in revenue should it expropriate the companies in order to ensure rural electrification, since provincial utilities were not subject to federal income taxes. Manning concluded firmly,

> The Government of Alberta would prefer to have the programme ... implemented by the present companies, but the development of the province has reached the stage where a comprehensive programme of rural electrification cannot longer be delayed.[10]

Doubtless relieved that any threat of a takeover seemed unlikely, the two private companies nonetheless, and not surprisingly, displayed little enthusiasm for such a scheme. How could the large sums required for extending service be raised when the returns would be so paltry? G. A. Gaherty complained that the proposed basic rate barely covered the cost of producing and transmitting the current and provided no return on the capital invested in the plant or insurance against risk. Calgary Power already faced the need to raise approximately $10 million to expand its generating capacity, but the real need was a subsidy to cover the heavy cost of extending rural lines, which was five or six times as high per customer as in the province's cities. While Ontario Hydro's rural lines had an average of 7.15 consumers per mile, the present rural lines in Alberta had but 1.3 users. With an average investment of $750 per additional customer required, the cost of adding over twenty-one thousand new connections would be more than $17 million. Instead, Gaherty proposed that rural electrical co-operatives be established to purchase current from Calgary Power and that the government agree to provide a subsidy equal to half the cost of the rural distribution systems constructed co-operatively.[11]

H. R. Milner of Canadian Utilities was equally unenthusiastic about the proposed rural electrification plan. He suggested that before the next provincial election, the government announce its commitment to action but point out to the electorate that the postwar boom had made it almost impossible to obtain the capital goods needed for such a massive scheme. Social Credit could thus reap the electoral advantage of its policy commitment, "even if it would have to remain in the wrapper for the next two or three years."[12]

The premier referred the issue back to the Alberta Power Commission. In a report rendered in October 1947, the commission argued that the private utilities were offering no more than to provide rural electric service in areas where they could earn a profit. By demanding hefty subsidies from the government to consumers, Calgary Power had eliminated any financial risk. The idea that shortages of material could justify the postponement of the entire program was exploded by pointing out that the Manitoba Power Commission was planning to make thirty-seven hundred rural connections in 1947 and another five thousand in 1948. In light of the foot dragging by the companies and the expense of constructing a rival public system, the report concluded:

> If it is the desire of the government to engage in expansion of distribution of electrical energy throughout the province, and with particular reference to the extension of rural electrification, it would be the view of your commission that such a policy can best be carried out by taking over the existing facilities of the power companies and operating the same as an integrated unit as a public utility through the Alberta Power Commission.

The first step recommended was the acquisition of Calgary Power, either by negotiation or expropriation.[13]

The issue would not go away because the Alberta government remained under pressure to take action to promote rural electrification. Pointing out that the number of electrified farms in the United States had risen from only 10 per cent in 1935 to over 60 per cent in 1947, mainly due to the New Deal program, Ken Reid of Islay argued that the time had come for the provincial government to take action:

> We believe in private enterprise when it's progressive. Otherwise we expect governments to wake them [sic] up or show them up.

You spent [$]7 million on main roads – and half a million on oil
sands – why not spend some to help the hard working farmer?[14]

Rural Albertans who shared these views and believed that private enterprise would not bring transmission lines to their farm gates for years to
come insisted that a plebiscite be held on the issue of public versus private ownership of electrical utilities on provincial election day, August 17,
1948. E. C. Manning, fearful that American oil explorers would be fright-
ened off by any "socialistic" extension of state enterprise, campaigned ac-
tively against any takeover of the utility companies. He argued that such
an experiment was "risky" and likely to lead to power shortages if undertaken. Predictions were made that it would cost $40 million to acquire
the existing companies, $40 million to extend rural transmission lines,
and another $25 million to build new generating stations. H. R. Milner of
Canadian Utilities reminded Albertans of the costs incurred in extending
Alberta Government Telephones into rural areas and warned against any
repetition of this extravagance.[15]

When the votes were counted, E. C. Manning had easily won another
term of office, and public power went down to defeat by the narrow margin of 139,991 to 139,840, largely because of strong opposition in southern
Alberta cities like Calgary (70% against), Lethbridge (65% against), and
Medicine Hat (81% against). Edmonton narrowly rejected the proposal by
only 51 per cent. In the aftermath, the premier laconically declared, "We
will just carry on as before."[16]

Even many rural dwellers agreed with the government's policy. The
executive of the new Alberta Rural Electrification Association, formed at
the time of the plebiscite, voted unanimously against public ownership:

Everyone felt that the private companies had given very satisfactory
service in the past, and their efforts for rural electrification were
all that could be expected under existing material and labour
conditions, and that no advantage would be gained by the
provincial government taking over.[17]

Attempts to persuade the government to call another plebiscite on the grounds that the results of the first one had been inconclusive seem to have elicited little enthusiasm.[18] Although the Alberta Rural Electrification Association reversed its position and voted in favour of a provincial utility in 1950, the government paid little attention. A 1951 article by the president of the Farmers' Union of Alberta condemned the rate of expansion of rural service by the power companies as "absolutely unsatisfactory," but the provincial minister of industries and labour hastened to defend the record of private enterprise. He claimed that twelve thousand farms had already received electrical service and another four thousand would be hooked up by the end of the year. An effort to have the provincial legislature order another plebiscite was stifled by the Social Credit government in 1952.[19]

The debate over establishing a public power system in Alberta effectively ended in 1948 with the plebiscite. Strong as the support for such a plan was in the traditional centres of Social Credit support, the voters in the booming cities of Calgary, Lethbridge, and Medicine Hat delivered a decisive verdict against the idea. Apart from a general satisfaction in those urban centres with the service provided by the private utility, Edmonton and Calgary residents perhaps sensed a threat to their own municipally owned distribution systems (and generating capability, in Edmonton's case). That was sufficient to convince Premier Manning that he could safely ignore the public power proponents, confident that Social Credit loyalists were unlikely to desert his government over this issue.

The failure of the rural supporters of a provincial utility to carry the day meant that the existing public-private hybrid would continue, with Calgary Power supplying a municipal distribution system in Calgary. Edmonton would be served by its own civic generating station. Most other urban areas were supplied by one of the two private companies. Premier Manning made it plain that the fight against socialism debarred his government from establishing a provincial utility without overwhelming support from the voters, and that had not been forthcoming.

The debate over public power in Alberta in the late 1940s caused Calgary Power to place its expansion plans on the back burner until the outcome was clear. I. W. Killam and G. A. Gaherty had no intention of undertaking any major expansion of generating capacity if a government takeover was a real possibility. With that issue settled, Calgary Power could resume planning in earnest to expand its generating capacity to meet sky-rocketing demand for electricity, which threatened severe shortages in the near future. That, in turn, would almost certainly entail the extension of its water storage capacity inside Banff National Park and bring the issue of wilderness preservation versus power development to the fore once more.

CHAPTER 10

Reversing Rivers

With the debate over public versus private enterprise settled in favour of the Calgary Power Company by the late 1940s and with a postwar economic boom fuelled by new oil discoveries under way, the federal and provincial governments once more found themselves under intense pressure to approve new power projects. The topography of southern Alberta made the Bow River the prime site for water storage for hydroelectric development. With the minister of mines and resources being from Edmonton, the demand for more power was bound to receive a sympathetic hearing. The federal government had already made an important concession to the Calgary Power Company in 1930 by carving the Spray Lakes out of the national park to permit their use as a reservoir. The company's power surplus during the 1930s and its focus on the more readily available Minnewanka option during the war effectively sidelined consideration of the Spray Lakes development. However, once looming shortages had aroused power users and provincial politicians, it was only a matter of time before Spray Lakes development proposals would resurface.

With the public power question settled once and for all, Calgary Power's enthusiasm for expanding its capacity to meet the demand revived. The company, with strong municipal and provincial backing, readily asked permission to proceed with the long-deferred Spray Lakes project. The territory had been cut out of the national park by the Parks Act of 1930. This meant that prime responsibility for approving development lay with the provincial government. But in the Canadian federal system, nothing is simple. The federal government remained a key player because the river whose waters would be rerouted and diverted for power production drained into Banff National Park. Moreover, revised plans for the development indicated that ever more land would have to be removed from the park to accommodate a larger reservoir.

After receiving permission to raise the dam at Lake Minnewanka in 1941, Calgary Power's energy requirements seemed to be met for the time being. However, no sooner had construction begun on the Cascade power plant in the summer of 1942 than the company revived its plans to use the Spray Lakes as a power reservoir. The revision of the National Parks Act in 1930 had, of course, removed the Spray basin itself from Banff National Park, but as we have seen, in the wartime emergency, Calgary Power opted instead for the less costly project at Lake Minnewanka. Now, with wartime demand straining generating capacity, the Spray development again began to look economically attractive.

Having conceded the removal of the Spray Lakes from the National Park system, the Lands, Parks, and Forests Branch (hereafter, the Parks Branch) of the Department of Mines and Resources was now simply concerned to ensure that the flow of the Spray River, which drained into the Bow at Banff, remained sufficient to preserve its scenic appearance. Calgary Power had lost its initial enthusiasm for the project in 1928 when Interior Minister Charles Stewart had insisted that the Spray River near its mouth must carry 500 cubic feet of water per second (cfs) since it entered the Bow right in the midst of the golf course at the CPR's Banff Springs Hotel. Because the Spray itself had no tributaries to swell its size for about fifteen miles below its headwaters, the flow demanded by Stewart would have required the release of a great deal of water over a dam at the Spray Lakes every summer. Every cubic foot flowing over the spillway would entail the loss of thirty-five hundred kilowatt hours of generating capacity to Calgary Power's Bow River plants during the ensuing winter. Company officials claimed that the whole storage project would be rendered uneconomical if more than 200 cfs had to be running at the mouth of the Spray in the tourist season.[1]

Despite the Spray Lakes having been removed from the park system in 1930, the agreement transferring natural resources to Alberta still empowered the federal government to fix the levels in watercourses like the Spray River that flowed into the parks so as to preserve their scenic beauty. When G. A. Gaherty once more raised the question of damming the Spray Lakes in the autumn of 1942, the superintendent of Banff National Park warned "that any move by his company to divert the flow of the Spray River would most assuredly be bitterly opposed by the Canadian Pacific Railway Company and by this Bureau."[2]

For its part, Calgary Power was considering altering its plans for the Spray Lakes development so as to mute such criticisms. Instead of channelling the stored water through a tunnel directly to a high-head plant on the Bow near Canmore, it was considering releasing it down the Spray River itself to be used at the existing Ghost, Horseshoe, and Kananaskis plants. Not only would this be much less costly, but it would avoid many of the problems created by low levels in the Spray in summer.[3] In the end, however, the company decided not to proceed with the development during the war and no formal application was presented, presumably because of the difficulty in raising capital and securing generating and other equipment under the circumstances.

It was obvious, however, that future growth in power demand would probably increase the need for more water storage in the Rocky Mountains. Near the end of 1944, Calgary Power suggested increasing the capacity of Lake Minnewanka by diverting Forty Mile Creek.[4] But company officials were aware of the problems likely to be created by more development inside Banff National Park, so in 1945 they began investigating a possible dam site lower down on the Bow near Cochrane, as well as on the upper Kananaskis River, both outside the park system and fully under provincial control. In addition, studies were made of an entirely new development in another watershed – across the Continental Divide in British Columbia near Canal Flats on the Kootenay River – that could be linked to the rest of the system by a transmission line running south of Banff National Park.[5] None of these schemes was undertaken, and the only addition to the system's capacity was Barrier, a small plant on the Kananaskis River, producing 16,000 hp with a head of 155 feet.[6]

While Albertans debated the possibility of establishing a provincial electrical utility, Calgary Power put on hold the undertaking of any new major projects. By mid-1947, however, it became clear that E. C. Manning did not favour public power when the premier asked the private utilities to submit plans for rural electrification. The plebiscite of 1948 demonstrated the lack of a strong consensus in favour of public ownership, and little more was heard of the matter thereafter. As a result, the company began to explore developing the Spray Lakes once again, starting in 1947. That brought a protest from the remnants of the wilderness preservation movement that had originally sprung into existence during the 1920s to defend the Spray Lakes against the depredations of the power developers.[7]

More significant were rumblings from the CPR reminding the federal government that the junction of the Spray and Bow Rivers was the scenic centre of the Banff townsite and that the Spray was heavily fished. Any move to reduce the flow in the Spray that would impair its scenic beauty or fish spawn would meet strong resistance from the railway and other tourist operators with heavy investments in the region. In response, the new deputy minister of mines and resources, H. L. Keenleyside, inquired confidentially how much money the railway actually had invested in the Banff region. The reply was $12.5 million, although the replacement value would obviously be much larger. Parks Branch bureaucrats were well aware of the value of such an ally:

> We should see that the Canadian Pacific Railway Company officials are kept advised of developments. No final decision on this proposition should be made without the Railway Company's approval, as their development at Banff involving many millions of dollars would be seriously affected if anything was allowed that would in any way spoil the beautiful Spray valley.[8]

But as in the past, the federal policy-makers quickly discovered that there were powerful interests who favoured going ahead with the proposed plan at top speed. The Calgary Electric Commissioner pointed out to the prime minister that power load in the city was rising almost 10 per cent annually and that additional capacity was needed to ensure continued industrial growth. Premier Manning also wrote to the acting minister of mines and resources, J. A. Mackinnon, to demand speedy action to deal with an increasingly serious power shortage in the province.[9]

When Calgary Power submitted its formal application to develop the Spray Lakes in the spring of 1948, it made a number of significant amendments to previous plans. Over the next five years, the company was prepared to invest up to $18 million in order to add about 100,000 hp annually to its generating capacity. Instead of a tunnel to carry the water from the Spray Lakes reservoir to a headpond above Canmore, it was now proposed to divert the water through a canal along the valley of Goat Creek. Flooding this valley would require a formal act of Parliament to alter the boundaries of Banff National Park in order to remove another twenty square miles of land for commercial purposes.

As for the flow of the Spray River, the company was now prepared to spill enough water from its reservoir to keep 180 cfs flowing out of the mouth of the river at Banff during the tourist season. G. A. Gaherty argued that releasing any more water would

> seriously detract from the economic value of the whole Bow River development including the Spray.... If there is an imaginative difference of opinion about this, the company claims that any possible adverse effect upon the scenery in a spot in this tremendous park is infinitesimal compared to the importance ... of the power which can be developed.[10]

The staff of the Parks Branch prepared to fight the good fight once more. At a meeting with Gaherty, the minister of mines and resources, and the deputy minister, Roy Gibson, director of the Parks Branch, insisted that both power development in the park and removal of more land from the park "would be resented by a great many people who have the interests of the park at heart." Furthermore, this would surely whet the company's appetite for more storage sites in the park. Gibson reiterated the familiar argument of his predecessor, J. B. Harkin, that Canadian parks must remain unspoiled if they were to compete successfully for the tourist trade with American parks, where development was banned. H. L. Keenleyside, the deputy minister, also urged the company to consider thermal power as an alternative.[11]

Unfortunately for those interested in wilderness preservation, the acting minister of mines and resources was not sympathetic to their case. J. A. Mackinnon (who assumed the portfolio on a permanent basis in June 1948), as the sole federal minister from Alberta, was naturally particularly sensitive to pressure from his home province.[12] Edmonton lawyer A. Fraser Duncan, who acted for Calgary Power, was on a "Dear Jim" basis in correspondence with Mackinnon. After meeting with company officials and staff, Mackinnon reported to Gaherty that he was giving the matter his "most sympathetic and earnest attention" to see if the necessary legislation could be rushed through Parliament before the end of the session with the concurrence of the opposition parties.[13]

Concern for Calgary Power's needs was fully shared by the powerful minister of trade and commerce, C. D. Howe.[14] Four days after Mackinnon took over as full-time minister of mines and resources, Howe advised him: "I have been looking into the power situation in Alberta, as it affects the development of that province, and find that you [i.e., Albertans] must have additional hydroelectric power if the industrial growth of the province is to be maintained."

The ammonia plant near Calgary, for which Howe had been so influential in obtaining power in 1940, was "a splendid producer of [US] dollar exchange, and there is a heavy demand for the output. It would, in my opinion, be a tragedy if its operation had to be curtailed." The only readily available source of energy was the Spray Lakes development, noted Howe. Parks Branch bureaucrats might object to the plans, fearing the impact on the scenery of the Spray valley, but surely, Howe argued, some scheme could be devised to release just enough water to maintain the flow of the river at an attractive level. "It seems to me," wrote Howe, "that the industrial growth of the province must be a first consideration. The province of Alberta is having a spectacular industrial expansion, and I would be sorry to see anything happen that would interfere with this very desirable development." He concluded, "I am giving you my views on account of my interest in industrial development throughout Canada," which was a polite way of saying, "My friends in the business community asked me to write to you."[15]

Certainly, the new minister's advisors on park policy remained hostile to the plans. In an elaborate memorandum entitled "A Further Projected Encroachment by Calgary Power Limited on the Natural Resources and Scenic Attractions of … Banff National Park …," T. E. Dunn set forth a full history of the company's activities in the area. The company was now proposing to build a dam at the head of the Spray River 740 feet long and 192 feet high. At the height of land between the Spray Lakes and Goat Creek would stand a control dam 2,100 feet long and 48 feet high to feed water into a canal flowing to a headpond of several hundred acres, contained in turn by an earth dike running diagonally across the Goat Valley. In an extensive section headed "Arguments Contra," Dunn noted that the company's annual earnings had almost doubled between 1941 and 1946. Under the heading "Gradual Encroachment," he pointed out:

> In the last thirty-six years the Calgary Power Limited has continually brought pressure to bear to establish storage reservoirs, power plants, canals and transmission lines within the park area.

And under *"Future Demands,"* he predicted:

> The demands by this corporation have never ceased. Three, five or ten years from now what further storage or power rights will they seek … and what assurance is there that the next will be the last?

Looking even further into the future, he saw a gradual demise of the very idea of national parks:

> There are many other industrial corporations that would like to gain a foothold in our national parks and … could … argue with equal weight that it is as much in the national interest that

they be granted a license to explore and develop mineral timber and oil resources.... Carried far enough, the eventual outcome of granting concessions is plain. Park areas will then be found to differ inappreciably from areas beyond their boundaries and the renowned purposes for which they were created will have vanished.[16]

On the day after his appointment as minister, Mackinnon wrote to Premier Manning to consult him on what to do. The premier urged immediate action in order to avoid power shortages that could arrive as early as 1950. Alberta officials considered a flow of 200 cfs in the Spray River adequate, as it would require twenty-five hundred acre-feet of storage capacity to maintain this flow during the tourist season. Increasing the flow by just 50 additional cfs, however, would require four times as much stored water, which, from Manning's perspective, served "to show that extravagance of endeavouring to improve the scenery at the expense of the power development."[17]

Consultations with the CPR indicated that the railway would not object provided that 200 cfs flowed out of the Spray in the summer. Armed with this assurance, Mackinnon tried to persuade his colleagues to rush through the necessary law amending the National Parks Act before the end of the 1948 session of Parliament. Other ministers, however, took note of the opposition to the scheme expressed by Mackinnon's own staff and refused to amend the parliamentary timetable. Despite Mackinnon's best efforts and a direct appeal to the prime minister from Premier Manning, any legislative change would have to wait until the following year.[18]

By mid-1948, it was clear that action to authorize the Spray Lakes development was almost certain in the near future. A memorandum summing up the current situation quoted Mines and Resources Minister Mackinnon as saying, "A good case was made out by the company from the standpoint of industrial needs, and a rather strong lobby was carried on in the company's behalf." With a federal election in the offing in the near future, Mackinnon wanted to be able to defend himself against criticism from Albertans that he was holding back economic development by

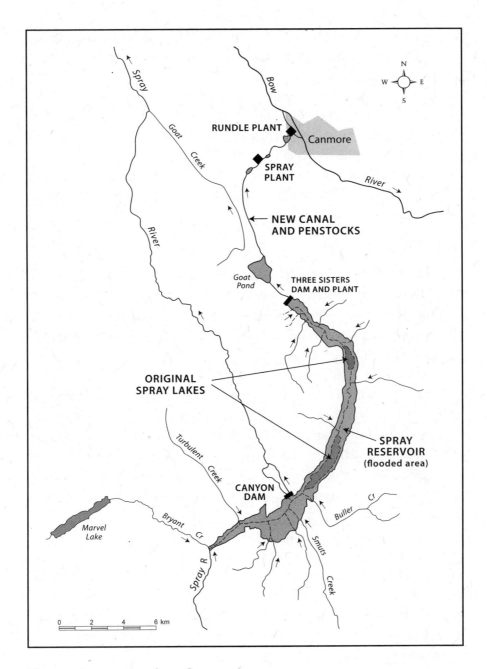

MAP OF THE COMPLETED SPRAY LAKES DEVELOPMENT.

failing to approve the immediate expansion of Calgary Power's capacity.[19] The acting deputy minister pressed the minister to give the Parks Branch "every opportunity to state its case before committing yourself to any policy of hydro power or the storage of water in national parks." Yet even before Mackinnon left for his Edmonton home, he told the parliamentary press that he would be considering Calgary Power's right to develop the Spray Lakes over the coming weeks.[20]

The director of the Parks Branch, R. A. Gibson, followed his minister to the West to consult with departmental officials and soon reported that support for additional power development was far from universal:

> There has been a disposition in the past to consider that the general interest was on the part of the Parks administration and the C.P.R. This is a short-sighted conception because many people in Banff and many people who are interested in Banff will immediately interest themselves in any proposition which they do not think is in the best interest of this park.

Other members of his staff attempted to convince James Mackinnon that using a single watershed like the Bow for a large hydroelectric system was unwise owing to the danger of sabotage or air attack. When the minister himself came to Banff, he was presented with a petition by the Town of Banff's advisory council opposing any development at the Spray Lakes as antithetical to the purposes for which the national park system had been established.[21]

Further discussion with Calgary Power officials about alternative schemes, however, proved fruitless. G. A. Gaherty, who had first devised the Spray Lakes storage scheme in the 1920s, remained firmly committed to the idea. Despite pressure to consider coal-fired thermal generating plants as an option, Gaherty continued "to press the Spray project by every means at his disposal," resisting any efforts to involve the wider public in the debate, according to Gibson:

Apparently it is the desire of the company that the argument on this question should be limited to the company and the departmental officials, and the company through every means at its disposal is endeavouring to have the matter dealt with as an emergency.[22]

In that, Calgary Power was successful. While at home in western Canada, the minister was persuaded to fix the flow at the mouth of the Spray River at 200 cfs during the tourist season, the order being drafted by the company solicitor. With the CPR being satisfied that the scenery around the Banff Springs Hotel would not be adversely affected, the decision was rushed through cabinet in early September 1948, as soon as the minister returned to Ottawa. Edmonton lawyer Fraser Duncan advised his friend Mackinnon privately that Gaherty was "particularly pleased" about the deal and had immediately set about ordering all the necessary generating equipment and planning construction, with the aim of commencing work before the autumn freeze-up.[23]

In the end, the officials of the Department of Mines and Resources were completely excluded from these final negotiations. The deputy minister and his assistant continued to oppose Calgary Power's demands but reported "that the minister was determined to grant the request and that he had received authority from Council [i.e., the cabinet] to do so." R. A. Gibson, the director of the Parks Branch, recognized defeat:

The minister is fully aware, and, I understand, has advised council that the officials concerned with the National Parks administration are unfavourable to the proposed action as they consider it a violation of section 4 of the National Parks Act. It is particularly unfortunate that a move of this kind should be made when there seems to be good ground for believing that the required power could be developed otherwise. However, we have failed in our argument on the general question of principle.

He asked plaintively to be allowed access to the minister's confidential files containing the correspondence between James Mackinnon and Fraser Duncan in order to find out what had been agreed to.[24]

Events had moved so rapidly that proponents of wilderness preservation had no opportunity to organize an effective protest against the Spray Lakes development, the threat to which had brought their movement into formally organized existence during the 1920s. One civil servant in the Parks Branch later confided to the executive secretary of the National Parks Association of the United States:

> The negotiations in connection with this ... withdrawal [of lands from the park system] did not cover a very long period, and there was not much time to work up any public interest in the matter before it was an accomplished fact. There is little use dwelling on the matter any further from our standpoint.... We, of course, hope that we will never be placed in a situation again where we will have to stand up to any further inroads on our National Park areas by outside interests.[25]

When the decision had already been made, W. J. Selby Walker (once executive secretary of the Canadian National Parks Association) wrote the Parks Branch to complain that wartime secrecy no longer prevented a full public airing of the issues, as had been the case when the damming of Lake Minnewanka had been approved in 1940. Mackinnon merely turned Walker's complaints aside with the response that as an Albertan, he, too, was "deeply concerned regarding the maintenance of the attraction of our National Parks," but that there was an acute shortage of power in the province and the Spray Lakes development was the "most expeditious" way of coping with that. Leaving 200 cfs flowing out of the Spray in the summer months would, he insisted, be quite sufficient to preserve the beauty of the scenery.[26]

Company officials, meanwhile, descended upon Ottawa, demanding approval to move heavy construction equipment into Banff National Park to begin road construction and the clearing of the dam site, even before the necessary legislation had been presented to Parliament. Mackinnon chafed at the reluctance of the Parks Branch to permit the company to commence work at once, but his officials seem to have continued a kind of low-level guerrilla warfare. When Mackinnon asked for a brief in favour of the concession to present to Parliament with the required bill in early 1949, R. A. Gibson replied that his staff had prepared plenty of material "but that our statements were hardly of the character to assist the minister with his bill."[27]

In the end, however, the bureaucrats had to bow to the will of their minister. James Mackinnon reached agreement with the Alberta government to compel Calgary Power to provide enough additional storage capacity to permit the release of 100 cfs down the Spray River during construction so that it would not become simply a dry riverbed along much of its upper reaches. Reluctantly, the company accepted this requirement, although with the following proviso:

> The company must be free to operate the power development and the reservoir as it may see fit, and in particular at all times to generate any such energy as it may require and to draw down the reservoir to the extent it may deem advisable.[28]

With this settled, the legislation to amend the National Parks Act by cutting more lands out of Banff National Park began to wend its way through Parliament. Having passed the Senate, the second reading debate in the House of Commons on March 23, 1949, lasted no more than about ten minutes. By the end of the month, the change had become law.[29]

The experience of the Parks Branch in overseeing the development of more energy from the Spray Lakes by Calgary Power proved as frustrating as previous dealings with the company. Faced with a steadily growing power demand even while the company waited for the new plants fed by the Spray Lakes to come into service, Calgary Power drew down the level of Lake Minnewanka to unprecedented levels during the summer of 1949, which was unfortunately a year when low precipitation made refilling the reservoir impossible. By the autumn, the lake contained only about one-third of the usual amount of water. Power demand was rising by more than 10 per cent annually, yet the company was able to generate significantly less hydroelectricity than under normal conditions.[30]

After visiting Banff, Parks Branch director R. A. Gibson complained that the shoreline of Lake Minnewanka reminded him

> ... strongly of the back view of the head[s] of some of the boys who used to come down from the Gatineau after a winter in the woods; ... the barber used to shave their neck[s] half way up the back of their heads. Long [mud]flats are noticeable, and while these are reasonably tidy they are certainly not attractive, and it is altogether a most unnatural layout.... It would seem that the action which was taken by parliament with respect to the Spray River has convinced the company that they can do about as they like in the National Park.

Was there nothing, he asked his officials, that they could do to control the level of Lake Minnewanka under Calgary Power's licence?[31]

Not much, as it turned out. The 1947 licence specified only maximum and minimum levels, and Lake Minnewanka was currently eleven feet higher than the minimum. Although the understanding had been that water would not be drawn off during the tourist season, only a change in the regulations by cabinet could ensure control over this matter. Despite some suspicions that Calgary Power might be drawing more heavily on Lake Minnewanka than on its other reservoirs, the Parks Branch decided not to pursue the matter in the hope that nature would rectify the problem with heavy precipitation.[32]

But the autumn rains were not heavy enough, and Calgary Power was soon requesting emergency permission to draw down Lake Minnewanka four feet below the previous minimum in the spring of 1950. All of the company's steam plants were running at capacity, and if, as hoped, the Spray development would be ready by the fall of 1950, no water would be released from that watershed into the Bow River during the coming winter. If nothing was done, bulk power supplies to the Canada Cement and Alberta Nitrogen would have to be curtailed, and there might even be general electricity rationing. Alberta Nitrogen was a particularly vital customer since it was a heavy earner of US dollar exchange: almost anything was justified to keep current flowing to its ammonia plant near Calgary.[33]

The superintendent of Banff National Park predicted that failure to accede to Calgary Power's demands was almost certain to spark a great public outcry once the news of a general power shortage leaked out. The provincial government would soon jump into the fray and attack Ottawa. He, therefore, recommended that the Parks Branch permit the emergency drawdown on the understanding that Calgary Power would run its thermal generating stations flat out during the summer of 1950 so as to permit Lake Minnewanka to refill. Company lawyer Fraser Duncan lobbied hard with the new minister of mines and resources, Colin Gibson (who had replaced James Mackinnon in the spring of 1949), and eventually, the company was granted permission to take the extra water if necessary.[34]

The unhappy relationship between the Parks Branch authorities and Calgary Power continued during the construction of the Spray project. The plan called for water from the Spray reservoir to be brought by canal to the head of Whiteman's Pass above Canmore and then released to generating equipment located in the Bow valley far below. Things rarely go according to plan, especially plans that involve moving mountains and reversing the flow of rivers. Errors of judgement and accidents happen. The canal dike was constructed along the steep side of Goat Creek valley in winter using frozen material. In November 1950, to meet rising power demands, the company raised the flow in the canal to feed its Bow River plants. Under this increased pressure, the dike melted and slid into the Goat Creek valley. In order to keep the water flowing into the Bow, the company then purposefully breached the dike in several places so that all the water running down Goat Creek would eventually reach the Bow River. That got the water to the Bow power plants, but it also moved a debris field into the valley, causing $100,000 worth of flood damage.[35] Re-engineering nature had precipitated a major environmental disaster, though it was not called that at the time.

The company then set about building a wooden flume to carry 700 cfs, but in January 1951, another breach in the dike led to the decision to abandon the canal plan. Instead, Calgary Power's engineers reverted to the more expensive Plan A and started drilling a fourteen-hundred-foot tunnel through Chinaman's Peak (now Ha Ling Peak). Until that was completed, the flow from the Spray reservoir into the Bow was cut off altogether. Construction errors then provoked a second environmental catastrophe. As the snow melted in the spring of 1951, the water began to pour over the spillway in the control dam at the head of the Spray River at the rate of 1,630 cfs. The valve in the diversion tunnel at the dam could have been opened to help cope with the problem, but the engineers were afraid to do so as they might not be able to close it again owing to the water pressure. Since the company had never expected to release more than the required 100 cfs over its dam each summer, no proper channel had been cut from the spillway to the Spray riverbed capable of carrying such a volume of water. The debris flow destroyed fish spawning beds in the river and inflicted an estimated $350,000 worth of damage upon the lands and buildings inside Banff National Park. Downstream, with the Spray in full spate because the Spray Lakes no longer acted as a natural reservoir, the CPR's golf course at the Banff Springs Hotel had to be closed for a time in the spring of 1951.[36]

Prolonged haggling ensued between the Parks Branch and Calgary Power over payment for the damages caused. A formal claim of $244,000 was countered by an offer from the company of only $103,000. A meeting in the office of the deputy minister of resources and development (as the portfolio was renamed in early 1950) finally produced an agreement from the company to pay $131,000 in compensation. G. A. Gaherty paid over this sum in May 1952, although he continued to grumble that Calgary Power should really be liable for less than $100,000 but would be magnanimous in light of its desire to continue a supposedly friendly relationship with the bureaucrats.[37]

These engineering problems forced Calgary Power to repeat its request to draw down Lake Minnewanka below the minimum fixed by licence early in 1951. The failure to complete the Spray project as planned and the redesign of the reservoir had left the company seriously short of electricity. Even with its thermal stations running flat out, both Alberta Nitrogen and Canada Cement had had to be cut back, and a series of radio advertisements were broadcast urging the public to curtail power use. The water that would come flooding down the Spray to the Bow in the spring might help somewhat, but further cutbacks to industry seemed inevitable. Fearful of the outcry that might arise, the Parks Branch again approved drawing down Lake Minnewanka by a further four feet.[38]

The growing power shortage in southern Alberta was finally dealt with later in 1951 when the Spray project came online, adding nearly 100,000 hp per annum to the capacity of Calgary Power's system. Not surprisingly, the CPR was soon complaining that a summer flow of only 200 cfs in the Spray River had created a small stream trickling down a wide, rocky riverbed through the golf course at the Banff Springs Hotel. The Parks Branch, which had predicted this result since the 1920s, could point out that the railway had agreed to the reduction in 1948. Because of the spring runoff, narrowing the streambed with landscaping seemed unwise; the only solution was to construct a series of weirs that would distribute the flow more evenly. Nature would have to be landscaped to disguise the effects of the diversion. Eventually, Calgary Power agreed to bear the cost of this work.[39]

That brought the wrangles over the Spray Lakes to an end after thirty years of controversy; henceforth, the lakes would function as a power reservoir. During those three decades, Banff National Park had its boundaries redrawn, its river flows manipulated, and its focal point marked by a hydroelectric storage and generating system. The battle had been long and drawn out, but it had been decisive. When Calgary Power applied to double the capacity of both the Spray and Cascade developments by installing additional generators in 1955, the Parks Branch had no objections.[40]

CHAPTER 11

Leaving the Bow

During its first forty years, Calgary Power generated its electricity from the Bow River.[1] Step by step, dam by dam, diversion by diversion, the company engineers extracted more and more power from the mountain river until in the 1950s, they began to run out of falling water. Eventually, to keep pace with the growth of southern Alberta, other primary energy sources would have to be found. Starting in the mid-1950s, Calgary Power management began investing heavily in the construction of mine-mouth thermal electric stations to meet a rising baseload. After having, over a half a century, exhausted the hydroelectric possibilities of the Bow and rearranged its unsuitable streamflow to increase its operational efficiency, the company virtually abandoned the river for new power development and adopted a policy long advocated by its critics.

Looking forward from the 1950s, then, the future seems to lead away from our subject: path dependence on a hydroelectric technology leading to conflicts with parks policy. Yes and no. Yes, because over the next thirty or more years the quantity of electricity produced from the Bow as a proportion of total electricity generated would become an insignificant fraction of the total. Thermal dependence would lead the company away from the Bow and relieve the pressure on Banff National Park. But the dams and diversions would stay. No, because the end of our book looks much like the beginning. A private utility company would organize itself around a low-cost method of producing electricity based upon a locally abundant natural resource, coal, which in turn would have profound environmental consequences. The company would no longer come into direct conflict with Parks policy, but it would – through its mines, emissions, and other disamenities associated with thermal production – strike a broader and entirely different bargain with the environment. And this time, almost all of Alberta would be locked into this dependence. So let us briefly fast forward through this second technological transformation so that we might, in our conclusion, look back through it to help put our primary narrative in perspective.

In the new scheme of things, the hydroelectric dams on the Bow would revert to the secondary role of meeting peak power needs. Yet the shift from hydroelectricity to thermal power could only occur gradually as the company neared the exhaustion of the Bow waterpowers. In 1950, Calgary Power had equipment installed sufficient to produce 82,800 kilowatts (kw) of hydro. In the next year alone, enough additional turbines, fed from the Spray Lakes, were brought online to almost double existing capacity. Water from the new reservoir leaving the Three Sisters control facilities fell 65 feet to produce 3,000 kw of electricity. It then dropped a further 900 feet to produce 49,900 kw at the Spray Plant above Canmore, and another 320 feet to the Rundle station in the bottom of the valley to turn out 17,000 kw. Adding to this total of 69,900 kw, the additional flow could be used downstream on the Bow for the expansion of the Kananaskis Falls plant by 8,900 kw, making an overall total of 78,800 kw: within a single year, these new additions almost equaled already installed capacity. (See Appendix.)

Over the next decade, the company would continue to try and squeeze as much hydraulic energy as possible out of the Bow watershed. To improve the efficiency of the plants at Horseshoe Falls (1911), Kananaskis Falls (1914), and Ghost River (1929), the company constructed additional storage outside the national park system on the Bow's principal tributary, the Kananaskis. This process had begun in 1933 with the building of the dams to raise both the Upper and Lower Kananaskis Lakes; in 1947, the Barrier dam created a head of 155 feet, which could produce 12,900 kw as well as store additional water for the Kananaskis and Horseshoe plants. In 1955, another storage dam was constructed at Pocaterra on the headwaters of the Kananaskis, which permitted the development of 14,900 kw under a head of 207 feet, and at the same time, the small Interlakes

G. A. GAHERTY, LONG-TIME
PRESIDENT OF CALGARY
POWER (TRANSALTA).

station was erected between Upper and Lower Kananaskis Lakes, which could turn out 5,000 kw from a 127-foot head.[2] After the late 1950s, hikers to this region would discover that for a short section, the entire Kananaskis River had been rerouted through the company's metal penstock and the former riverbed – a smooth, sculpted marble canyon – had been turned into a trail.

Meanwhile, with the demand for power increasing steadily, the Ghost plant on the Bow was expanded by 22,900 kw in 1954, bringing its total capacity to 50,900 kw. The same year, the provincial government manoeuvred Calgary Power into building a fifty-foot high dam at Bearspaw, just outside the western limits of Calgary, to alleviate the winter floods apparently caused by the increased winter streamflow.[3] Though the company was reluctant to do this, it was able to recoup some of the cost by installing a 16,900 kw generating station there. Upstream, the Cascade plant in Banff National Park, built to meet an emergency wartime power shortage, was expanded in 1957 to add 17,900 kw of new capacity. Finally, further gains from the Spray Lakes project were achieved in 1960 that more than doubled the output of the Spray powerhouse with an additional 52,900 kw, while a second unit was added at the Rundle station lower down to bring its potential from 17,000 kw to 49,900 kw.[4] Overall, by 1960, the company had added hydroelectric capacity of 163,400 kw to the 161,600 kw that had existed on the Bow in 1951 when the Spray plants had first come online.[5]

Naturally, each of these sizable construction projects had lead times of many months before the turbines came into service. As early as 1955, president G. A. Gaherty reported to shareholders that the company must begin building thermal generating stations if future load growth were to be met.[6] This represented a fundamental strategic shift for the company, one that an old hydroelectric champion such as Gaherty must have found difficult to swallow. Initially, the company hoped to use Alberta's abundant supplies of natural gas to produce steam, a plan that it began testing in 1955 with a 25,000 kw gas turbine located in the Joarcam gas field. Eventually, however, the experiment determined that this supply of gas was inadequate to produce sustained baseload power.[7]

Calgary Power began, therefore, to focus instead upon a large thermal development at a site forty miles west of Edmonton. At first glance, this location seemed a curious choice since the company's principal markets were in southern Alberta and it did not supply wholesale power to the provincial capital, which had its own municipal generating system.[8] What attracted Calgary Power to the Lake Wabamun area, which was outside of its market area, was a huge deposit of sub-bituminous coal. This fuel could be strip-mined, ground to powder, and used to fire large boilers that would draw water directly from the lake and return it there for cooling. Moreover, this plant would not require elaborate pollution-control equipment on its exhaust stacks because the coal had an unusually low sulphur content averaging just 0.3 per cent.[9] At this site, the company believed, thermal electricity could be produced at the lowest possible cost. In 1956, Calgary Power therefore purchased the shares of the Alberta Southern Coal Company, which owned the Wabamun site, securing control of fifty million tons of coal reserves.[10]

What made the scheme economical was the fact that as early as 1930, Calgary Power had constructed a 138 kilovolt (kv) transmission line over the 190 miles from its new Ghost plant on the Bow to Edmonton. This tie line permitted exchanges of current with the municipal system in the provincial capital as required, and that link was twinned in 1951.[11] Starting in 1956, the company upgraded this transmission system – including the key links between Ghost, Wabamun, Edmonton, and Calgary – to carry 230 kv, which made it possible for the company to switch power efficiently from all its stations throughout the southern part of the province.[12]

Obviously, some time would be required to open up the strip mine at Lake Wabamun and begin producing sizable amounts of coal, so Gaherty and his engineers devised a scheme that would provide the greatest flexibility in expanding Calgary Power's capacity. In 1955, Calgary Power decided to build a 69,000 kw thermal station at Lake Wabamun but to use gas while making it convertible to coal later, "[a]gainst the day when the use of natural gas as a 'premium' fuel, both locally and for export, may make its cost prohibitive for power plant use." This plant came into production in 1956, followed two years later by a second unit of the same type and size.[13] One Wabamun generator was converted to run on coal in 1963, but the second was not changed over until twenty years later.

Four factors worked together to leave Calgary Power well positioned to meet future demand: the company's rapid expansion of capacity outlined above; a slight slowing of load growth as a result of the recession in Canada, which began in the late 1950s; the sizable additions to the Spray hydro plants in 1960; and a marked reduction in line losses owing to the higher voltage tie lines to the Ghost plant. As Gaherty told the shareholders in 1959, "A few years ago your Company's system was supplied entirely by hydro, but already half of its energy requirements are met from thermal plants." And he went on to point out the advantages of the new set-up: as fuel charges declined with rising coal production, generating costs would be among the lowest in North America; at the same time, the additions to the Spray plants to meet peak needs were an extremely economical way to produce more power, costing only $83 per additional kilowatt since the capital charges for those dams and reservoirs had already been covered. Furthermore, hydraulic plants could be switched on and off as demand fluctuated without the time lag required to raise steam at the thermal stations. The following year, Gaherty reported that Calgary Power was selling 139,000 kw to meet the power requirements of the city of Calgary, accounting for 18.6 per cent of its revenues, and had just signed a new contract to supply the city's entire power requirements until 1973, which might then total 300,000 kw.[14] In 1961, G. H. Thompson, who had taken over as president from Gaherty, was able to report that projections of higher power demand now justified the opening of a third coal-fired unit at Wabamun, this one capable of producing 147,000 kw, or more than twice as much as each of the earlier plants there.[15]

Four decades after the Horseshoe plant opened, Calgary Power was finally able to end its reliance upon hydroelectricity from the Bow watershed for its baseload requirements. Nonetheless, hydraulic energy still had an important place in the company's plans. In his penultimate report to shareholders, Gaherty had observed that there were still several sites along the Bow, such as Russell, which could be developed to meet peaking requirements but that "other considerations" made it desirable to look elsewhere for future hydro developments. In fact, the government of Alberta was already pressing the company to consider a large dam project on the Brazeau River, ninety miles southwest of Edmonton, not initially for power purposes but to reduce sharp seasonal fluctuations in the flow of the North Saskatchewan at Edmonton to alleviate pollution problems and supply water for industry.[16] Eventually, the province agreed to finance a dam on the Brazeau capable of storing one million acre-feet of water at a cost of $14.5 million; the company would only be required to purchase the dam once it had installed generating equipment there to meet its peak needs. As load growth surged upward in the early 1960s, construction got under way on the Big Bend plant on the Brazeau; the plant was ready to turn out 165,000 kw by 1965, followed by an expansion of another 190,000 kw in 1967.[17]

At the same time, Calgary Power began investigations, in co-operation with the government, on the future hydroelectric potential of the Athabasca River in northern Alberta, with the possibility of using Lesser Slave Lake to store water for a plant on the Lesser Slave River. Longer-range assessments also started into the use of oil from the Alberta tar sands for thermal units and even into the construction of a nuclear plant.

All in all, the company seemed to be in an enviable situation in the early 1960s. Thompson pointed out to the shareholders that the low price of the coal from the new Whitewood mine at Wabamun would keep the cost of the baseload under control. He observed that although the eleven hydro plants on the Bow were comparatively small, and two of them more than a half century old, now that they had been converted to remote control they could be switched on and off as required, so they could "be operated and maintained almost indefinitely at a low cost."[18]

One danger to which the company had to be alert was public agitation against a single private power producer serving most of southwestern Alberta. Management always argued that fulminations against its "monopoly" were misguided since many of its wholesale contracts with municipalities and industrial users were the result of competition and could be terminated after notice. Barriers to entry by rivals were always weakened by the availability of abundant natural gas supplies at the lowest rates anywhere in Canada. In 1964, the city bureaucrats of Calgary, Edmonton and Red Deer began discussing a municipally owned thermal station on the Ardley coalfield near Red Deer. Calgary Power was convinced that there was not enough coal to fuel the station but comforted itself with the thought that cost estimates for the new plant would demonstrate how economical was its wholesale power supply contract with the City of Calgary, which accounted for about 20 per cent of total revenues. Eventually, interest in the Ardley plan evaporated, and by the autumn of 1966, a contract had been signed with the city for up to 550,000 kv of power, with rates good until 1980, after which either party could terminate with ten years' notice. At the same time, Red Deer also signed a ten-year contract, which generated 2 per cent of company revenues, and Edmonton decided to build a gas-fired plant for its own municipal system. In 1970, the City of Lethbridge also signed a twelve-year contract for bulk power and, four years later, sold its municipal station to the company. Meanwhile, industrial load was growing by 10 per cent per annum, so Calgary Power continued to investigate nuclear generation as a future possibility.[19]

Management remained convinced that for the near term, reliance upon thermal generation for the baseload, reserving the hydro plants for peak demand, was the proper business strategy. In 1968, a fourth and final unit was constructed at Wabamun capable of producing 286,000 kw, nearly twice as large as its immediate predecessor. As early as 1960, Calgary Power had begun considering another huge strip mine on the south side of Lake Wabamun to fuel a number of additional stations, and by 1965, a drilling program had revealed reserves of a hundred million tons of coal at Highvale in addition to the seventy million–ton reserve at the existing Whitewood mine to the north. In 1972–73, rights to an additional

WABAMUN POWER PLANT (TRANSALTA).

eighty-eight million tons of reserves were acquired near Highvale. The first generating unit at a new mine-generating site called Sundance, with a capacity of 286,000 kw, came into operation at the end of 1970, followed by another one of similar size in 1973.[20]

Though the Bow seemed unable to yield any more power, the company remained interested in developing as much additional hydroelectric capacity as possible to meet peak requirements. In the late 1960s, discussions began with Alberta about a dam at Bighorn on the headwaters of the North Saskatchewan about eighty miles upstream from Rocky Mountain House, "the largest known storage possibility in the province on the eastern slopes of the Rocky Mountains." The provincial government was eager to support the project because, like the Brazeau scheme, it would further increase the winter flow of the river to alleviate flooding and to use for industrial purposes. While the company claimed that the capital cost of generating power at Bighorn would be greater than expanding its thermal plants nearer Edmonton, it was willing to make a deal since "hydro power does offer certain inherent advantages over thermal power, such as operating flexibility and stable long term operating costs." Eventually, agreement was arrived at for Calgary Power to construct a three-hundred-foot-high dam, fourteen hundred feet long, that would permit storage of 1.165 million acre-feet of water in the 13,700-acre Lake Abraham, the largest man-made body of water in Alberta, and to install equipment that could produce up to 120,000 kw. Calgary Power drove a fairly hard bargain with the province, extracting a subsidy to compensate for the higher costs of developing hydro-power as compared to thermal electricity.[21]

The completion of Bighorn left Calgary Power with a potential capacity of up to 800,000 kw of hydroelectricity,[22] but it effectively brought an end to any sizable future hydraulic schemes in the southern part of Alberta. Investigations had revealed that another 1.5 million kw might be developed at Fort Fitzgerald on the Slave River in the far north of the province, but the high cost of the project and the need to transmit current 460 miles to link up with the company's high voltage grid at Edmonton rendered the plan uneconomical in the current circumstances. When the second of the two large stations at Sundance was added to the four units at Wabamun in 1973, Calgary Power, with 1,141,000 kw available from its coal-fired plants, now had much more thermal than hydraulic capacity available. Future growth would rest upon adding to its steam plants.[23]

The relationship of Calgary Power to the Government of Alberta within a broader Canadian context remained anomalous. Some other provinces – in the interests of accelerating economic growth, developing resources to the fullest extent, and equalizing economic opportunity – had nationalized their electric utilities in the postwar era. Neighbouring British Columbia was among the last of the provinces to go this route. As we have seen, Alberta, under Social Credit management, had decisively rejected that option after the war. As long as the private companies kept ahead of demand and maintained relatively low prices, the province, both ideologically and fiscally, preferred a lightly regulated private sector to a quantum increase in the role and size of the public sector. Still, there were issues to be resolved. At the end of the 1960s, the company began to concern itself with its long-term relations with government. In 1968, Alberta municipalities pressured the province to bring municipally owned systems under a revised Power Commission Act that would grant them exclusive franchises in their service areas. Calgary Power successfully opposed such a change, arguing that it would make it possible for a local government to expropriate private power producers if permitted to annex new territory.[24]

The company then turned its attention to trying to simplify and regularize its relations with the province. For the first thirty years of its existence, Calgary Power had dealt exclusively with the federal Department of the Interior for land leases and water rights, whether on provincial land or Indian reserves, or inside the national park system. In 1929, however, a federal-provincial agreement transferred all remaining lands and natural resources to Alberta, which was confirmed by concurrent legislation the following year. When Calgary Power applied to begin construction of the dams at the Kananaskis Lakes in 1931, it procured its first water storage licence from the province. Yet Ottawa remained intimately involved in the company's affairs: the overlap of land ownership, water rights, national park territory, and Indian reserves continued. For instance, the 1942 Cascade project required a licence from the federal Department of Mines and Resources and the passage of the Natural Resources Transfer (Amendment) Act of 1941, as well as Alberta's approval to divert the upper Ghost River into Lake Minnewanka to store more water. While the original federal licences to use water at Horseshoe and Kananaskis were for terms of twenty-one years, renewable for additional twenty-one-year periods, this Cascade licence, like several other provincial ones, ran for a term of fifty years.[25] A new federal-provincial agreement in September 1945, later confirmed by concurrent legislation in both Ottawa and Edmonton, transferred all the rights and obligations of the federal government to Alberta but still left a situation of Byzantine complexity that seemed to favour nobody except a few lawyers.[26]

Inflation brought the pressure for change to a head. By 1970, Calgary Power was becoming concerned that the rising cost of new generating capacity might render it very difficult to earn a decent rate of return on its investment. Power rates fixed around the time of World War II had been reduced significantly owing to large plants using low-cost coal, but management now concluded that an across-the-board rate increase was required in order to raise additional capital from outside investors instead of continuing to rely upon retained earnings.[27] In 1969, an advisory committee recommended to the Alberta government that the company should be treated in the same way as all other utilities, and negotiations were entered into that would make the terms of its various agreements and licences with Ottawa and Edmonton more or less uniform. In September 1972, Calgary Power signed an agreement with the Alberta Department of the Environment that would make it subject only to the provincial Water Power Regulations in order to facilitate future rate hearings.[28]

The company hastened to apply to the Alberta Public Utilities Board for a large rate increase. Within two years, Calgary Power had been granted a rise of 20.5 per cent over its 1972 rates, and the company immediately requested an additional 17.6 per cent rise, which was allowed on an interim basis pending further hearings. The decision to rely upon coal-fired thermal stations seemed to be confirmed by the rapid rise in oil and natural gas prices sparked by OPEC during the 1970s. With millions of tons of reserves in its strip mines around Lake Wabamun, Calgary Power management authorized the construction of four new generating stations at Sundance, each with an unprecedented capacity of more than 350,000 kw; the new stations came into service between 1976 and 1980. (See Appendix.)

The scale of these operations created new pressures on the company. In 1923, management had attempted to convince Parks Branch bureaucrats that the unsightly mudflats and decaying vegetation that would surround Lake Minnewanka when its level was drawn down to produce power would "resemble a bold seacoast at low tide."[29] During the next quarter century, Calgary Power wrangled with the Parks Branch lobby and wilderness preservationists over plans to transform the Spray Lakes into a power reservoir. The company eventually got its way with both Lake Minnewanka and the Spray Lakes development by arguing that the growing demand for hydroelectricity in southern Alberta must be met. But the development of half a dozen huge new thermal stations around Lake Wabamun, along with the growing sensitivity of public opinion concerning the environmental impact of economic activity, had begun to change the situation. A. W. Howard's 1970 report to shareholders described for the first time a plan to minimize air pollution from the plants at Sundance by constructing five-hundred-foot exhaust stacks to disperse nitrogen oxides higher into the atmosphere. Beginning the following year, for the first time, the company's annual report contained a section headed "The Environment," in which the president admitted that such large thermal stations could not be operated without "some prejudicial effects."[30] Tighter regulation by the Alberta Health Department soon required the company to take other steps to control the environmental impact of thermal generation. Electrostatic fly ash precipitators installed on the stacks were designed to capture nearly all the solid particulates in the exhaust gases.[31] Calgary Power sought to recoup part of the cost of these devices by creating a subsidiary called Western Fly Ash, which marketed some of the ash to manufacturers of concrete blocks and the like. By 1970, the company was mining about two million tons of coal for the Wabamun plant alone, with huge draglines stripping topsoil off hundreds of acres, and, recognizing that damage to the environment was likely to arouse criticism, it began restoring 250 acres at the Whitewood mine. By 1980, the Highvale mine was producing an additional 6.5 million tons of coal, and the topsoil had been replaced on over fourteen hundred acres at the two mines; the reclaimed land was seeded with alfalfa with yields comparable to other areas of the province.[32]

As power production increased from the power plants around the shores of Lake Wabamun, protests began to be heard from cottage owners and fishing enthusiasts that the discharge of millions of gallons of heated water was promoting the growth of aquatic weeds. The company started harvesting weeds in 1972, while arguing that more time and research on nutrient supply and penetration by sunlight was required to solve the problem. The following year, however, the Alberta Energy Resources Conservation Board shifted the onus to Calgary Power for showing that the heat added to the lake was not having an adverse effect; the board ordered the immediate construction of a twelve-hundred-acre cooling pond fed by water brought from the North Saskatchewan River by an eight-mile pipeline at a cost of $23 million, to be completed by 1975. Meanwhile, the company promised to spend $80 million over the next three years on ecological research on the lake, including a study with the Department of Agriculture on whether warm water irrigation would enhance crop yields. In an effort to fend off critics, management argued that its hydroelectric plants already contributed

> ... significantly towards abatement of pollution on the North Saskatchewan and Bow Rivers. Water stored in our reservoirs from the spring and summer runoff is released during the period of low natural flow in winter. In addition to providing water for communities, industry and others, the dilution of industrial and municipal wastes by this additional water is an important factor in preventing serious pollution problems to downstream users in winter months.

Eventually, the ecological studies of Lake Wabamun failed to produce conclusive evidence that discharge water from the company's plants needed to be cooled, and the Energy Resources Conservation Board was persuaded not to order expensive remedial measures; instead, the board allowed the company to deal with the problem through weed harvesting, pending a final board decision in 1979.[33]

With inflation becoming a serious concern for such a capital-intensive industry, Calgary Power convinced the Public Utilities Board in 1975 to fix its power rates for a two-year test period at a level to provide a return on common shares of $3.40 for the first year and $3.75 for the second. This rise gave a boost to investor confidence, which permitted the sale of 1.3 million new common shares in a sales campaign entitled "Opportunity for Albertans." At another round of hearings before the Public Utilities Board, the company sought to demonstrate that the capital cost of Sundance units #1 and #2 had been $184 per kw, while units #3 and #4, which were expected to come onstream over the next two years, would require $288 per kw, an increase of 57 per cent. The company therefore asked for further increases in rates to raise its per share earnings to $4.18 in 1977 and $4.57 in 1978.[34]

With world petroleum prices continuing to rise during the 1970s, Calgary Power became even more firmly committed to increasing its coal-fired generating capacity;[35] the company completed the Sundance development with a sixth unit, opened in 1980, bringing that station's potential output up to 1,987,000 kw. Exploratory work meanwhile revealed another sizable deposit of low-sulphur, non-bituminous coal only five miles away at Keephills. In addition, the company purchased additional coal reserves near Lake Wabamun from both PanCanadian Petroleum and Fording Coal, adding over 65 million tons to its supplies, and in the early 1980s, Calgary Power acquired over 90 per cent of Dome Petroleum's coal holdings near the existing Highvale mine, increasing its reserves to more than one billion tons. With economical fuel supplies assured, Calgary Power began the construction of the first of two 377,000 kw units at Keephills, one of which opened in 1983, the second the following year.[36]

In 1980, seeking to consolidate its position in Alberta's electricity supply industry, Calgary Power split its common shares on a three-for-one basis and purchased a 40 per cent interest in Canadian Utilities Limited, which controlled a group of utilities that supplied most of the northern and eastern regions of the province with whom interconnections had already been established at several points. To reflect its expansion, the company changed its name to TransAlta Utilities Corporation in 1981; at the same time, it created a subsidiary called TransAlta Resources to hold this equity interest since these earnings were not directly regulated by the province. The following year, however, in an effort to block a complete takeover, Canadian Utilities acquired a 21 per cent interest in TransAlta Utilities. A few weeks later, the two companies signed an agreement concerning the future divestiture of their interlocking ownership positions in each other: for the next three years, neither TransAlta nor Canadian Utilities would attempt to gain voting control of each other or of ATCO (which controlled Canadian Utilities). This standstill arrangement led to a decision by TransAlta in November 1984 to negotiate the sale of its interest in Canadian Utilities and unlock their equity interests in one another.[37]

While these corporate manoeuvres were under way, demand for electricity in Alberta was predicted to continue to grow rapidly. In response,

TransAlta began planning for a large new thermal generating station near Hanna on the Sheerness coalfield, about one hundred miles northeast of Calgary, to be jointly owned with Alberta Power Limited (as Canadian Utilities Limited had been renamed). Although load growth was slowed by the economic recession of the late 1980s, the two units at Sheerness, each capable of turning out 366,000 kw, were brought into production in 1986 and 1990, with TransAlta's half interest in the project giving it a total thermal generating capacity of 3,676 kw. (See Appendix.) In 1983, the company built its first 500 kv transmission line from Keephills (at Lake Wabamun) to Edmonton and, two years later, added another 500 kv line from Calgary through the Crowsnest Pass to link up with the British Columbia power grid. Since BC Hydro was already connected to other very large systems in the Pacific Northwest, all of which produced their baseload from hydroelectric plants, this tie permitted TransAlta to use its coal-fired plants for more efficient load management and to bank energy credits by taking off-peak hydroelectricity from outside Alberta.[38]

With power supplies now almost totally generated by three producers (TransAlta, Alberta Power, and Edmonton Power), the Alberta government decided to try and eliminate rate disparities between various types of customers in different parts of the province.[39] On September 1, 1982, the Alberta Electric Energy Marketing Agency (EEMA) began to purchase all current at prices approved by the Public Utilities Board. The costs of the three generating systems were then averaged and an EEMA price established for the utilities companies to resell power to their customers over the coming year.[40] Since TransAlta was the lowest-cost producer, it repurchased its power from EEMA at a premium, which had to be passed on to its customers, leading to rate increases that were phased in over a five-year period.[41] By 1990, TransAlta was generating over 70 per cent of Alberta's electricity, 93 per cent of which came from coal-fired plants. The three huge strip mines at Whitewood, Highvale, and the Montgomery mine at Sheerness (co-owned with Alberta Power) were producing 15.7 million tons of coal – equal to 23 per cent of total Canadian production.[42]

Although hydroelectricity accounted for a mere 7 per cent of TransAlta's power production in 1990, the company still had every reason to value its hydraulic plants. Even the small stations on the Bow River could be turned on with little delay to meet peak power needs, and a symbol of their complete integration into the wider system was the shift of the control of hydro generation from its historical location at the Kananaskis dam at Seebe to a broader Systems Control Centre in Calgary in 1985. Furthermore, in that same year, rather than being the focus of criticism for its impact on the environment, as had often been the case in earlier decades, the company could advertise that it had received the Bighorn Award, Alberta's highest commendation for wildlife conservation, as a result of eight years of co-operation with the Stony Plain Fish and Game Association.[43]

Yet the environmental issues raised by hydroelectric generation still had the potential to arouse controversy. On this occasion, the anxiety arose downstream rather than upstream. In 1984, the Alberta Water Resources Commission convened a series of public hearings on its South Saskatchewan River Basin Planning Program dealing with water use priorities in the entire watershed south of Red Deer. A whole range of interested parties testified at sessions held across southern Alberta concerning the use of water for purposes such as irrigation, industry, power production, and recreation. TransAlta officials seized the opportunity to point out that there were plenty of potential conflicts and to defend its water utilization policies. The need for water storage to generate electricity during the winter often clashed with summer irrigation requirements, since farmers downstream were likely to demand more releases in a dry year even though lower precipitation in the mountains might cut down the flow of the Bow at the same time. Hydroelectricity probably supplied one-third of Calgary's winter power needs as a source of speedy, flexible supplies to meet peak fluctuations. Yet the Bearspaw dam, just to the west of the city, also had to be managed to even out large seasonal fluctuations in the river's flow to dilute pollution, provide water supply, and control flooding, while providing enough volume to satisfy the irrigators along the lower Bow.[44]

In a written brief to the Alberta Water Resources Commission, TransAlta contended that any changes required to the company's pattern of reservoir management on the Bow that could affect generating capacity would result in higher power rates. The most efficient possible use should be made of scarce water supplies, but power consumers ought not to have to finance benefits enjoyed by irrigators. The company also downplayed the recreational potential of its reservoirs on the upper river for fishing and boating, noting that shifting water levels on the shorelines were an impediment to such activities.[45] The dams may have lost much of their importance as primary energy producers, but they rose in importance as recreational resources. The surges in flow downstream from the dam when the turbines were suddenly turned on attracted whitewater kayakers, and the mountain reservoirs had become magnets for campers and canoeists.

That the conflict between users of the reservoirs remained a lively and contentious issue was clear from the testimony of Jim Blake, mayor of the Ghost Lake Summer Village, which sprang into existence at the Ghost dam each year. Blake reported that TransAlta virtually drained the lake each winter and spring down to a level of 3,884 feet above sea level (asl), only starting to refill it in the first week of July. The summer residents, who since 1952 had joined the eight or nine permanent families to make up a seasonal population of 189, needed the lake filled to the brim at 3,906 feet asl for safe boating and swimming. In 1983, the company had promised that the water would stay at 3,906 from July 1 on, but when Blake went to look, he discovered that the level had been lowered between four and six feet, leaving a wide band of mud and rock exposed around the shoreline. The next year, TransAlta had not even started to raise the lake level until August 1, and then only to 3,904 feet asl. With a serious frost putting an end to most recreational uses in the second week of September, Blake noted, "this makes a very short summer." He demanded that the refilling of Ghost Lake be started earlier and be held at the promised maximum throughout the swimming and boating season.[46]

Other witnesses expressed fears about schemes to build more dams along the Bow. For the previous two decades, there had been rumours that the government intended to build a new barrier east of Calgary. The likeliest site was downstream from the point at which the Highwood River joined the Bow near Dalemead: this would create a huge reservoir that would back up the water as far as the eastern suburbs of the city. This dam, which would be constructed mainly for irrigation purposes, might also permit an interbasin transfer as part of a larger scheme to redistribute water supplies across southern Alberta. At the Water Resources Commission hearings in November 1984, Neil Jennings of the Bow River Protection Society expressed fears that the plan was "almost inescapable," though "that possibility frightens us, it angers us, and it saddens us beyond words."[47] Should it be built, the dam would sound the "death knell" for the world-famous fishery on the Bow below Calgary, creating instead "an enormous sewage lagoon."[48]

From TransAlta's point of view, the Bow plants existed primarily to be turned on and off to meet peaks in demand. Other uses – recreation, sanitation, irrigation – might be accommodated from time to time, but conflicts between optimization of operations within the TransAlta distribution system received the highest priority. However, as the Bow River's contribution to the grid declined to virtual insignificance, it became harder and harder to defend such a position.

By the late twentieth century, ninety years after entrepreneurs like Max Aitken had begun to eye the hydroelectric potential of the Bow, the flow of the river below Banff was almost entirely the product of engineering. The dam operators for TransAlta Utilities, the water and sewage managers of the City of Calgary and other cities, the fish biologists, and the irrigation co-operatives determined how many cubic metres of water passed any given point. Some things had not changed all that much: in 1955 (before the dramatic expansion of the three stations fed by the Spray Lakes), Calgary Power generated 1.728 billion kwh of hydroelectric current, while by 1994 (with those additions in the late 1950s plus the two large hydraulic developments in the North Saskatchewan watershed at Big Bend and Brazeau in the 1960s), TransAlta produced 1.574 billion kwh of hydro to meet peak power needs.[49] The only variables not subject to human control seemed to be the level and timing of precipitation in Alberta, the size of the snowpack in the mountains along the upper Bow, and the warmth of the weather during the spring runoff, although some people had already suggested trying cloud-seeding to increase available water supplies.[50]

WILDERNESS AND WATERPOWER

The engineered river had become such an accepted fact of life that the town manager of Cochrane, just west of Calgary, told the Alberta Water Resources Commission during the 1984 hearings that his main concern was that TransAlta's Ghost dam might cease to be used to generate electricity. Should this occur, the seasonal fluctuations that had kept the Bow ice-free in winter would end, and a steady flow "would undoubtedly result in much of the river freezing solid during extended cold spells. Our raw water intake for the municipal water supply has been constructed on the basis of daily fluctuations." A rise in the river level would harm recreational uses and reduce economic benefits to the town by reducing visitor traffic to the area.[51] Humans had adjusted their behaviour to this "second nature" of the engineered Bow, especially its recreation potential and its altered flow behaviour.

Meanwhile, upriver near Banff each spring and early summer, boaters and fishers would continue to raise their eyes to the mountains encircling Lake Minnewanka, trying to ignore the broad mudflats littered with stumps that the drawdown of the power reservoir for TransAlta's Cascade plant still required. In winter, Calgarians could sleep more soundly in the knowledge that the engineers at the Bearspaw dam were attempting to manage the ice buildup along the Bow so as to prevent any disastrous floods. Down below the city, the fishers would return each spring to cast for wild trout, which now bred naturally among the plants that grew there thanks to the nutrient loads flowing out of Calgary's sewage plants. Over the past ninety-odd years, a new kind of "natural" waterway had evolved out of the wilderness river that had first attracted the hydraulic engineers soon after the turn of the century.

CHAPTER 12

Conclusion

With great effort and ingenuity – not to mention expense – Calgary Power had managed to make the Bow River a much more efficient producer of hydroelectricity by the 1960s. At that point, driven by the unbottled genie of Alberta's oil-fuelled economic growth, the company turned from the province's rivers to its coalfields for a source of primary energy to meet the demand for electricity. In this new dispensation, the Bow's role reverted to that of spot power producer to meet peak demand and backup in the event of emergencies within the core thermal system.

Dammed and plumbed to hold back water until it was needed by the generators, the Bow had been redesigned during the first half of the twentieth century to surrender more power than nature had originally intended. It was subsequently eclipsed as a source of electricity. It remains, by way of conclusion, to ask what this hydroelectric engineering meant for the river and the national park. And, now that waterpower has shrunk to relative insignificance, what has kept all of those dams, diversion works, and reservoirs in place?

The history of the electrification of Edmonton and Calgary presents contrasting experiences of system development. Both actually began in a similar fashion, supplying civic, commercial, residential, and industrial needs from centrally located thermal electric stations. Edmonton continued down that path, generating electricity from locally available coal and gas and distributing it to the city and, with surplus capacity, to the surrounding region. Power lines radiated out to the region from the city of Edmonton. Calgary's municipal utility, by contrast, gave up generating its own power in the 1920s, preferring instead to perform retail distribution of wholesale power purchased from the Calgary Power hydroelectric system. Edmonton paid a price for its electrical autarchy in power rates significantly higher than those prevailing throughout the period in Calgary.

Geography explains part of the divergence. Edmonton, located astride the large North Saskatchewan River, nevertheless lacked convenient waterpower of the necessary scale, situated as it was further east from the foothills and the mountains on the open prairie. The nearest industrial-scale waterpowers lay hundreds of kilometres to the west, high up in the mountains. In that context, owning and operating a municipal plant in the city made sense. Calgary, however, had what appeared to be industrial-strength waterpower close at hand, although as we have seen, that appearance proved illusory. Nevertheless, as the power company succeeded in re-engineering the river, producing electricity at prices lower than the city could generate at its thermal station, the city retreated to urban distribution functions. Meanwhile, Calgary Power's system grew around the city as a regional grid, with the city as the core demand source.

Alberta thus developed with two dominant electric utilities employing different energy sources and based upon different business models. These two systems would remain geographically isolated until the 1950s, when system growth and provincial utilities regulation brought the two utilities into physical and institutional contact. As Calgary Power moved its generating capacity north to the coalfields closer to Edmonton, co-operative upstream hydroelectric development of expensive waterpower sites on the tributaries of the North Saskatchewan River became financially possible, and provincial regulation smoothed the way to intersystem grid management.

In theory, at any point before the mid 1950s, Calgary Power could have given up on hydroelectricity and opted for thermal electric production. Alberta had lots of coal begging for markets; that's why the coal operators joined the parks advocates in opposing the Spray Lakes development in the 1920s. The technology was available and, when adapted at scale, produced reasonably priced electricity. The publicly owned Edmonton electric utility took this thermal power route from the outset. Later, oil and gas presented power-generating possibilities. But Calgary Power could not bring itself to take that step until it ran out of river to plumb.

Nothing absolutely constrained the company. No iron shackles bound it to the river. Rather, the company managers' own imagination limited their reasoning to the hydroelectric option. Technological momentum or path dependence – this phenomenon has been called both – put blinkers on management thinking.[1] This reflex was partly a justification of past decisions that had set the company on the hydroelectric path, but it was also due to professional bias. The managers were all hydroelectric engineers, true believers in the superior cleanliness and efficiency of hydroelectricity. It was partly, too, an economic quest, a search for electricity at the lowest possible operating cost. And it was a conventional modernist way of thinking about costs being restricted to certain kinds of things, a type of accounting that excluded aesthetic, scenic, and environmental considerations from the cost calculation. Convenience figured in the equation as well: it was always easier, faster, and possibly cheaper, right up until the end, to continue machining the river than it was rethinking the whole process and investing in an entirely different way of doing things. Calgary Power became a captive of an early technological choice. A perverse rationality drove it, in the face of opposition and viable alternatives, to continue to invest in redesigning and machining a mountain river. A very Canadian obsession with hydroelectricity possessed the management of Calgary Power for three generations. Ultimately, the force behind the redesign of a river and a national park emanated from the grooved thinking of a power corporation.

Corporate strategy may also have played a part in this Bow River fixation: occupying territory and thus denying important assets to competitors took priority. However, there are limits to this line of thought. After the early elimination of a rival bidder on Kananaskis Falls, the provincial government itself remained the most likely competitor for waterpower resources and for the electric utility business. That made for a very delicate dance between the government and the company, who were at once potential competitors, controller of the resource and supplicant, regulator and regulated, and allies in negotiations with the federal government. The power company had to finesse its way forward in a situation where the province might at any time enter its business as a rival and takeover threat, or where the provincial government might back the company as its policy instrument of choice.

In the playing out of this drama, nothing appears to have been inevitable or predetermined. The Province of Alberta explored the possibility of creating a provincial electric system in the 1920s, just as it had earlier created a provincial telephone system. The Hydro-Electric Power Commission of Ontario had famously – or notoriously – paved the way. But then the Great Depression, followed by a world war, crushed any thoughts of state expansion for a generation by drying up revenues, freezing provincial credit, and seizing taxation room (especially, during the war, by the federal government). After the war, "provincialization" of the electric industry once again loomed as a real possibility. A more traditional conservative provincial government might well have gone forward with such a project. Manitoba and Saskatchewan had already gone this route, as had Nova Scotia, New Brunswick, and Quebec. Besides, an out-of-province, eastern-controlled public utility seemed particularly vulnerable to Alberta's populist politics. But the Social Credit government of Ernest Manning was not a conventional conservative government. Its ideological obsession with communism and the Cold War raised ideological barriers against this kind of statism even though public ownership of electricity had strong support in Social Credit's strong populist constituencies and within Calgary and Edmonton – both of which had municipal-owned systems. But the timing of things mattered. Who could have predicted that the province would take a self-denying ordinance in this critical period? A conservative government like that of W.A.C. Bennett in British Columbia, or a more consciously province-building progressive conservative government like that of Peter Lougheed in Alberta in the 1970s, might have followed a different course. But Calgary Power survived in the postwar era by virtue of Premier Manning's Cold War ideological abhorrence of state enterprise. As a result, an investor-owned, private utility flourished in Alberta, a lone holdout against the pattern of provincial hydro companies

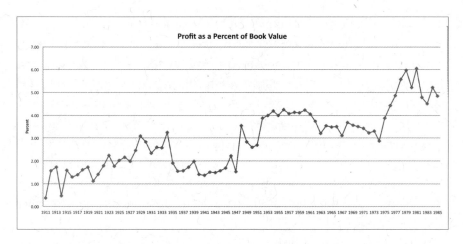

Profit as a Percent of Book Value

Graph 12.1. Long-term profitability of Calgary Power TransAlta Utilities, 1911–1985. Source: Compiled from data obtained from Calgary Power and TransAlta Annual Reports.

that characterized postwar Canada. Political events far from Alberta had a profound influence upon the structure of its electricity industry.

The private versus public ownership debate complicated power issues in Alberta, but it did not have much influence on whether the waterpower resources of the upper Bow would be developed. The resolution of this debate would determine who would be in charge of development. After protracted negotiations interrupted and influenced by extraneous events – the Depression, World War II, and the Cold War – Calgary Power was able, with provincial backing, to complete its program of Bow River remediation to maximize its hydroelectric output.

The combination of an ability to produce more power more efficiently and to sell more power at lower prices made for a much more profitable company. Graph 12.1 attempts to capture the gradually improving profitability of the Calgary Power Company over time. The measure – reported net surplus as a proportion of book value of assets – is not the best measure, but it is the only one at our disposal for an extended period. Nor should the specific figures be given too much weight: the longer term trends are more significant. Accounting legerdemain and very lax financial regulation gave management the ability to manipulate financials to some extent. Nonetheless, the trend lines show that over time, management was gradually able to improve the financial performance of the company up to the late 1920s. The Great Depression and World War II had a deep impact on profitability, but in the postwar era, on the strength of a much more efficient hydroelectric generating system, rapid growth in southern Alberta followed by extremely low-cost thermal electric production at mine-mouth plants raised the company to new and sustained levels of profitability in the 6 per cent range. It took time, an enormous investment, and almost half a century of struggle to stabilize the fortunes of Calgary Power.

Upon completion in the late 1950s, Calgary Power's river management system consisted of the following:

- Three diversions: the Upper Ghost into Lake Minnewanka, the Spray River into the Bow at Canmore, and Smith-Dorrien Creek into the Spray Lakes

- Eight storage reservoirs: Lake Minnewanka, two at Spray Lakes, two at Kananaskis Lakes, Barrier Lake, Ghost Lake, and Bearspaw Lake

- Eleven hydroelectric generating stations: Cascade (36 mw), Rundle (50 mw), Spray (103 mw), Three Sisters (3 mw), Pocaterra (15 mw), Interlakes (5 mw), Barrier (13 mw), Kananaskis (19 mw), Horseshoe (14 mw), Ghost (51 mw), and Bearspaw (17 mw)[2]

Together, these facilities, rated at 326 megawatts (mw), made possible the generation of 837 gigawatt hours of electricity annually. After these facilities were in place, no significant waterpower sites remained undeveloped on the upper river. Two possible locations below Calgary would be costly to develop and would destroy the most popular trout-fishing reaches.[3] For all intents and purposes, the Bow was tapped out as a power source by the mid-1950s.

The Bow had become, in the words of environmental historian Richard White, an "organic machine."[4] Not only had its power been captured for use, but the river itself had been re-engineered to make more power and more reliable power. Nature and technology had become so intertwined as to be inseparable. The Bow remained a natural phenomenon, beloved by tourists and residents alike, much visited, used, and photographed, but it was "second nature" reworked by human ingenuity to serve human needs.

Over the course of half a century, through the addition of upper watershed storage reservoirs, the flow of the river had been significantly altered. Early summer peak flows had been shaved by storing water upstream for release in the fall and winter, which effectively doubled the "natural" streamflow during those periods.

It is not possible, given the state of the data, to compare streamflow before hydroelectric storage with streamflow after the system became operational. First, as noted earlier, detailed streamflow data were not collected before 1911. Reliable and comparable data exist only from 1912 onward. But by that time, the first Lake Minnewanka dam had already gone into service, slightly modifying streamflow patterns. Thus, our comparison shows not before and after, but rather minimal streamflow regulation against full management. It is quite likely that the differences between unregulated and regulated regimes would have been even greater had we been able to obtain recorded levels of unimpeded river flow, but we must make do with a best approximation. Second, the river never flows in exactly the same quantity or with the same pattern of variability, thus skewing year-to-year comparisons. The graphs presented in this chapter, therefore, should be thought of as suggestive and illustrative rather than definitive. They are also more of a statistical artefact than a precise representation of an observed phenomenon. Averages often mask large differences within the period, and they certainly do so in mountain river measurement.

The graphs are based upon average actual weekly mean flow records in cubic metres per second (m³/s) for the Bow River at Calgary.[5] The numbers are averages of a series of means. To compare two periods, we have averaged these means in two series, the 1910s (1912–20) and the 1960s (1960–69). To compare the flow at different times of the year, we have selected two periods: April to July (weeks 18 to 30) to capture peak flow trends and January to March (weeks 1 to 12) to register low flow perform-ance. During these two periods, the total flow of the river was compar-able but not identical, an average of 3,409,022 dam^3 (1 dam^3 = 1,000 cubic metres) in the 1910s and 3,116,798 dam^3 in the 1960s. It should be borne in mind, therefore, that the total average flow during the earlier period slightly exceeded that of the later period. Nevertheless, the changes in streamflow are quite clear.

Graphs 12.2a and 12.2b show that in the 1910s, streamflow after week 23 substantially exceeded streamflow recorded during the 1960s. Early peak flows were higher, or, alternatively, the 1960s summer peaks were much lower than before. In the interim, and especially after the 1940s, the missing water (the area between the two lines on the graph) was retained upstream in the company's reservoirs to be released as needed. The graph covering the first three months of the year, shows the effects of releasing stored water in the winter months during periods of traditionally low flow. Storage effectively doubled the "natural" flow of the river in the 1960s. The next graph (12.3) compares two years of almost identical quantities of streamflow, 1912 and 1966. Here, the shaving of the peak and the doubling of winter streamflow can also be seen in the much lower curve in summer for the 1960s and the much higher winter flows on the tails of the curve on either side of the peak. On the left side of the chart, 1960s flow levels were approximately twice those of 1912 until week 19. Then the 1912 flow peaked at much higher levels and stayed higher until week 45, when stor-age releases in 1966 resumed.

Storage smoothed out the variation, but not completely. In its stream-flow profile, the Bow remained a mountain river, but one of moderated extremes. Graphs 12.4a and 12.4b profile streamflow during two periods: 1912 to 1942 with minimal storage capability and 1960 to 1990 when the storage system was fully operational. In outline, both are quite similar pro-files of a mountain river with highly seasonal variations in streamflow. A close comparison of the scale of the vertical axis on the graphs measuring flow in cubic metres per second reveals, however, that the maximum (over 1,000), median (900), and minimum (600) levels of the peaks were much

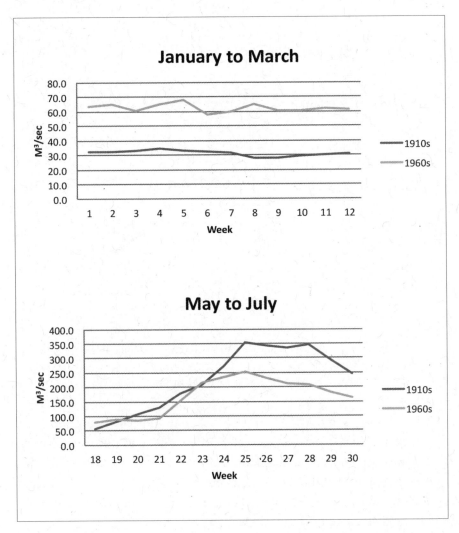

Graphs 12.2a and 12.2b. A comparison of the winter and summer flow of the Bow River at Calgary before upstream storage (1910s) and with storage in full operation (1960s). Source: Environment Alberta, South Saskatchewan River Basin Historical Natural Flows, 1912–1995, CD-ROM version 2.02.

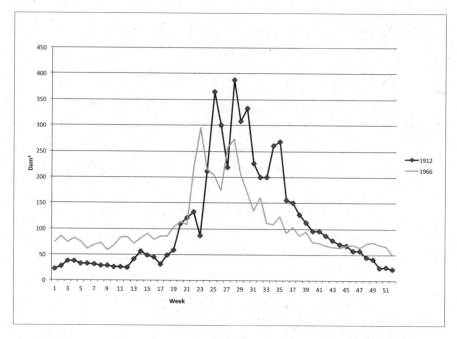

Graph 12.3. Bow River weekly flow at Calgary in two years of comparable volume before storage (1912) and after 1966. Source: Environment Alberta, South Saskatchewan River Basin Historical Natural Flows, 1912–1995, CD-ROM version 2.02.

higher in the earlier period than later – 700, 600, and 400, respectively. In contrast, maximum, median, and minimum flows were much higher (between 100 and 200) later in the twentieth century than in the earlier period (all under 100). The curve had been flattened somewhat: the peaks had been lowered and the tails raised.

Calgary's growing demand for electricity, combined with capital and hydroelectric technology following the logic of path dependence, created a "second nature" on the Bow River. In the sense best described by William Cronon in the case of Chicago, commodity flows into and out of the city altered the landscape, shaping a new ecology that, over time, came to be thought of as a natural landscape.[6] This phenomenon was not limited to the river. The ranches, farms, irrigated fields, and feedlots, and the coal mines, drilling rigs, pump jacks, and pipelines of the energy economy

WILDERNESS AND WATERPOWER

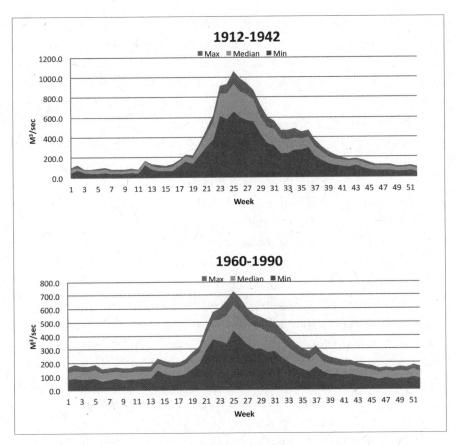

Graphs 12.4a and 12.4b. Maximum, mean, and minimum flows of the Bow River at Calgary under relatively small-scale (1912–1942) and extensive (1960-90) storage regimes. Source: Environment Alberta, South Saskatchewan River Basin Historical Natural Flows, 1912–1995, CD-ROM version 2.02.

also represented nature transformed by capital, technology, labour, and public policy into commodity flows directed through the city of Calgary. Here, we see how the metabolism of a growing city operating within a hydroelectric technological regime changed the nature of a river – and a national park. We will return to this point in a moment.

First, however, we must explore some of the broader implications of second nature on the Bow River. The river had been changed, but that was nothing new: the river changed itself all the time. Its flow varied; it meandered in its bed, each year cutting away banks and piling up new banks and bars. What was different was the role of humans in driving change. On the one hand, summer floods gradually diminished, until they became a distant memory.[7] On the other hand, for a period, the increased winter flow produced brief but alarming mid-winter floods during the 1940s and 1950s, until the provincial government ordered the power company to build the Bearspaw dam to minimize the possibility of winter ice jam recurrence under artificially elevated flow levels. The moderated river carried less debris, worked less vigorously against its banks, and stayed more regularly in its bed. On the stabilized banks, vegetation thickened. In time, beavers colonized new reaches of the river that now provided abundant shrubbery for food, even in Calgary. The less extreme river became more verdant.

Certainly, people living by the river noticed the changes. They responded by changing their attitudes toward the newly well-behaved river and reconceptualizing land use along its banks. Public hearings in the 1950s looking into winter flooding and a participatory democracy insurgency in the early 1970s against floodplain clearance demonstrated how closely people in Calgary observed changes in "their" river, disregarded flood risks in the new flow regime, and valued its new attributes. The banks of the Bow as it flowed through Calgary – once the home of lumber yards, auto shops, and junkyards – became the location for manicured parks, trails, and condominium and commercial complexes. Trees, flourishing in the floodplain, became an urban forest worthy of preservation on an otherwise treeless prairie. The river gradually became the focus of outdoor recreation and a centre of civic pride.[8] Second nature became the new normal. As the river became domesticated, no longer running rogue in summer and winter, people, without thinking about it too much, came to prefer the new river to the old, or rather, what existed in their experience compared to some imagined earlier state.

Although hydroelectric development of the Bow reshaped not only the boundaries of Banff National Park but also the park's internal ecology, it must be noted that aesthetic considerations trumped development

– even among hydroelectric engineers – at what was considered one of the most scenic spots in the park, Bow Falls. Engineers excluded this potential hydroelectric site from development calculations right from the very beginning. "Highest use" thinking reserved it for other human revenue-producing pleasures. Bow Falls would remain untouched by electricity developers, though not completely untouched: for fifty years it would live an underground existence as the sewerage outfall for the town of Banff.

Parks do not exist in isolation but in a broader politics in which different "rights" compete in the formation of public policy. The particular fate of Banff National Park with respect to hydroelectric storage and generation hinged upon the intricate interplay of federal and provincial politics over a fairly long period of time. The power company, driven by its own technological and capitalist imperatives, eventually achieved its objectives, but not according to its own timetable or under its own steam. It could only do so with the powerful support of provincial and municipal officials who themselves made choices about how electricity would be developed and distributed.

Similarly, historians who write of "the state" as if it were a singular, coherent, purposeful entity will be cautioned by this story, noting how internally divided the "state structure" actually is on something as straightforward as hydroelectric development of a western Canadian river. The internal pluralism of the state – not just the separate federal, provincial, and municipal orders of government, but also the diversity within those orders – needs to be taken into account. The conflicts within the state were as intense as those between interest groups. Officials from Parks, Waterpower, Fisheries, Indian Affairs, and Munitions and Supply contended with one another with an intensity and tenacity comparable to that of the Alpine Club and the Canadian National Parks Association with Calgary Power. The state was not of one mind; its internal divisions had to be brokered. Readers may be inured to stories of overriding capitalist power or the iron rule of bureaucracies, but in this particular story, elected politicians do the decisive deciding. Whatever happened to Banff National Park happened because complex political forces came into alignment. It is broadly a democratic story, however much nature and parks purism were compromised.

As the ideology of parks hardened, Banff, as we have seen, necessarily shrank in size to exclude development sites. Nonetheless, hydroelectric development changed nature within Banff as well. The "Doctrine of Usefulness" accommodated an initial storage project at Lake Minnewanka, which Parks Branch officials opportunistically used to build their own hydroelectric generating system to serve the park. But once the camel's nose had crept into the metaphorical tent, the camel itself – larger, more effective storage – was not far behind. This force could be, and would be, resisted during both the Roaring Twenties and the Dirty Thirties, but it could not hold out against a world war.

Storage and electricity generation within the park and on its eastern border had implications for the environment of the park itself. Storage at Lake Minnewanka after 1912, but especially after 1942, created a much different kind of lake than the old Devil's Lake. It was a much larger, deeper, more integrated body as the retained water pushed back into the mountains and up former canyons. The annual six- to ten-metre raising and lowering of water levels lent a bathtub ring effect, first where the forest had been stripped and then in the form of a 294-hectare dead zone of alternately exposed and sunken earth. But the raised water levels also improved boating and sustained a popular service industry. On the debit side, however, important fish spawning zones were drowned in deep water, and the artificial raising and lowering of water levels also interfered with fish reproduction. Of course, the fish themselves were partly products of human intervention, an introduced species having been stocked in the lake from the park's own fish hatchery.

The needs of war planted a hydroelectric station in one of the most visible sites within the park, right beside the highway, and a large power canal cut a geometric line through the park angling from the lake to penstocks leading down to the generators. Did this diminish the "park experience" for the millions of postwar visitors? That is an impossible question to answer, particularly as mass automotive-based tourism overwhelmed the park. The new tourists had quite different aesthetic sensibilities from those of the trail riders, mountain climbers, and spa goers of an earlier era. Were the visitors to the tour boats and campgrounds of Lake Minnewanka offended by the berm and head gates and power canal of the storage reservoir? Did the generating station on the highway just past the hoodoos jar the mood of autotourists threading their way into the mountains at Banff? For some perhaps. But for most, these intrusions were rendered invisible by the more obvious splendours. The equipment creating Lake Minnewanka did not normally crowd its way into the photographs of the mountain scenery reflected in the water. It is more likely that, in time, visitors came to live with the incongruities – and these were not the only ones on offer. Time turned earlier intrusions into romantic relics: the site of Bankhead, for example, had to be imagined from the ghostly concrete remnants of the mine.

The Spray development, though removed from the park, nevertheless had important consequences for the park. Water levels were raised sixty-one metres, drowning forty-four hundred acres of subalpine terrain and creating a fifteen-mile lake. The lake filled up, as we have seen, when the natural outflow into the Spray River was dammed up to divert water through a tunnel through a mountain toward a much higher fall through an intricate series of interconnected generating stations. The Spray River, as a result, virtually dried up during some months of the year and, for the benefit of the golfers and tourists at Banff Springs Hotel, carried just enough water in high season to be scenic. This regulation of the river was, of course, fatal to the fish in the stream. The Spray River was once the main focus of fishing within the park, but the sport fishery on the river became a victim of Bow River hydroelectric development downstream. To the extent that fishing continued as a pastime for visitors, its focus shifted from the rivers to the lakes of the park, which were, of course, stocked with vigorously fighting introduced species much beloved by anglers.

The Kananaskis Lakes and the Spray Lakes experienced the same increase in surface area and the same annual cycle of fill up and draw down as Lake Minnewanka. The fish faced the same reproductive difficulties in their changed environment. But the constantly restocked introduced species did survive in sufficient numbers as to satisfy anglers. These larger lakes that resulted from hydroelectric development, fully filled in the summer months and newly accessible with logging roads and provincial parks, created new recreational opportunities for canoeists, kayakers, and campers. Boaters and sailors, too, colonized the ponds behind the dams, and whitewater enthusiasts capitalized on the surging increased flows below the dams when the turbines sprang to life.

Several recent studies have surveyed the environmental impact of hydroelectric storage and development in Banff National Park and on the Bow generally.[9] Dams on the mainstem and in the mountains have prevented the migration of fish populations. Flooding and dewatering of the reservoirs has interfered with the spring and fall spawning of certain fish species and favoured the reproduction of species preferring deeper water. Fluctuations in lake levels has changed the structure of aquatic communities and altered food sources for some species. The Cascade and Spray Rivers have virtually vanished as a result of damming. The flow of the Cascade has been almost entirely redirected through the power station, and the lowest sections of the river have disappeared completely. The Spray River, too, has been dramatically altered, as we have seen, although minimal flows have been maintained in summer for golfers and tourists. The original 14 m³/s flow has been reduced to an annual average of 3 m³/s. This regulation eliminated the annual spring floods, changed the stream channel, and permitted vegetation to encroach on the bed. It also decimated populations of cutthroat trout, Dolly Varden trout, rainbow trout, and mountain whitefish. The overall net effect of altered streamflows within the park for hydroelectric storage has been to reduce species diversity and biomass.

Downstream on the Bow, the dams and their periodic on/off operation have had an impact upon aquatic and terrestrial ecosystems as well. Daily water-level fluctuations complicate the reproductive activities of some species of fish. Slack water created by the dams affects native species requiring fast-running cold water. River management has, to some degree, contributed to the stabilization of riverbanks and a concomitant thickening of streamside vegetation. This, in turn, has diminished the habitat for some species and improved it for others – in particular, beavers and muskrats. Overall, however, it is difficult to measure whether the ecological impact of the modification of the river for hydroelectric production has had a greater or lesser effect than introduced fish species and nutrient loading as a result of sewage effluent. In many places, native species have been virtually extirpated by introduced sport fish, one of which, the rainbow trout, has flourished in the nutrient-rich reaches below Calgary.

Undeniably, the nature of Banff National Park changed in response to hydroelectric development of the Bow River. It is important to note, however, that this was a relative rather than an absolute change. The new dispensation simply represented a different mix of the human and the natural world. Banff before hydroelectric storage was not an Eden before the Fall.

The city, with its growing appetite for energy, continued to act on nature far beyond its own city limits, but the nature being incorporated was coal, and the consequences of its metabolism were felt by the atmosphere and climate. But that is another story. With the growth in electricity demand being satisfied by other energy sources within the province, and with the capitalist imperative thus relaxed, what kept these elaborate engineering works on the Bow River in existence? They required costly maintenance. Why not tear them down, let the river revert to its wild state?[10] Some people argued for such an outcome. But surprisingly, long after these hydroelectric works had outlived their functional usefulness, an unusual coalition of interests formed to keep the dams in place. Indeed, when proposed, the idea of removing the dams – as has been done in dozens of rivers in the United States – would be dismissed out of hand as "socially unacceptable."[11]

From an industry point of view, the Bow plants existed primarily to be turned on and off to meet peaks in demand. Other uses – recreation, sanitation, irrigation – might be accommodated from time to time, but conflicts between optimization of operations within the TransAlta distribution system received the highest priority, as its brief to the Alberta Water Resources Commission hearings in the 1980s contended that it should. However, as the Bow River contribution to the grid declined to virtual insignificance, it became harder and harder to defend such a position.

For half a century, TransAlta – née Calgary Power – had enjoyed the run of the river. The electricity company designed and operated it to suit itself – though not without persistent opposition, as we have seen. However, as the company withdrew from the river as its primary energy source after the 1960s, the power of other users over river management grew. Over the last thirty years, TransAlta has lost control of the river and even of its own works. Put another way, it has had to learn to share management of the river and its facilities with a broader coalition of interests. While, for the most part, they have all agreed upon maintaining the river as a managed resource, they have differed on management principles.

Through several rounds of analysis, public consultation, and reporting, it became apparent that the river would in future be managed to serve a number of needs, not just hydroelectric production. Through the South Saskatchewan River Basin Study and the Alberta Water Resources Commission hearings of the 1980s, the Bow River Water Quality Council State of the River reports and the Banff–Bow Valley Task Force consultations of the 1990s, and the Alberta Water for Life legislation and the creation of the South Saskatchewan Water Basin Council during the last decade, the principle of co-management of the river to meet a broader range of social and environmental objectives has gradually been established. The electric company, in the operation of its dams and reservoirs, must comply with government regulation intended to serve the sometimes conflicting objectives of a broad constellation of interests: Native peoples, irrigators, duck hunters, fishers, ecologists, water experts, canoeists, boaters, recreationists, environmentalists, business groups, labour unions, tourist promoters, park authorities, and municipal councils, to mention only the organized interests. Through consultation processes, it became clear that irrigators wanted the storage reservoirs to release water in late summer when they most needed it rather than in the winter. Boaters and recreational users wanted water levels behind the dams to be maintained at steadier levels. Fishers insisted that river levels be managed to promote fish-spawning activities. Fisheries biologists and environmental scientists, studying the impact of human interference on the ecology of the river, sought measures to restore natural habitat. The higher needs to be served that have emerged from these consultations are maintaining safe and secure domestic water supplies, meeting inflow stream needs for aquatic ecosystems, mimicking natural streamflow behaviour to restore terrestrial and aquatic ecologies, and providing adequate water supplies to irrigation districts to meet the minimum flow requirements of the Master Agreement between Alberta and Saskatchewan. Water storage and release by the power company must now be managed to take these requirements into consideration.

TransAlta, too, had its own reasons for keeping its Bow River system in working order, even if it had to share management of it. After the Kyoto Protocol was adopted in December 1997, TransAlta, whose electricity came from coal-fired generators, needed "green" offsets to compensate for the heavy atmospheric carbon emissions from its coal-fired thermal generating stations. Hydroelectric capacity, having been deemed to be "green," served a strategic purpose in the calculus of carbon credits. The existence of this legacy hydroelectric system to some degree made up for greenhouse gas emissions from those thermal generators. The new value of the Bow to the company derived from what its waterpower permitted elsewhere. The same was true of the wind farms sprouting under TransAlta sponsorship in the southern Alberta foothills and as far away from Calgary as rural Ontario.

The reign of the power company over the river had effectively ended by the beginning of the twenty-first century. Its works in the river would remain, but they would be operated to serve priorities other than maximum hydroelectric output. Some environmental purists would campaign for a return of the river to a "wild" state, but a new coalition of interests enshrined in public policy ensured that for quite different reasons, it would remain an organic machine.

Time matters in the telling of stories. Different timeframes afford opportunities for quite different narrative arcs. Imagine what this story would have looked like had it ended in 1929, or 1949. Similarly, the transition to coal-fired energy production looked different in the 1970s than it does in an era of carbon emissions–induced climate change. And, of course, time has not stood still, nor has Alberta's appetite for electricity diminished. So the story continues to unfold.

This is not a moral tale. We have not told this story to cheer on corporate capitalism, to discourage environmental protest – or vice versa. We have written this account to demonstrate how historically contingent public policy outcomes can be in a democratic society. The players do not always have equal access to power, to be sure, but in this case, corporate power on its own was not enough. The power of the respective players, too, is influenced by context and circumstances – rising or falling electricity demand, war or depression, economic growth, and the salience of aesthetic and environmental concerns. Calgary Power achieved its objectives on the Bow River, but it was a surprisingly long and convoluted struggle ruled by path dependence. While, to a degree, the company's hydraulic needs were a surrogate for the demands of southern Alberta electricity consumers, there were other means of producing that primary power. And those residents, too, were the people with the greatest direct interest in the management of Banff National Park, being its largest users. The development of waterpower on the Bow and the implications for a wilderness national park involved complex tradeoffs, managed by the politics of a federal system, in shifting economic and ideological circumstances over more than half a century. At each stage, the forces engaged with uncertain outcomes.

Nor, in taking the humans-in-nature approach, do we seek to justify every form of alteration to parks and natural systems. Quite the contrary. This is not an apologia for what happened to the Bow and Banff National Park; rather, we want to understand the social and political processes of human-induced environmental change. Nor is it our intention to license with this narrative any modification of rivers or national parks to suit human needs. Principles are worth fighting for, usually against other principles. But we do not believe that there is some absolute principle whose rigorous application should everywhere and always prevail. We do not believe that there is some prelapsarian nature to return to. Rather, these are matters for debate, contestation, and resolution in their time as interests and ideals compete. The tension built into the original legislation for Rocky Mountains National Park promoting "use and enjoyment," on the one hand, and the injunction of the 1930s Parks Act to pass on parks "unimpaired for the enjoyment of future generations," on the other, opens space for a politics of parks rather than a theology of parks – a politics in which choices are publicly debated and democratically decided. With this story, we affirm that the game is always worth playing and that outcomes are never predetermined.

Appendix

Calgary Power Generating Capability, 1911–90

Hydroelectric Capability in 1951

Station	Date	Net Capability (Kilowatts)
Horseshoe	1911	13,900
Kananaskis	1914	10,000
	1951	8,900
Ghost	1929	28,000
Cascade	1942	18,000
Barrier	1947	12,900
Spray	1951	49,900
Rundle	1951	17,000
Three Sisters	1951	3,000
Total		161,600

Hydroelectric Capability added after 1951

Station	Date	Net Capability (Kilowatts)
Ghost	1954	22,900
Bearspaw	1954	16,900
Pocaterra	1955	14,900
Interlakes	1955	5,000
Cascade	1957	17,900
Spray	1960	102,800
Rundle	1960	32,900
Big Bend (Brazeau)	1959	165,000
	1967	190,000
Bighorn	1972	120,000

Total Hydroelectric Capability		849,900

Calgary Power Generating Capability, 1911–90 cont'd

Thermal Generating Capability		
Station	Date	Net Capability (Kilowatts)
Wabamun # 1	1956	69,000
Wabamun # 2	1958	67,000
Wabamun # 3	1962	147,000
Wabamun # 4	1968	286,000
Sundance # 1	1970	286,000
Sundance # 2	1973	286,000
Sundance # 3	1976	352,000
Sundance # 4	1977	352,000
Sundance # 5	1978	352,000
Sundance # 6	1980	359,000
Keephills # 1	1983	377,000
Keephills # 2	1984	377,000
Sheerness # 1 *	1986	366,000
Sheerness # 2 *	1990	366,000
Total Thermal Capability		3,676,000

* 50% owned by Alberta Power

Notes

ABBREVIATIONS

CPC	Calgary Power Company Fonds, Glenbow Archives, Calgary
GA	Glenbow Archives
HLRO	House of Lords Record Office, London
LAC	Library and Archives Canada
MB	Calgary Water Power Company Minutebook
PAA	Provincial Archives of Alberta
UAA	University of Alberta Archives
Whyte Museum	Whyte Museum of the Canadian Rockies, Banff

INTRODUCTION

1 Martin V. Melosi, "Path Dependence and Urban History: Is a Marriage Possible?" in *Resources of the City: Contributions to an Environmental History of Modern Europe*, ed. Dieter Schott, Bill Luckin, and Genevieve Massard-Guilbaud (Aldershot: Ashgate, 2005), 262. A major debate within the economic profession unfolded over whether "history matters" after Paul David's essay on the subject, "Clio and the Economics of QWERTY," *American Economic Review* 75, no. 2 (1985), 332–37.

2 R. C. Brown, "The Doctrine of Usefulness," in *Canadian Parks in Perspective*, ed. J. G. Nelson and R. C. Scace (Montreal: Harvest House, 1970), 46–62.

3 The standard account of Canada's national parks policy is Fergus Lothian's four-volume *A History of Canada's National Parks* (Ottawa: Parks Canada, 1976). Despite its length, it is a narrowly constructed compendium of the administrative histories of each park. At the polemical end of the spectrum, Leslie Bella proffers a history of parks policy centred on the thesis that rather than promoting preservation, they leaned toward making a profit from tourism.

Leslie Bella, *Parks for Profit* (Montreal: Harvest House, 1987). For the development of national park policy from a political science perspective, see Paul Kopas, *Taking the Air: Ideas and Change in Canada's National Parks* (Vancouver: University of British Columbia Press, 2007). Although Kopas focuses on the rise of ecological influences after the 1950s, he does offer a brief overview of the earlier evolution of policy development. Ecological integrity, the main principle underlying the 1988 National Parks Act, is an example of the elevation of an abstraction to a policy goal. E. J. Hart's recent biography, *J. B. Harkin: Father of Canada's National Parks* (Edmonton: University of Alberta Press, 2011), is a de facto history of parks policy from 1911 to 1936. For focused studies of the application of policy in individual cases, see the Parks Canada centennial collection of essays edited by Claire Campbell, *A Century of Parks Canada, 1911–2011* (Calgary: University of Calgary Press, 2011). As for Banff National Park per se, E. J. Hart's two volumes, *The Place of the Bows* and *The Battle for Banff* (Banff: EJH Literary Enterprises, 1999 and 2003) is the place to start. Walter Hildebrandt's insightful study of park history for the Banff-Bow Valley Task Force is the best brief guide: *An Historical Analysis of Parks Canada and Banff National Park, 1968–1995* (Banff: Banff-Bow Valley Task Force, 1995).

4   William Cronon launched the debate in a provocative essay, "The Problem with Wilderness; or, Getting Back to the Wrong Nature," published in a collection that he edited, *Uncommon Ground: Rethinking the Human Place in Nature* (New York: Norton, 1995), 69–90. The first issue of *Environmental History* republished this essay along with surprisingly intense responses from Thomas Dunlap, Sam Hays, and Michael Cohen, and Cronon's reply.

Environmental History 1 (1996): 7–55. For the influence of Cronon's essay, see Char Miller, "An Open Field," *Pacific Historical Review* 70 (2001): 71–74, and Thomas R. Dunlap, *Faith in Nature: Environmentalism as Religious Quest* (Seattle: University of Washington Press, 2004), ch. 3.

5   J. G. Nelson set things in motion with his early paper "Man and Landscape Change in Banff National Park: A National Park Problem in Perspective," in Nelson and Scace, *Canadian Parks in Perspective*, 63–98.

6   On Native-set fires, the role of humans in shaping the ecology, and the removal of Native people and settlers from the area designated to be Jasper National Park, see I. S. MacLaren, "Cultured Wilderness in Jasper National Park," *Journal of Canadian Studies* 34 (1999): 7–58. Ted Binnema and Melanie Niemi argue that hunters' organizations and elite sportsmen, rather than wilderness enthusiasts, played a leading role in the removal of Native people from national parks. "Let the Line Be Drawn Now: Wilderness, Conservation, and the Exclusion of Aboriginal People from Banff National Park," *Environmental History* 11 (2006): 724–50. Mark David Spence could be said to have begun this re-evaluation of the impact of park-making on Native peoples with his book *Dispossessing the Wilderness: Indian Removal and the Making of National Parks* (New York: Oxford University Press, 1999). Karl Jacoby followed with the more sensational *Crimes against Nature: Squatters, Poachers, Thieves and the Hidden History of American Conservation* (Berkeley: University of California Press, 2001). In Canada, Bruce Hodgins and Kerry Cannon first broached this subject in "The Aboriginal Presence in Ontario Parks and Other Protected Places," in *Changing Parks: The History, Future and Cultural Context of Parks and Heritage Landscapes,*

ed. John Marsh and Bruce Hodgins (Toronto: Natural Heritage, 1998), 50–76. John Sandlos explores a similar theme within the wildlife conservation movement in *Hunters at the Margin: Native People and Wildlife Conservation in the Northwest Territories* (Vancouver: University of British Columbia Press, 2007).

7   The Alberta Wilderness Association keeps the idea alive (www. AlbertaWilderness.ca), as does the Canadian Parks and Wilderness Society (www.cpaws.org) and a contemporary RV motorhome brand that goes by the name "Wilderness."

8   This amiable contradiction is reflected in the titles of two recent books on the subject that examine the role of the automobile at both ends of the "wilderness" spectrum: David Loutor, *Windshield Wilderness: Cars, Roads and Nature in Washington's National Parks* (Seattle: University of Washington Press, 2006), and *Driven Wild: How the Fight against Automobiles Launched the Modern Wilderness Movement* (Seattle: University of Washington Press, 2002). We contributed a paper on the role of the automobile in the shaping of Banff National Park to the 2008 T2M (Transportation, Technology, and Mobility) Conference in Ottawa: "Car Park: The Influence of Auto Tourism on Banff National Park." See also Amy Larin, "A Rough Ride: Automobiles in Banff National Park, 1905–1918," *Alberta History* (Winter 2008): 2–9. Several of the essays in I. S. MacLaren's edited collection on the fur trade, homesteading, tourism, and ecological restoration expand on the theme of prior occupation and human landscape modification: *Culturing Wilderness in Jasper National Park* (Edmonton: University of Alberta Press, 2007).

9   Whyte Museum, National Parks Papers, M317, file 3, Changes in Boundaries and Areas of National Parks. For a brief history of national park policy, see Ian Attridge, "Canadian Parks Legislation: Past, Present and Prospects," in Marsh and Hodgins, *Changing Parks*, 221–37.

10   Joel Tarr's books and essays over the years have applied the concept of path dependence and urban metabolism. See, for example, "Sewerage and the Development of the Networked City in the United States, 1850–1930," in *Technology and the Rise of the Networked City in Europe and America*, ed. Joel Tarr and Gabriel Dupuy (Philadelphia: Temple University Press, 1988), 159–85; *The Search for the Ultimate Sink: Urban Pollution in Historical Perspective* (Akron: University of Akron Press, 1996); "The Metabolism of the Industrial City: The Case of Pittsburgh," *Journal of Urban History* 28 (2002): 511–45; with Terry F. Yosie, "Critical Decisions in Pittsburgh Water and Wastewater Treatment," in *Devastation and Renewal*, ed. Joel Tarr (Pittsburgh, University of Pittsburgh, 2003), 64–88; with Clay McShane, *The Horse in the City: Living Machines in the Nineteenth Century* (Baltimore: Johns Hopkins University Press, 2007).

11   In addition to the essay referenced in note 1 above, see Melosi's *Garbage in the Cities: Refuse Reform and the Environment* (Pittsburgh: University of Pittsburgh Press, 1988); *The Sanitary City: Urban Infrastructure in America from Colonial Times to the Present* (Baltimore: Johns Hopkins University Press, 2000); *Effluent America: Cities, Industry, Energy and the Environment* (Pittsburgh: University of Pittsburgh Press, 2001); with Joseph Pratt, eds., *Energy Metropolis: An Environmental History of Houston and the Gulf Coast* (Pittsburgh: University of Pittsburgh Press, 2007).

12   Donald Worster, *Rivers of Empire: Water, Aridity, and the Growth of the*

American West (New York: Oxford University Press, 1985); *The Wealth of Nature: Environmental History and the Ecological Imagination* (New York: Oxford University Press, 1993).

13 William Cronon, *Nature's Metropolis: Chicago and the Great West* (New York: Norton, 1996). It is a pleasure to acknowledge the influence of this book, inspired as it is in part by the "metropolitanism" tradition of Canadian historiography.

14 Richard White, *The Organic Machine: The Remaking of the Columbia River* (New York: Hill and Wang, 1995). One observation that White made in passing about taking a moral approach to railroad businessmen in his most recent book confirms our feelings about the utilities magnates: "If the goal is to have great villains or powerful heroes, don't read the mail of the men who ran the transcontinentals." *Railroaded: The Transcontinentals and the Making of Modern America* (New York: Norton, 2011), 233.

15 C. Armstrong and H. V. Nelles, "Competition vs. Convenience: Federal Administration of Bow River Waterpowers, 1906–1913," in *The Canadian West*, ed. Henry Klassen (Calgary: University of Calgary Press, 1977), 163–80; *Monopoly's Moment: The Organization and Regulation of Canadian Utilities, 1830–1930* (Philadelphia: Temple University Press, 1986); *Southern Exposure: Canadian Promoters in Latin America and the Caribbean, 1896–1930* (Toronto: University of Toronto Press, 1988); and with Matthew Evenden, *The River Returns: An Environmental History of the Bow* (Montreal and Kingston: McGill-Queen's University Press, 2009). As this book was in press we received a copy of *Powering Generations: The TransAlta Story, 1911–2011* (Calgary: TransAlta, 2011),

written by Dr. Robert Page and David A French. We had supplied the authors with pre-publication drafts of earlier versions of this account which assisted them in their project. Their beautifully illustrated account of the whole range of company activities provides context for our focused examination of hydroelectric development by the company on the Bow.

CHAPTER 1: WATER FALLS

1 Vaclav Smil's primer, *Energy in World History* (Boulder: Westview Press, 1994), places the development of waterpower and, subsequently, hydroelectricity in the context of the broader energy-use patterns of Western civilization. Louis Hunter documents changing waterpower technology and applications in America in *Waterpower: A History of Industrial Power in America, 1780–1930* (Charlottesville: University of Virginia Press, 1979).

2 There is a vast literature on electrification, to which we have contributed our mite. Peter Hertner, Will Haussman, and Mira Wilkins provide a global view of the process, emphasizing the role of multinational enterprise, in *Global Electrification* (New York: Cambridge University Press, 2008), which contains an excellent bibliography. For the development of electric technology, the most accessible account is Jill Jones, *Empires of Light* (New York: Random House, 2004). Thomas P. Hughes analyzes system development in the United States, Britain, and Germany in *Networks of Power* (Baltimore: Johns Hopkins University Press, 1983). Harold C. Passer's *The Electrical Manufacturers* (Cambridge: Harvard University Press, 1953) remains the best treatment of the rise of the equipment industry. David E. Nye examines the social processes

and implications of electrification in *Electrifying America: Social Meanings of a New Technology* (Cambridge: MIT Press, 1992); Harold L. Platt's *The Electric City* (Chicago: University of Chicago Press, 1991) offers the best account of the electrification of a city, Chicago. The most comprehensive but daunting national history of electricity, the electrical industry, and electrification is the three-volume compendium edited by François Caron, Fabienne Cardot, Henri Morsel, and Maurice Lévy-Leboyer, *Histoire de l'Électricité en France* (Paris: Fayard, 1991, 1994, 1996). We have written a history of the rise of the domestic Canadian electric industry, *Monopoly's Moment: The Organization and Regulation of Canadian Utilities* (Philadelphia: Temple University Press, 1986), and of electric enterprises abroad, *Southern Exposure: Canadian Promoters in Latin America and the Caribbean* (Toronto: University of Toronto Press, 1988). No one has attempted an assessment of the Canadian electric industry over the entire twentieth century, though H. V. Nelles has made a gesture at it: "Hydro and After: The Canadian Experience with the Organization, Nationalization and Deregulation of Electrical Utilities," *Annales Historique de l'électricité* 1 (Juin 2003): 117–32.

3   Until recently, Canada was the world leader in total hydroelectric production, but within the last few years, it has been overtaken by China, with its massive river projects. For details, see the US Energy Information Administration website: www.eia.gov/emeu/international/ electricitygeneration.html.

4   Leo G. Denis and Arther V. White, *Water-Powers of Canada* (Ottawa: Commission of Conservation, 1911).

5   On the early history of Calgary, see George A. Nader, *Profiles of Fifteen*

Metropolitan Centres, vol. 2 of *Cities of Canada* (Toronto: Macmillan, 1976), 333ff; Max Foran, *Calgary: An Illustrated History* (Toronto: Lorimer, 1978); A. Rasporich and H. Klassen, eds., *Frontier Calgary: Town, City and Region 1875–1914* (Calgary: University of Calgary Press, 1976).

6   The convoluted history of the early electrification of Calgary is dealt with in impressive documentary detail in W. E. Hawkins, *Electrifying Calgary: A Century of Public and Private Power* (Calgary: University of Calgary Press, 1987), 1–72.

7   GA, CPC, box 1, MB, June 1890–July 1920; box 4, file 8, Ordinance of Incorporation, Calgary Water Power Company, 1889–94; box 1, Licence, Department of the Interior, December 15, 1897, for right to divert water for use of steam engine; box 3, Map of the Mill and Its Water System, undated; GA M1565, Incorporation Document and Plan for the Proposed Bow River Dam at Calgary, November 11, 1889; GA, Peter A. Prince Fonds; Hawkins, *Electrifying Calgary,* ch. 2.

8   C. Armstrong, M. Evenden, and H. V. Nelles, *The River Returns: An Environmental History of the Bow* (Montreal and Kingston: McGill-Queen's University Press, 2009), chs. 4 and 5; Hawkins, *Electrifying Calgary,* ch. 2.

9   GA, CPC, box 1, file 1, shareholders' meeting, Calgary Water Power Company, July 17, 1903; MB, June 10, 1905; GA, Calgary Council minutes, July 16, 1903, September 24, 1904, March 20, July 13, 1905.

10 Ted Binnema offers the most sophisticated analysis of pre-contact land use in *Common and Contested Ground: A Human and Environmental History of the Northwestern Plains* (Toronto: University of Toronto Press, 2001).

11 Armstrong, Evenden, and Nelles, *River Returns*, chs. 2, 3, and 4.

12 The most accessible and comprehensive description of the Bow River can be found in Bow River Basin Council, *The 2005 Report on the State of the Bow River Basin* (Calgary: Bow River Basin Council, 2005), also available at www.brbc.ab.ca.

13 Walter Hildebrandt, Treaty 7 Elders and Tribal Council, Dorothy First Rider, and Sarah Carter, eds., *The True Spirit and Original Intent of Treaty 7* (Montreal and Kingston: McGill-Queen's University Press, 1996); GA, Map Collection, G3503 IR 142, 1889, 1890 C212.

14 Quoted in Armstrong, Evenden, and Nelles, *River Returns*, 271ff; E. J. Hart, fleshes out the story with lots of local detail in *The Place of Bows: Exploring the Heritage of the Banff-Bow Valley, Part 1 to 1830* (Banff: EJH Literary Enterprises, 1999), 9–114; Whyte Museum, M317, Canadian Parks Service Papers, F17, L. A. Taylor, "The Cave and Basin – Birthplace of National Parks," Background Information Document, March 31, 1978; University of Alberta Archives, William Pearce Papers, acc. 74–169, vol. 51, files 473–74, Letterbooks, 1886.

15 For a map, see Armstrong, Evenden, and Nelles, *River Returns*, 284; see also Geoffrey Wall, "Recreational Lands," in *Addressing the Twentieth Century*, vol. 3 of *Historical Atlas of Canada*, ed. Donald Kerr and Derek Holdsworth (Toronto: University of Toronto, 1990), plate 36; Whyte Museum, M317, Canadian Parks Service Papers, F3, memorandum from S. F. Kun to Maryalice Stewart, October 9, 1974, enclosing a memo by J .E. Spero on boundary changes at Banff. See also F4, a manuscript history of the park, 1975.

16 Armstrong, Evenden, and Nelles, *River Returns*, ch. 10; Hart, *Place of Bows*, 114–230; Bart Robinson, *Banff Springs: The Story of a Hotel* (Banff: Summerthought, 1988); E. J. Hart, *The Selling of Canada: The CPR and the Beginning of Canadian Tourism* (Banff: Altitude, 1983).

17 Leo Denis and J. B. Challies, *Water Powers of Manitoba, Saskatchewan and Alberta* (Ottawa: Commission of Conservation, 1914), 197.

CHAPTER 2: POWER STRUGGLE

1 See William Cronon, *Nature's Metropolis* (New York: Norton, 1992) for the classic development of this idea using Chicago as the example.

2 For 1903 and 1905 episodes of investigation, see W. E. Hawkins, *Electrifying Calgary: A Century of Public and Private Power* (Calgary: University of Calgary Press, 1987), 108.

3 LAC, RG 85, vol. 737, file R1436-3-5, W. M. Alexander and W. J. Budd to the Minister of the Interior, December 21, 1906.

4 For a fuller discussion of the North West Irrigation Act, its adoption, implementation and subsequent modification, see C. Armstrong, M. Evenden, and H. V. Nelles, *The River Returns: An Environmental History of the Bow* (Montreal and Kingston: McGill-Queen's University Press, 2009), 155–56, 329–30.

5 LAC, RG 10, vol. 3563, file 82, part 16, C10099, Frank Oliver to Clifford Sifton, July 1, 1903.

6 In one of those ironies of politics, Frank Oliver, as the newly appointed minister of the interior in 1905, ruled that waterpower licences on Indian reserves could be granted under the North West Irrigation Act (1894). LAC, RG 89, vol. 605, file 1514, memorandum "Re Jurisdiction, Bow River Licenses," March 2, 1944 [unsigned but initialed by J. M. W(ardle) of the Water Power Branch].

7   LAC, RG 10, vol. 3686, file 13119-2, 3, 4, C10120, memorandum July 14, 1903; H. E. Sibbald to Indian Commissioner, August 17, 1903; Deputy Superintendent General of Indian Affairs to Frank Oliver, August 31, 1903; Secretary of the Calgary Board of Trade to Department of the Interior, October 10, 1903; Guardian Insurance Company to Department of Indian Affairs, September 30, 1904; Johnson and Johnson, Barristers on behalf of E. R. Wood, to Department of Indian Affairs, September 15, 1905.

8   The following correspondence recapitulates the matter: LAC, RG 85, vol. 737, file 1436-3-5 (1), J. B. Challies to Mr. Young, copy to Wm Cory, Deputy Minister, January 4, 1907.

9   LAC, RG 10, vol. 3686, file 13119-2, 3, 4, C10120, Frank Pedley, Superintendent General of Indian Affairs, to Rev. John McDougall, May 23, 1906; McDougall to Pedley, May 25, 1906; Pedley to McDougall, June 6, 1906 and June 12, 1906; McDougall to Pedley, June 6, 1906, reporting the asking price. The minister, Frank Oliver, replied to McDougall himself on July 24, 1906, stating the price to be "unjustified by the value of the power in its undeveloped state."

10 LAC, RG 85, vol. 737, file 1436-3-5 (1), W. M. Alexander and W. J. Budd to the Minister of the Interior, December 21, 1906; C. H. Mitchell to Secretary, Department of the Interior, December 21, 1906; J. B. Challies to Mr. Young, copy to Mr. Cory (DM), January 4, 1907. The creation of a provincial government in 1905 caused this confusion: the bureaucrats thought the land under the river was "under the jurisdiction of the local government" (i.e., the province). Authority to grant diversion or waterpower permits, however, rested with the Department of the Interior, but the authorities were not certain and added a phrase about possible jurisdiction by "local government if rights have been passed on to the province." LAC, RG 85, vol. 737, file 1436-3-5 (1), Lands and Timber Branch to Deputy Minister Cory, January 30, 1907.

11 LAC, RG 85, vol. 737, file 1436-3-5 (1), Charles Mitchell (engineer for Alexander and Budd) to Department of the Interior, February 26, 1907; R. E. Secretary, Department of the Interior to J. B. Challies, March 1, 1907.

12 LAC, RG 85, vol. 737, file 1436-3-5 (1), Surrender Agreement with T. I. Fleetham, Agent; Moses Bearspaw, Chief; Peter Wesley, Chief; Jonas Two Young Man, Chief; and James Swampy, Amos Big Stony, John Mark, Hector Crawler, George McLean, Councillors, March 22, 1907; Draft Lease, April 1, 1907. See also GA, CPC, M1546, vol. 4, file 11, material relating to the development of the Horseshoe Falls, and vol. 4, file 12, Quit Claim, Stoney Indians, Morley, 1907, sale of 1,000 acres adjacent to Horseshoe Falls.

13 This position was adopted despite the fact that the office of superintendent general was usually, though not always, occupied by the minister of the interior.

14 LAC, RG 85, vol. 737, file 1436-3-5 (1), J. B. Challies to R. E. Young, memorandum, March 13, 1909; J. D. McLean, Secretary, Department of Indian Affairs, to R. E. Young, April 6, 1909; Water Power Regulations under the Dominion Lands Act, passed by order-in-council, June 2, 1909. Probably as a result of these negotiations and to ensure greater certainty and clarity, the federal government amended section 35 of the Dominion Lands Act in 1908 to assert its rights to control and license the use of water for power purposes, establish a regulatory framework, and create the Water Power Branch in the Department of the Interior to identify

locations, conduct hydrographic surveys, issue licences, and regulate the construction and operation of hydroelectric works. The minister of the interior was specifically granted authority to make regulations governing "the diversion, taking or use of water for power purposes" and "for fixing the fees ... to be paid for the use of water for power purposes, and the rates to be charged for power or energy derived therefrom." The amendments to the Dominion Lands Act and the regulations respecting water allocation and development are printed in Leo G. Denis and Arthur V. White, *Water-Powers of Canada* (Ottawa: Commission of Conservation, 1911), 275ff, and again in Leo G. Denis and J. B. Challies, *Water-Power Resources of Manitoba, Saskatchewan and Alberta* (Ottawa: Commission of Conservation, 1916), 302ff. This latter volume contains detailed hydrographical analysis of the Bow River and its flow conducted by J. B. Challies, superintendent of the Water Power Branch (178–226). The records of the Water Power Branch are to be found in LAC, RG 89.

15 LAC, Kerry and Chace Papers, Report No. 839 on Hydro-Electric Development on Bow River Horseshoe Falls near Calgary, Alberta, November 2, 1907, by C. B. Smith; RG 85, vol. 737, Garnet P. Grant to Secretary, Department of Interior, August 30, 1907.

16 GA, CPC, box 4, file 11, Agreement between Calgary Power and Transmission and Western Canada Cement and Coal Company, May 17, 1909; Agreement of Smith and Royal Securities, October 4, 1909.

17 On Aitken's early career in Canada, see C. Armstrong and H. V. Nelles, *Southern Exposure: Canadian Promoters in Latin America and the Caribbean, 1896–1930* (Toronto: University of Toronto Press, 1988),

chs. 6 and 7, and Greg Marchildon, *Profits and Politics: Beaverbrook and the Gilded Age of Canadian Finance* (Toronto: University of Toronto Press, 1996). A.J.P. Taylor skips over this aspect of Aitken's career in his biography *Beaverbrook* (London: Hamish Hamilton, 1972).

18 HLRO, Lord Beaverbrook Papers, series A, vol. 19, W. M. Aitken to R.T.D. Aitken, September 3, 1908; R.T.D. Aitken to W. M. Aitken, September 8, 1908. Correspondence regarding the abortive attempt to secure the Calgary street railway franchise can be found in series A, vol. 26.

19 HLRO, series G, vol. 18, W. M. Aitken to R.T.D. Aitken, April 23, 1909; R.T.D. Aitken to W. M. Aitken, April 28, 1909.

20 HLRO, Lord Beaverbrook Papers, series A, vol. 42, E. R. Wood to G. A. Morrow, September 29, 1909, E. R. Wood to W. J. Campbell, September 29, 1909, E. R. Wood to J. W. Mitchell, September 30, 1909; series A, vol. 65, W. M. Aitken to R. B. Bennett, October 6, 1909; GA, CPC, Minutebook No. 1, January 4, 1910.

21 HLRO, Lord Beaverbrook Papers, series A, vol. 49, C. C. Giles to W. M. Aitken, April 11, 1910.

22 LAC, Kerry and Chace Papers, vol. 14, Report No. 839, November 2, 1907.

23 GA, CPC, box 4, file 17, report to W. M. Aitken on Calgary Power Development by Western Canada Power Company, Stave Falls, Rusking, BC, December 7, 1909. Aitken was also investigating the promotion of Western Canada Power.

24 LAC, Kerry and Chace, vol. 14, Report No. 838 on Construction of Hydro-Electric Power Plant at Horseshoe Falls on the Bow River, 50 Miles West of Calgary, Alberta, n.d. [1910?]; GA, CPC, MB, December 23, 1910, May 2, 1911.

25 LAC, Kerry and Chace, vol. 14, Report No. 839, November 2, 1907; RG 85, vol.

734, Arthur L. Ford to J. T. Johnston, March 10, 1921.

26 Hawkins provides abundant detail on this negotiation in *Electrifying Calgary*, 147–61. Aitken grudgingly congratulated Bennett on his achievement, which, Bennett admitted, "has been one of the most annoying and difficult matters I have dealt with since I came here."

27 Quoted in Hawkins, *Electrifying Calgary*, 95.

28 Lord Beaverbrook, *Lord Beaverbrook: My Early Life* (Fredericton, NB: Brunswick Press, 1965), 128.

29 This is the conclusion of Marchildon, who has made the closest study of the available documentation on the Canada Cement merger. Marchildon, *Profits and Politics*, 143–80. The Mount Royal Club incident is reported on p. 152.

30 In 1918, Aitken sold his interest in Calgary Power and the Montreal Engineering Company to his old partner, I. W. Killam, and the Montreal financier, Ward Pitman.

CHAPTER 3: DOUBLING DOWN

1   LAC, RG 85, 737, engineering report of C. H. Mitchell on Kananaskis Falls, September 8, 1911.

2   LAC, RG 85, 737, application of the Calgary Power Company to develop Kananaskis Falls, January 12, 1910; Fred C. Clarke to Secretary, Department of Interior, April 6, 1910, May 3, 1910, August 17, 1910; memorandum from J. B. Challies to R. E. Young, May 26, 1910; Carl Giles to Secretary, Department of Interior, October 6, 1910.

3   On Macphail and his application, see C. Armstrong and H. V. Nelles, "Competition vs. Convenience: Federal Administration of Bow River Waterpowers, 1906–1913," in *The

Canadian West, ed. Henry Klassen (Calgary: University of Calgary Press, 1977), 170–76. See also Ian Robertson, *Sir Andrew Macphail: The Life and Legacy of a Canadian Man of Letters* (Montreal and Kingston: McGill-Queen's University Press, 2008).

4   LAC, RG 85, 737, Andrew Haydon to W. W. Cory, January 19, 1911; Haydon to Secretary, Department of Interior, August 8, 1911; John B. McRae to Macphail, March 13, 1911.

5   LAC, RG 85, 737, engineering report of C. H. Mitchell on Kananaskis Falls, September 8, 1911.

6   LAC, RG 85, 737, memorandum from J. B. Challies to R. E. Young, September 28, 1911; Final Agreement re: Kananaskis Falls, October 14, 1912.

7   GA, CPC, MB, August 3, 1911; HLRO, Lord Beaverbrook Papers, series A, box 65, R. B. Bennett to Aitken, February 16, 1912, and September 19, 1912.

8   LAC, RG 85, 737, file 1436-3-5, J. B. Challies to R. E. Young, December 29, 1910; E. F. Drake to J. B. Challies, January 18, 1911; House of Commons, *Debates*, April 28, May 9 and 17, 1911, cols. 8084–6, 8606–41, 8650–74, 9345–7; *Statutes of Canada*, 1911, 1–2 Geo V, ch. 10, s. 17.

9   LAC, RG 10, 8057, R. E. Young to Frank Pedley, February 7, 1911.

10 See Canada, House of Commons, *Debates*, April 10 and 26, May 4, 1911, cols. 7019–21, 7825–69, 8403–8 (Oliver's speech is at 7825–6); *Statutes of Canada*, 1911, 1–2 Geo V, ch. 14, s. 46.

11 Canada, *Sessional Papers*, 1913, No. 25, Department of the Interior, *Annual Report*, 1912, Report No. 35, report of Water Power Branch, pp. 210–20; RG 85, 737, memorandum from Challies to W. W. Cory, April 16, 1912.

12 LAC, RG 85, 737, K. M. Perry, Calgary Power, to Challies, November 20, 1912;

Challies to Perry, November 22, 1912; RG 10, 8507, L. Pereira to McLean, November 22, 1912; McLean to Pereira, November 23, 1912; Challies to Perry, November 25, 1912; J. W. Waddy to McLean, December 14, 1912.

13 LAC, RG 10, 8057, McLean to Waddy, December 24, 1912, January 24, 1913; Waddy to McLean, January 11, 1913, April 18, 1913; RG 85, 737, memorandum for file by J. B. Challies, April 16, 1913.

14 LAC, RG 10, 8507, Waddy to McLean, May 1, 1913 (quoted); Bennett to McLean, May 28, 1913; Waddy to Constable A. J. Barber, June 30, 1913; Inspector G. S. Worsley to Superintendent R. B. Deane, July 6, 1913; Crime Report of Constable Barber, July 7, 1913. Worsley thought that local storekeepers were urging the Indians not to give up hopes of benefitting from a larger cash payment. For police response to the summer of 1913 discontents on the Nakoda Reserve, see also William M. Baker, ed., *Pioneer Policing in Southern Alberta* (Calgary: Alberta Records Publication Board, 1993), 219. We owe this reference to Don Smith.

15 LAC, RG 10, 8057, memorandum from J. B. Challies to W. W. Cory, July 10, 1913.

16 LAC, RG 10, 8057, Campbell to McLean, July 8, 1913.

17 LAC, RG 10, 8057, H. A. Moore to McLean, August 7, 1913; Campbell to McLean, August 29, 1913.

18 LAC, RG 10, 8057, McLean to H. A. Moore, September 10, 1913; Moore to McLean, October 4, 1913.

19 LAC, RG 10, 8057, Moore to McLean, October 3, 1913. When the deputy minister of justice advised that the company lacked the expropriation powers that it claimed to have, that suggestion was dropped. See LAC, RG 10, 8057, W. S. Edwards to McLean,

October 16, 1913; D. C. Scott to Moore, October 16, 1913.

20 LAC, RG 10, 8057, Moore to Waddy, October 25, 1913; McLean to Waddy, November 10, 1913.

21 LAC, RG 10, 8057, Scott to Moore, November 18, 1913; Moore to Scott, December 4, 1913; S. Bray to Scott, December 5, 1913 (quoted). GA, CPC, box 13, file 172, Agreement between Calgary Power and City of Calgary, December 1, 1913. Under the agreement, the price of power over 10,000 hp would fall to twenty dollars.

22 LAC, RG 10, 8057, Waddy to McLean, December 16, 1913, January 9, 1914 ; McLean to Waddy, December 17, 1913; W. A. Thompson to McLean, December 16 and 29, 1913.

23 LAC, RG 10, 8057, Moore to McLean, February 14, 1914; Waddy to McLean, February 21, 1914, enclosing clipping from *Calgary News-Telegram*, February 20, 1914; Campbell to Scott, March 25, 1914.

24 LAC, RG 10, 8057, Campbell to Scott, May 1 and 6, 1914.

25 LAC, RG 10, 8057, Scott to Campbell, May 7, 1914; Campbell to Scott, May 7, 1914.

26 LAC, RG 85, 737, [J. B. Challies] to D. C. Scott, May 12, 1914.

27 LAC, RG 10, 8057, Scott to James Muir, April 27, 1914.

28 LAC, RG 10, 8057, Scott to V. M. Drury, May 23, 1914, enclosing memorandum regarding settlement of differences between the Stoney Indians and the Calgary Power Company. Geo. Maclean, Jonas Benjamin, and Dan Wildman for the Indians; V. M. Drury for the Power Company; and witnesses Duncan C. Scott and J. W. Waddy, Ottawa, May 20, 1914.

29 LAC, RG 10, 8057, memorandum from Scott, May 23, 1914; Drury to Scott, May 30, 1914.

30   LAC, RG 10, 8057, memorandum from Scott to F. W. Paget, May 23, 1914; Drury to Scott, May 30, 1914; J. D. McLean to Drury, September 7, 1915; S. B. Hammond to Indian Affairs, September 11, 1915.

31   LAC, RG 10, 8057, Scott to Calgary Power, November 2, 1915; E. W. Robinson to Scott, November 30, 1915.

32   LAC, RG 10, 8057, Scott to Calgary Power, October 12, 1916; S. B. Hammond to Scott, October 17, 1916; Hammond to Indian Affairs, August 20, 1917, October 3, 1917; memorandum from F. W. Paget re: amounts owing on Kananaskis, August 27, 1917.

33   Our analysis of the waterpower story on the Nakoda Reserve largely corresponds with the conclusion arrived at by Kenichi Matsui in *Native Peoples and Water Rights: Irrigation, Dams and the Law in Western Canada* (Montreal and Kingston: McGill-Queen's University Press, 2009): "Under these circumstances, what the Stoney Nakoda people achieved was remarkable, especially in a matter related to Native water rights. Today, experts in Aboriginal rights tend to emphasize court decisions and statutes, but the history of Stoney Nakoda water rights highlights the need to consider the political, social and economic contexts of the hydroelectric developments" (139). Matsui's book appeared at about the same time as our *The River Returns*, which contained our short account of the story. He arrived at his interpretation apparently without the benefit of consulting the Waterpower Branch records or our article on the subject: "Competition vs. Convenience: Federal Administration of Bow River Waterpowers, 1906–1913," in *The Canadian West*, ed. Henry Klassen (Calgary: University of Calgary Com-Print, 1977).

CHAPTER 4: DOWNSTREAM BENEFITS

1   Two projects, both joint enterprises of Calgary Power and the Alberta government, were built on the upper tributaries of the North Saskatchewan River in the 1960s. Big Bend on the Brazeau River and Bighorn on the upper mainstem of the North Saskatchewan were constructed at sites that allowed for extensive storage capacity behind the dams, which effectively evened out streamflow to the generators.

2   HLRO, Lord Beaverbrook Papers, series A, vol. 19, W. M. Aitken to R.T.D. Aitken, September 3, 1908, R.T.D. Aitken to W. M. Aitken, September 8, 1908.

3   GA, CPC, box 4, file 17, report to W. M. Aitken on Calgary Power Development, December 7, 1909.

4   M. C. Hendry, Bow River Power and Storage Investigations, 1914, Water Resources Paper No. 2, Glenbow Library and Canada, Sessional Papers, Department of the Interior Annual Report, Sessional Paper No. 25e, 1914. This paper informs J. B. Challies's two chapters on the Bow River in L. G. Denis and J. B. Challies, *Water-Power Resources of Manitoba, Saskatchewan and Alberta* (Toronto: Commission of Conservation, 1916).

5   Denis and Challies, *Water-Power Resources of Manitoba, Saskatchewan and Alberta*, 207.

6   Ibid., 194–95.

7   HLRO, Lord Beaverbrook Papers, series A, box 65, R. B. Bennett to Sir Max Aitken, February 16, 1912.

8   Hendry, Bow River Water Power and Storage Investigations, 1914.

9   Denis and Challies, *Water-Power Resources of Manitoba, Saskatchewan and Alberta*, 196–205.

10   LAC, RG 84, file B39-5, P. M. Sauder to R. H. Campbell, February 6, 1911; A. B.

Macdonald to Campbell, February 20, 1911.

11 For a local history of Lake Minnewanka and its community, illustrated with many charming photographs, see R. W. Sanford, *Lake Minnewanka: The Spirit of the Waters* (Banff: Lake Minnewanka Boat Tours, 1999).

12 LAC, RG 84, file B39-5, John Standly to R. H. Campbell, May 15, 1911; Campbell to Standly, May 22, 1911.

13 LAC, RG 84, file B39-8, vol. 1, Harkin to W. W. Cory, December 24, 1912; memorandum from M. C. Hendry to J. B. Challies, December 14, 1912; memorandum from Challies to Harkin, March 26, 1913; memorandum from Harkin to Challies, April 3, 1913.

14 LAC, Harkin Papers, memorandum, March 20, 1914.

15 The beginning point for critical analysis is R. C. Brown, "The Doctrine of Usefulness: Natural Resources and National Park Policy in Canada, 1887–1914," in *The Canadian National Parks: Today and Tomorrow*, vol. 1, ed. J. G. Nelson and R. C. Scace (Calgary: National and Provincial Parks Association and University of Calgary, 1969), 94–110. Leslie Bella subsequently took the extreme point of view that parks policy always placed revenue generation above other goals in *Parks for Profit* (Montreal: Harvester House, 1986). Alan MacEachern reasserted the balance between use and preservation in *Natural Selections: National Parks in Atlantic Canada, 1935–1970* (Montreal and Kingston: McGill-Queen's University Press, 2001). E. J. Hart's recent magisterial biography, *J. B. Harkin: Father of Canada's National Parks* (Edmonton: University of Alberta Press, 2011), also emphasizes the complicated balancing act required to reconcile these two objectives; Hart focuses on Harkin's inspired leadership in difficult times.

16 W. E. Hawkins, *Electrifying Calgary: A Century of Public and Private Power* (Calgary: University of Calgary Press, 1987), 94–97, 156–57.

17 LAC, RG 84, file B39-8, memorandum from Harkin to W. W. Cory, December 24, 1912.

18 LAC, RG 84, file B 39-8, memorandum from J. B. Challies to Harkin, March 26, 1913; memorandum from Harkin to Challies, April 3, 1913.

19 Calculated from the streamflow data reported in Denis and Challies, *Water-Power Resources of Manitoba, Saskatchewan and Alberta*, 179–81.

20 LAC, RG 84, file B39-5, "Montreal Engineering Company, Limited, Proposed Cascade Development," August 28, 1922; file R39-8, memorandum from J. B. Harkin to W. W. Cory, May 22, 1926.

21 Sandford, *Lake Minnewanka*. See p. 23 for a photograph.

22 LAC, RG 84, file B39-5, memorandum from M. C. Hendry to J. B. Challies, December 3, 1914; memorandum from J. T. Johnston to Challies, December 7, 1914; W. W. Cory to W. A. Found, December 30, 1914; G. F. Desbarats to Cory, January 11, 1915; memorandum from Cory to Challies, January 20, 1915.

23 LAC, RG 85, 734, memorandum re: "The Power Situation in Calgary," March 1920. The Calgary Water Power Company continued to turn out small amounts of thermal power that met about 10 per cent of local demand. The city also considered purchasing this undertaking, but its owners wanted to include its sawmill and timber limits in the sale, at which the municipal authorities balked.

24 On the Stairs-Aitken-Killam relationship, see C. Armstrong and H. V. Nelles, *Southern Exposure: Canadian Promoters in Latin America and the Caribbean, 1896–1930*

WILDERNESS AND WATERPOWER

(Toronto: University of Toronto Press, 1988), 107–47. On the sale of Royal Securities to Killam and Pitfield, see also A.J.P. Taylor, *Beaverbrook* (London: Hamish Hamilton, 1972), 79; Greg Marchildon, *Profits and Politics: Beaverbrook and the Gilded Age of Canadian Finance* (Toronto: University of Toronto Press, 1996), 236; and James D. Frost, *Merchant Princes: Halifax's First Family of Finance, Ships and Steel* (Toronto: Lorimer, 2003), 278.

25 LAC, RG 85, 734, memorandum re: "The Power Situation in Calgary," March 1920; A. L. Ford to J. T. Johnston, March 10, 1921; RG 84, file B39-5, memorandum from J. T. Johnston to F.H.H. Williamson, March 3, 1921.

26 LAC, RG 84, file B39-5, memorandum from Norman Marr to J. B. Challies, March 3, 1921; memorandum from Challies to J. B. Harkin, February 23, 1921.

27 LAC, RG 84, file B39-5, memorandum from Challies to Harkin, March 3, 1921.

28 LAC, RG 84, file B39-5, memorandum from Harkin to W. W. Cory, September 23, 1930. On Harkin's changing attitude toward power development see Hart, *J. B. Harkin*, 241–47. Hart also covers this Minnewanka episode (259–64).

29 LAC, RG 84, file B39-5, Harkin to W. A. Found, March 5, 1921; R. S. Stronach to Harkin, March 5, 1921; memorandum from Harkin to Challies, March 9, 1921; memorandum from Challies to Harkin, March 14, 1921.

30 LAC, RG 84, file B39-5, Montreal Engineering Company to Minister of the Interior, July 31, 1922.

31 LAC, RG 84, file R39-5, "Montreal Engineering Company Limited, Proposed Cascade Development," August 28, 1922.

32 LAC, RG 84, file B39-5, Montreal Engineering Company to Minister of the Interior, July 31, 1922.

33 LAC, RG 85, 734, "Memorandum Re: Cascade Water Power Project," G. A. Gaherty, September 15, 1922.

34 The other branches reporting to Deputy Minister W. W. Cory were Parks, Dominion Lands, Timber and Grazing, Irrigation, Forestry, Yukon, Surveys, Immigration, and Dominion Astronomer. The interior minister was also responsible for Indian affairs.

35 LAC, RG 84, file U321, memorandum from H. W. Grunsky to Challies, February 12, 1919.

36 These consultations are documented in LAC, RG 85, file R-1430-1, and the first draft of the new regulations is in RG 84, file U321, Department of the Interior-Canada, Dominion Water-Power Branch, *Proposed New Dominion Water-Power Regulations with Explanation* (Ottawa: Government Printing Bureau, 1916): confidential, not released for publication.

37 LAC, RG 85, file R-1430-1, J. B. Challies to W. W. Cory, February 14, 1919; *Statutes of Canada*, 1919, 9–10 Geo V, ch. 19.

38 LAC, RG 84, file U321, memorandum from J. B. Harkin to J. B. Challies, May 16, 1919; memorandum to Harkin, December 30, 1921. The proclamation was Order-in-Council, P.C. 4034, October 31, 1921.

39 LAC, RG 85, vol. 734, J. T. Johnston to W. W. Cory, August 3, 1922; RG 84, file B39-8, memorandum from Johnston to Cory, August 8, 1923.

40 LAC, RG 84, file B39-5, Harkin to R. S. Stronach, January 13, 1922.

41 LAC, RG 84, file B39-5, memorandum from Harkin to J. B. Challies, February 13, 1922. The determination of Harkin and Stronach (the superintendent of Rocky Mountains National Park) to

oppose the company was redoubled by a wrangle in February and March of 1922, when the release of water from Lake Minnewanka caused a tremendous ice buildup on the Cascade that threatened to carry away the highway bridge. The company and its allies in the Water Power Branch refused to accept responsibility and insisted that the whole problem was caused by unusual weather conditions, although Stronach pointed out that such problems had never been experienced until Lake Minnewanka had been used for water storage. See RG 84, file B39-5, for the correspondence on this subject during February and March, 1922, and file R39-5, Stronach to F. J. Robertson, March 24, 1922.

42   LAC, RG 94, file B39-5, R. S. Stronach to F.H.H. Williamson, August 9, 1922; J. M. Wardle to Harkin, August 28, 1922, marked "Confidential."

43   LAC, RG 84, file R39-5, memorandum from J. M. Wardle, August 18, 1922; file B39-5, Banff Citizens Council to Harkin, September 12, 1922.

44   LAC, RG 84, file B39-5, memorandum from Harkin to W. W. Cory, October 7, 1922; file R39-5, clipping from *Calgary Morning Albertan*, January 29, 1923.

45   LAC, RG 84, file B39-5, Harkin to V. M. Drury, January 23, 1922.

46   LAC, RG 84, file B39-9, Harkin to Drury, April 20, 1923; file B39-5, Harkin to W. W. Cory, October 7, 1922. Hart, in *J. B. Harkin*, also has difficulty squaring this action with Harkin's rhetoric (322–23).

47   LAC, RG 84, file B39-5, memorandum from J. T. Johnston to J. B. Challies, November 9, 1922: "From the standpoint of conservation of water power in southern Alberta, I am strongly of the opinion that the larger scheme of development proposed for the Cascade River should be disproved, both from the engineering

and economic aspects, before the smaller scheme of the Parks Branch is proceeded with, and I hope that there will be no departmental commitment thereto until my views have been received and considered."

48   LAC, RG 84, file B39-9, memorandum re: purchase of power for Banff from Calgary Power Company, March 8, 1923.

49   LAC, RG 84, file B39-5, J. B. Harkin to V. M. Drury, January 23, 1923; RG 85, vol. 734, Mitchell to Stewart, February 21, 1922; Drury to Mitchell, March 7, 1922.

50   LAC, RG 85, vol. 734, memorandum from R. A. Gibson to J. B. Challies, March 15, 1923; RG 84, file B39-5, V. M. Drury to Minister of the Interior, April 12, 1923.

51   LAC, RG 84, file B39-5, memorandum to W. W. Cory, October 13, 1922.

52   LAC, RG 84, file B39-8, memorandum from W. W. Cory to J. B. Challies, November 23, 1922.

53   LAC, RG 85, vol. 733, memorandum from J. T. Johnston to J. B. Challies, March 16, 1923.

CHAPTER 5: SELLING SCENERY

1   LAC, RG 84, file B39-8, memorandum from M. C. Hendry to J. B. Challies, December 14, 1912; RG 85, 737, K. H. Smith to J. B. Challies, October 2, 1912. M. C. Hendry made an extensive study of the storage capabilities in *Water Resources Paper No. 2* (Ottawa: Department of the Interior, 1914). Leo G. Denis and J. B. Challies provided a lengthy summary of this work in chapter 11 of *Water-Power Resources of Manitoba, Saskatchewan and Alberta* (Ottawa: Commission of Conservation, 1916), 193–226. The detailed map series accompanying this analysis of upriver storage can be found in the Glenbow Library under the call number G3502

B785N33 1912 C212 and following. The Spray Lakes surveys can be found at G3502 B785N33 svar 19, sheets D to I.

2   LAC, RG 84, file B39-8, memorandum from J. T. Johnston to J. B. Harkin, October 29, 1920; memorandum from J. B. Challies to Harkin, November 12, 1920. This diversion project may have been inspired by a similar venture being simultaneously undertaken by Canadian financiers and engineers for Brazilian Traction. In Brazil, above the port of Santos, engineers reversed the flow of several rivers, creating a huge reservoir on the Serra do Mar plateau. This impounded water was thus reversed and diverted over the coastal escarpment to the Cubatão power station more than seven hundred metres below. In this dramatic fall, the water would be made to generate 20,000 hp on a year-round basis for the power-hungry city of São Paulo. The project, financed and managed by Canadians in Montreal and employing Canadian engineers, would have been well known in Montreal engineering circles and certainly within the Montreal Engineering Company. See Duncan McDowall, *The Light: Brazilian Traction, Light, and Power Company Limited, 1899–1945* (Toronto: University of Toronto Press, 1988), 250–61. Calgary Power outlined the technical aspects of the Spray Lakes project in *The Canadian Engineer* 48, no. 11 (1925), 316.

3   James D. Frost, *Merchant Princes: Halifax's First Family of Finance, Ships and Steel* (Toronto: Lorimer, 2003), 196, 239, 265, 278–81; *Dictionary of Canadian Biography*, vol. 13, John Fitzwilliam Stairs, http://www.biographi.ca; *Canadian Who's Who*, 1961–63, vol. 9 (Toronto: University of Toronto Press, 1963), 390.

4   LAC, RG 84, file B39-5, Montreal Engineering Company to the Minister of the Interior, July 31, 1922; file R39-5,

"Montreal Engineering Company, Proposed Cascade Development," August 28, 1922.

5   LAC, RG 84, file B39-5, Montreal Engineering Company (per Gaherty) to Stewart, July 31, 1922.

6   LAC, RG 84, file B39-8, memorandum from J. M. Wardle, February 3, 1923.

7   LAC, RG 84, file B39-8, memorandum to W. W. Cory, October 13, 1922. Changes to parks regulation first excluded quartz mining in 1916, and during the 1920s, it became clear that coal mining would be soon be prohibited – and it was, under the 1930 Parks Act revision. Bankhead, a coal-mining community within Rocky Mountains National Park, under the threat of exclusion, closed down in 1922. Many of the buildings were removed for use in the town of Banff. The coal mine at Anthracite continued to operate but eventually shut down as well. See Ben Gadd, *Bankhead: The Twenty-Year Town* (Banff: Friends of Banff National Park, 1989).

8   LAC, RG 84, file B39-5, V. M. Drury to Charles Stewart, April 12, 1923; memorandum from Harkin to W. W. Cory, October 7, 1922; April 12, 1923.

9   LAC, RG 85, vol. 733, memorandum from J. T. Johnston to J. B. Challies, March 16, 1923, from which the quotations that follow are taken.

10 LAC, RG 84, file B39-8, Mayor G. H. Webster to Charles Stewart, March 29, 1923; D. E. Black, president, Board of Trade, to Stewart, March 29, 1923.

11 LAC, RG 84, file B39-8, Drury to Stewart, May 17, 1923.

12 LAC, RG 84, file B39-8, Greenfield to Stewart, April 17, 1923; Stewart to Greenfield, May 3, 1923.

13 PAA, acc. 69.289, file 467, record of interview with Mayor Webster, June 27, 1923; Greenfield to Stewart, August 24, 1923.

14 PAA, acc. 69.289, file 467, Greenfield to Sir Adam Beck, December 5, 1923.

15 LAC, RG 84, file B39-5, T. B. Moffatt to Stewart, March 27, 1923. In her work on these events, PearlAnn Reichwein focuses on the role of the Alpine Club of Canada in the opposition to the Spray Lakes development and its role in the formation of the Canadian National Parks Association but Reichwein did not have direct access to the Parks and Water Power Branch records. PearlAnn Reichwein, "Beyond the Visionary Mountains: The Alpine Club of Canada and the Canadian Park Idea, 1909 to 1969" (PhD dissertation, Carleton University, 1996), and "'Hands Off Our National Parks': The Alpine Club of Canada and Hydro-Development Controversies in the Canadian Rockies, 1922–1930," *Journal of the Canadian Historical Association* 6, no. 1 (1995): 129–55. E. J. Hart deals with the Spray Lakes episode in *J. B. Harkin: Father of Canada's National Parks* (Edmonton: University of Alberta Press, 2011). In a chapter entitled "Hands Off Our National Parks," Hart places the Banff controversy in the broader context of economic pressure on park lands (241–70). For a condensed account, see also Leslie Bella, *Parks for Profit* (Montreal: Harvester House, 1986), 50–58.

16 LAC, RG 84, file B39-8, J. B. Harkin to A. B. MacKay, March 28, 1913 (quoted below). Harkin was careful to protect himself with his bureaucratic superiors, explaining to the deputy minister that he intended only to give "friends of the parks some specific information which will help them understand the situation from the parks' standpoint." Memorandum from Harkin to W. W. Cory, March 28, 1923. E. J. Hart, in *J. B. Harkin* (262–65), expands upon Harkin's hardening position against hydroelectric development in this particular case.

17 See LAC, RG 84, file 39-8, which includes letters from the Banff Citizens' Association (April 2, 1923), the Brandon Rotary Club (June 12, 1923), the Brandon Canadian Club (June 13, 1923), the Natural History Society of Manitoba (June 13, 1923), and the Edmonton branch of the Alpine Club of Canada (June 14, 1923); see also PAA, Attorney General's Papers, box 7, file 535, clipping of editorial from *Ottawa Journal*, June 11, 1923.

18 LAC, RG 84, file B39-8, Arthur O. Wheeler to William Pearce, May 24, 1923. For a discussion of Wheeler's prickly, obstinate, autocratic temperament, see Bella, *Parks for Profit*, 40–46, and Hart, *J. B. Harkin*, 266–68. In "Beyond the Visionary Mountains" (207–20), PearlAnn Reichwein gives an account of the wrangle.

19 LAC, RG 84, reel T12877, series A-2-a, vol. 102, file U36-1, part 2, Wheeler to Harkin, March 26, May 6 and 12, 1921; Harkin to Wheeler, April 13, May 17 and 26, 1921. Banff Superintendent R. S. Stronach had to come up with already scarce funds and suggested concealing the grant under the line item "Clearing Hay Meadows," but Harkin instructed him simply to use some of the money allotted for constructing trails in the park to pay Wheeler. LAC, RG 84, reel T12877, series A-2-a, vol. 102, file U36-1, part 2, Stronach to Harkin, June 6, 1921; Harkin to Stronach, June 29, 1921.

20 LAC, RG 84, reel T12877, series A-2-a, vol. 102, file U36-1, part 2, clipping from *Calgary Daily Herald*, June 30, 1921; Wheeler to Harkin, September 26, October 19 (quoted), 1921.

21 LAC, RG 84, reel T12877, series A-2-a, vol. 102, file U36-1, part 2, Wheeler to Harkin, May 12, 1921; Harkin to Wheeler, November 25, 1921; letters to the minister, Sir James Lougheed, included C. E. Fortier, Winnipeg,

December 6, 1921, and Andrew J. Gilmour, New York, December 7, 1921; ACC circular, January 1, 1922 (quoted), which produced many more letters to the Interior Department, and, on February 20, 1922, Professor N. W. Tyler of MIT (who was also the secretary of the National Association of University Professors) sent Wheeler a list of "College Men" from universities across the United States and a draft letter by Tyler for which he hoped to secure signatories.

22 LAC, RG 84, reel T12877, series A-2-a, vol. 102, file U36-1, part 2, memoranda from J. M. Wardle to Deputy Minister W. W. Cory, January 3, March 23, 1922, memorandum from Harkin to Cory, February 14, 1922; Wheeler to Cory, February 4,1922; Harkin to Wheeler, February 18 and 28, and May 16, 1922; Cory to Wheeler, March 8, 1922, Wheeler to R. A. Gibson, March 8, 1922; Wheeler to Harkin, April 3, May 25, 1922. Leslie Bella, in *Parks for Profit* (41–43), discusses this incident, stressing Wheeler's volatile character. In *J. B. Harkin* (254–57), E. J. Hart treats Wheeler as a difficult ally.

23 LAC, RG 84, reel T12877, vol. 102, file U36-1, part 3, Wheeler to Harkin, December 14, 1923; Harkin to Wheeler, December 28, 1923, April 24, 1924. In the end, the minister approved a grant of only $800.

24 LAC, RG 84, file B39-8, minutes of the first meeting of the National Parks Association of Canada, August 2, 1923. The executive consisted of the following:

President: Lt.-Col. W. W. Foster, Vancouver

Vice-presidents: Charles Hanbury-Williams, Aylmer, Quebec

A. A. McCoubrey, Winnipeg

Treasurer: Major J.W.S. Walker, Calgary

Executive secretary: Andrew S. Sibbald, Saskatoon

Arthur O. Wheeler, Calgary

Executive committee members: Dr. W.J.A. Hickson, McGill University; Professor R. B. Thomson, University of Toronto; F. M. Black, MPP, Winnipeg; Mrs. W. C. McKillican, Brandon; H. E. Sampson, Regina; John Blue, Edmonton; Mrs. J. W. Henshaw, Vancouver; Col. F. C. Bell, Vancouver; and Major F. V. Longstaff, Victoria.

See letterhead of open letter from Wheeler to Premier Herbert Greenfield, January 21, 1924 (PAA, acc. 69.289, file 467), which quotes Harkin.

25 LAC, RG 84, file B39-8, A. S. Sibbald to Stewart, August 14, 1923.

26 These letters may be found in LAC, RG 84, files B39-8 and R39-8. Somebody, probably A. S. Sibbald, organized a big push in Saskatoon to attack the Spray scheme, ultimately using a mimeographed petition form.

27 See LAC, RG 84, file R39-8, memorandum re: proposed Spray Lakes project, December 4, 1926, *"List of Organizations protesting against the above project,"* which listed the following: Canadian National Parks Association (representing over 150,000 people); Banff Citizens' Council; Alpine Clubs of Vancouver Island, Vancouver, Saskatoon, Winnipeg, Toronto, Calgary, and Edmonton; Calgary Anglers Association; Calgary Automobile Club; Canadian Clubs of Winnipeg and Brandon; Women's Canadian Clubs of Winnipeg and Brandon; Brandon Board of Trade and Civics; Brandon Rotary Club; Natural History Society of Manitoba; Royal Society of Canada, Saskatoon Motor Club; Toronto Field Naturalists Club; Western Canada Coal Operators Association; Drumheller Board of Trade; Manitoba Motor League; Kiwanis Clubs of Brandon

and Victoria; Young Women's Auxiliary, St. Paul's Church, Brandon; Brandon Local Council of Women; Manitoba Horticultural and Forestry Association; Alumni Association, Manitoba Agricultural College; Victoria Gyro Club; Natural History Society of BC; American Institute of Park Executives; Alberta Provincial Liberal Association; Vancouver Institute; Association of Chief Engineers, Calgary. Obviously, Mrs. W. C. McKillican of Brandon, who was on the board of the CNPA, helped engender many of these resolutions.

28 Susan E. Markham-Starr, "W.J.S. Walker and the Canadian National Parks Association: Protectors of Canadian Leisure Interests," *Leisure/Loisir* 32 (2008): 649–80.

29 LAC, RG 84, file B39-8, Walker to R. S. Stronach, Superintendent, Rocky Mountains National Park, August 22, 1923. Stronach answered cautiously that he felt the local people already knew all they needed to about the project. See also GA, Western Coal Operators Association Records, box 17, file 110, Walker to R. M. Young, December 11, 1923.

30 GA, Western Canada Coal Operators Association Records, box 17, file 110, Young to Walker, January 5, 1924; Walker to Young, January 5, 1924.

31 GA, Western Canada Coal Operators Association Records, box 17, file 110, Walker to Young, April 22, 1924. See the list of opponents of the Spray scheme in note 27 above. Eventually, the association petitioned the premier of Alberta not to spend public funds on the development of the Spray Lakes or any other hydroelectric scheme before a full investigation of the possibility of generating thermal power from small coal had been completed. See GA, Western Canada Coal Operators Association Records, box 17, file

110, Resolution of the Association, December 21, 1926.

32 UAA, Pearce Papers, file 421.1, Pearce to R. B. Bennett, May 12, 1923; Pearce to the editor of the *Herald*, May 19, 1923; memorandum by Pearce, May 23, 1923; Pearce to the Minister of the Interior, June 7, 1923. Pearce's intervention caused the CPR "some embarrassment" in Ottawa and the company asked him, once he had expressed his opinion, to "desist from further controversy." Pearce to D. C. Coleman, CPR Vice President, June 25, 1923, quoting the instructions he had received. See also Bella, *Parks for Profit*, 48–51.

33 GA, CPC, box 13, file 172, agreement between CPC and the City of Calgary, August 6, 1923.

34 PAA, Premier's Papers, box 43, Stewart to Greenfield, December 22, 1923.

35 Canada, House of Commons, *Debates*, April 10, 1924, 1259–60.

36 PAA, acc. 69.289, file 467, V. M. Drury to Herbert Greenfield, May 19, 1924; I. W. Killam to Greenfield, May 28, 1924.

37 PAA, acc. 69.289, file 467, Mayor G. H. Webster to Greenfield, August 7, 1924; memorandum of interview with Stewart, December 13, 1924; LAC, RG 84, file B39-8, report tabled in the Alberta legislature by Greenfield, April 8, 1925.

38 PAA, acc. 70.414, Alberta Sessional Papers, Sessional Paper No. 15, 1925, Report on the Development and Distribution of Hydro-Electric Power in the Province of Alberta by the Hydro-Electric Power Commission of Ontario, 2 vols.

39 LAC, RG 84, file B39-8, report to the Alberta legislature by Greenfield, April 8, 1925; PAA, acc. 69.289, file 467, Greenfield to Director of Reclamation and Water Power, April 24, 1925.

40 See PAA, acc. 69.287, file 467, J. H. Hanna, secretary, Calgary Board of Trade, to Greenfield, January 30, 1925; Secretary, Calgary TLC, to Greenfield, May 5, 1925.

41 PAA, acc. 69.289, file 467, Hoadley to Greenfield, June 21, 1925; PAA, Premier's Papers, box 42, Vernon Pearson and John Haddin to Public Works Minister Alex Ross, August 28, 1925.

42 Canada, House of Commons, *Debates*, June 26, 1925, col. 5008-11.

43 LAC, RG 84, file B39-8, J. M. Wardle to J. B. Harkin, July 2, 1925.

44 PAA, acc. 69.289, file 467, George Hoadley to Greenfield, June 21, 1925; Greenfield to Charles Stewart, July 30, 1925.

45 LAC, RG 84, file B39-8, Stewart to Greenfield, August 19, 1925; Greenfield to Stewart, August 25, 1925; memorandum from J. B. Harkin to R. A. Gibson, August 29, 1925.

46 PAA, acc. 69.289, file 467, clipping from *Calgary Daily Herald*, December 11, 1925; LAC, RG 84, file B39-8, Brownlee to Stewart, December 16, 1925; Stewart to Brownlee, December 29, 1925.

47 PAA, Attorney General's Records, box 7, file S35, clippings from *Calgary Albertan*, June 16, 1923; January 24, 1924.

CHAPTER 6: POLITICAL LOGIC

1 On the 1925 election, see H. B. Neatby, *William Lyon Mackenzie King, 1924–1932: The Lonely Heights* (Toronto: University of Toronto Press, 1963), 68–76.

2 J. A. Maxwell, *Federal Subsidies to the Provincial Governments in Canada* (Cambridge: Harvard University Press, 1937), 152. In 1924, Alberta Premier Greenfield finally accepted the federal offer to return the resources without the subsidy, but King had done

nothing to reach a final agreement. See Neatby, *William Lyon Mackenzie King*, 100–102.

3 Neatby, *William Lyon Mackenzie King*, 127–29.

4 PAA, acc. 69.289, file 467, Premier Greenfield to the Director of Reclamation and Water Power Branch, Ottawa, April 24, 1925: "There is a very strong sentiment in this province in favour of the development of the natural waterpower resources of the Province under public ownership or Government control, and the Government is now carrying on negotiations with the larger municipalities, with a view to determining in what way the Spray River power should be developed, having regard to the best interests of the Province."

5 PAA, acc. 69.289, file 466, statement tabled in the Alberta legislature, March 10, 1926; Brownlee to Stewart, March 22, 1926; Brownlee to King, March 22, 1926; Brownlee to H. E. Spencer, March 22, 1926.

6 PAA, acc. 69.289, file 466, Killam to Brownlee, May 3, 1926, marked "Private and Confidential."

7 LAC, RG 84, file B39-8, Webster to Stewart, March 25, 1926; R39-8, Calgary Board of Trade to Stewart, May 6, 1926.

8 LAC, RG 84, file B39-8, Stewart to Brownlee, March 25, 1926; memorandum from Harkin to R. A. Gibson, March 25, 1926.

9 LAC, RG 84, file B39-8, memorandum from Johnston to R. A. Gibson, March 31, 1926.

10 There are two very similar versions of this reply in LAC, RG 84, file B39-8, "Draft notes on the memorandum dated March 31, 1926 of Mr. J. T. Johnston to the Acting Deputy Minister of the Interior," April 21, 1926, and the memorandum from

Harkin to W. W. Cory, May 22, 1926. Quotations that follow are from the latter.

11   PAA, acc. 69.287, file 466, Brownlee to Stewart, May 6, 1922; Stewart to Brownlee, June 5, 1926; NAC, RG 84, file R39-8, Stewart to J. H. Hanna, Secretary, Calgary Board of Trade, June 5, 1926.

12   For an account of these events see Neatby, *William Lyon Mackenzie King*, 130–57.

13   PAA, Premiers' Papers, box 43, Killam to Brownlee, July 23, 1926.

14   LAC, RG 84, R 39-8, R. C. Marshall to Charles Stewart, 21 November 21, 1926, marked "Personal."

15   LAC, RG 84, file R39-8, Brownlee to Stewart, November 29, 1926; circular from Arthur O. Wheeler, Executive Secretary, Canadian National Parks Association, November 29, 1926; Walker to Stewart, December 8, 1926, marked "Personal."

16   LAC, RG 84, file R39-8, memorandum from J. B. Harkin to W. W. Cory, November 30, December 22, 1926; Stewart to Brownlee, November 29, December 2, 1926; Brownlee to Stewart, December 2, 1926; GA, City of Calgary Papers, box 241, file 1351, City Clerk to Mayor, December 23, 1926, transmitting council resolution to apply pressure to Stewart to get him to meet with Brownlee.

17   LAC, RG 84, file R39-8, memorandum from Harkin to W. W. Cory, January 11, 1927.

18   LAC, RG 84, file R39-8, memorandum from Harkin to Cory, January 7, 1927.

19   PAA, Premiers' Papers, box 43, Solicitor General to Brownlee, December 26, 1926.

20   NAC, RG 84, file R39-8, George Webster to Mayor Fred E. Osborne, Calgary, February 2, 1927.

21   LAC, RG 84, file R39-8, Resolution of the National Council of Women, n.d., and Henrietta L. Wilson and Lydia M. Parsons to Charles Stewart, January 19, 1927, which contains another resolution in similar terms: "*Attention! Most Important!* The Spray Lakes in Banff National Park," circular from Arthur O. Wheeler, Executive Secretary, CNPA, February 15, 1927.

22   PAA, Premiers' Papers, box 22, Bulletins Nos. 1–4, Alberta Power Research Association, January 3, 1927, January 17, 1927, Spring 1927, May 14, 1927.

23   NAC, RG 84, file R39-8, A. B. MacKay, Chairman, APRA, to Stewart, January 3, February 3, 1927; Stewart to MacKay, January 9, February 9, 1927.

24   NAC, RG 84, file R39-8, memorandum from J. T. Johnston to W. W. Cory, February 5, 1927, which also contains a copy of this pamphlet.

25   NAC, RG 84, file R39-8, memorandum from Johnston to W. W. Cory, February 5, 1927; memorandum from J. B. Harkin, February 9, 1927.

26   NAC, RG 84, file R39-8, memorandum from Harkin to W. W. Cory, February 10, 1927; Harkin to R. A. Gibson, March 3, 1927. NAC, RG 84, file B39-8 is full of correspondence dated March–April 1927 from groups such as the Toronto Field Naturalists opposing the exploitation of national parks for commercial purposes; the correspondence was sparked by a circular from the Canadian National Parks Association with the heading "*Attention! Most Important!* The Spray Lakes in Banff National Park," February 15, 1927.

27   NAC, RG 84, file B39-8, Brownlee to Stewart, March 2, 1927.

28   Although there was no announcement of Stewart's decision, in September 1928, he advised an official of the Calgary Board of Trade that he had

made up his mind eighteen months earlier to order the resurvey of the Spray Lakes to permit their removal from Rocky Mountains National Park. See NAC, RG 84, file B39-8, Stewart to T. M. Carlyle, September 6, 1928; NAC, RG 84, file B39-5, memorandum from J. B. Harkin to W. W. Cory, October 25, 1930.

29 LAC, RG 84, file B39-8, Walker to Stewart, October 24, 1927; Stewart to Walker, November 18, 1927.

30 The other question was a redrawing of the eastern boundary near Jasper where it crossed the Athabasca River.

31 These conditions are discussed in PAA, acc. 69.289, file 465, Brownlee to Stewart, February 14, 1928 and Stewart to Brownlee, February 28, 1928.

32 LAC, RG 84, file B39-8, Mayor F. E. Osborne to Stewart, June 7, 1928; memorandum from J. B. Harkin to W. W. Cory, July 6, 1928; Stewart to T. M. Carlyle, Calgary Board of Trade, September 6, 1928; Canada, House of Commons, *Debates*, June 6, 1928, 3854.

33 Neatby, *William Lyon Mackenzie King*, 294–95; PAA, Premiers' Papers, box 42, Stewart to Brownlee, March 11, 1929.

34 Canada, House of Commons, *Debates*, May 28, 1929, 2883–84.

35 E. J. Hart, *J. B. Harkin: Father of Canada's National Parks* (Edmonton: University of Alberta Press, 2011), 319–20.

36 LAC, R. B. Bennett Papers, series E, 48, CNPA, *Bulletin*, No. 8, "Support the Parks Bill," January 1, 1930 (quoting Stewart) ; series F, 469, CNPA, *Bulletin*, No. 9, July 1, 1930; RG 84, file B39-5, clipping from *Calgary Daily Herald*, July 5, 1930. For the debate on the National Parks Act, see Canada, House of Commons, *Debates*, 1930, 2, May 9, 1930; *Statutes of Canada*, 1930, 20–21 Geo V, c. 33. A more detailed account of the legislation can be found in C. J. Taylor, "Legislating Nature: The

National Parks Act of 1930," in *To See Ourselves/To Save Ourselves: Ecology and Culture in Canada*, ed. Roland Lorimer et al., proceedings of the Annual Conference of the Association for Canadian Studies, University of Victoria, May 31–June 1, 1990 (Montreal: Association for Canadian Studies, 1991), 125–37. Hart provides a comprehensive account of the passage of the National Parks Act in *J. B. Harkin*, 381–86. In a masterful piece of political legerdemain the boundary changes actually added to the area of Banff National Park: the excisions on the south east for power development were more than compensated for by additions in the northwest.

CHAPTER 7: MINNEWANKA REDUX

1 LAC, RG 84, file B93-5, J. O. Apps to Charles Stewart, April 17, 1930.

2 The summer flow of the Spray averaged about 556 cfs, and the Alberta government and the Parks Branch agreed that it should be maintained at roughly that level. See LAC, RG 84, file B 39-8, memorandum re: Spray River flow, February 28, 1928.

3 LAC, RG 84, file B39-8, memorandum from J. M. Wardle, April 13, 1928; memorandum, April 13, 1928.

4 LAC, RG 84, file B39-8, Mayor F. E. Osborne to Stewart, June 7, 1928; memorandum from Harkin to W. W. Cory, July 6, 1928.

5 W. E. Hawkins, *Electrifying Calgary, A Century of Public and Private Power* (Calgary: University of Calgary Press, 1987), 168–69; PAA, Premiers' Papers, box 43, Stewart to Brownlee, April 14, 1928; PAA, Premier's Papers, 69.289, file 476, Calgary Power Plants, correspondence and documents relating to the Ghost/Radnor licence; GA, Calgary Council minutes, May 12, 1928, proposed agreement with Calgary Power; May 15, 1928,

memorandum of agreement; GA, CPC, box 1, file 1, directors' minutebook, July 31, 1928.

6 Killam had replaced Bennett as president in the spring of 1928 and then became chairman of the board. See GA, CPC, box 2, directors minutebook, December 16, 1927, March 12, October 18 and 25, 1928; box 3, shareholders minutebook, October 18, 1928.

7 LAC, RG 84, file B39-8, Mayor Fred Osborne to Stewart, August 9, 1928; T. M. Carlyle, Calgary Board of Trade, to Stewart, August 20, 1928.

8 LAC, RG 84, file B39-8, resolution passed at the UFA convention, January 17–20, 1928.

9 See the collection of clippings on electricity supply from *The U.F.A.* in GA, Norman Smith Papers, file 188.

10 PAA, Premiers' Papers, box 42, R. P. Baxter to V. M. Smith, Minister of Telephones, February 20, 1928, marked "Confidential"; memorandum, April 4, 1928.

11 PAA, Premiers' Papers, box 42, R. P. Baxter to V. M. Smith, Minister of Railways and Telephones, August 1, 1928.

12 A similar attitude was expressed by H. R. Milner, local counsel for Midwest Utilities Limited, an American firm that had just begun to buy up small municipal electric systems in the southeastern part of Alberta. "We already have the reputation of being inclined to socialism," warned Milner, predicting that private capitalists would refuse to invest in the province if public ownership were adopted. Nor would rates be lowered while scarce provincial resources were stretched thin due to the cost of electrical systems. See PAA, Premiers' Papers, box 42, Milner to Brownlee, September 20, 1928, marked "Confidential."

13 PAA, Premiers' Papers, box 42, Brownlee to C. A. Magrath, June 18, 1929.

14 PAA, Premiers' Papers, box 42, R. G. Reid to Brownlee, August 15, 1929. In April 1929, Calgary city council established a five-man special committee to examine the power situation, which retained Acres.

15 See the collection of clippings on this subject from *The U.F.A.* in GA, Norman Smith Papers, file 188.

16 PAA, Premiers' Papers, box 42, memorandum "Re Calgary Power and the Right of the Province to Expropriate," from W. S. Gray to Brownlee, August 19, 1929.

17 LAC, RG 84, file B39-5, clipping from *Calgary Herald*, December 20, 1929; Mayor F. E. Osborne and R. C. Thomas to Charles Stewart, December 21, 1929.

18 LAC, RG 84, file B39-5, memorandum from Harkin to R. A. Gibson, December 23, 1929.

19 GA, Calgary Council Papers, Stewart to R. C. Thomas, December 23, 1929; resolution of TLC and CCU, January 2, 1930; LAC, RG 84, file B39-5, Mayor Andrew Davison to Stewart, January 4, 1930; PAA, Premiers' Papers, box 42, J. H. Hanna to John Brownlee, January 25, 1930.

20 LAC, RG 84, file B39-5, memorandum from Harkin to R. A. Gibson, December 23, 1929; LAC, RG 84, file B39-5, R. B. Bennett Papers, J. H. Hanna to Bennett, February 20, 1930.

21 LAC, RG 84, file B39-5, Stewart to Mayor Andrew Davison, March 1, 1930; memorandum from W. W. Cory to Harkin, April 11, 1930; Harkin to R. A. Gibson, April 25, 1930; Harkin to Cory, June 5, 1930.

22 LAC, RG 84, file B39-5, clipping from *Calgary Herald*, June 23, 1930; clipping from *Calgary Herald*, August 22, 1930; LAC, RG 84, file B39-5, R. B. Bennett

Papers, series F, vol. 106, J. H. Hanna to Bennett, August 7, 1930, 70700; series F, vol. 469, W.J.S. Walker to CNPA members, August 18, 1930, 296314. See also RG 84, file B39-5, Resolution of the Alpine Club of Canada, August 13, 1930.

23 LAC, RG 84, file B39-5, memorandum from Cory to Murphy, September 11, 1930; memorandum from J. T. Johnston to Cory, October 17, 1930; LAC, RG 85, file R-1436-3-3, E. J. Chambers, solicitor for Calgary Power, to Murphy, September 16, 1930.

24 Hart, *J. B. Harkin*, 287.

25 LAC, RG 84, file B39-5, memorandum from Harkin to Cory, October 25, 1930.

26 LAC, R. B. Bennett Papers, series F, Murphy to Gaherty, February 23, 1931; Gaherty to Murphy, March 13, 1931, 70767, 70773-4; RG 84, file R39-5, T. H. Hogg to Calgary Power, March 5, 1931; RG 84, file B 39-5, memorandum from Johnston to R. A. Gibson, March 21, 1931.

27 E. J. Hart, *J. B. Harkin: Father of Canada's National Parks* (Edmonton: University of Alberta Press, 2011), 189.

CHAPTER 8: WAR MEASURES

1 LAC, RG 84, file B39-5, extract of paper by Gaherty, February 15, 1939.

2 The Alberta Nitrogen Company was a subsidiary of Allied War Supplies Corporation.

3 The portfolios of Mines, Immigration, and Colonization and the Interior, as well as the office of Superintendent General of Indian Affairs were combined under Mines and Resources by *Statutes of Canada*, 1936, I Edw. VIII, c. 33, which came into force on December 1, 1936.

4 LAC, RG 84, file B39-5, C. M. Walker to T. S. Mills, September 9, 1940.

5 Ibid.

6 LAC, RG 84, file B39-5, G. A. Gaherty to R. A. Gibson, October 10, 1940.

7 LAC, RG 84, file B39-5, P. J. Jennings to F.H.H. Williamson, September 7, 1940; C. M. Walker to T. S. Mills, September 16, 1940.

8 LAC, RG 84, file B39-5, Jennings to F.H.H. Williamson, September 7, 1940.

9 LAC, RG 84, file B39-5, memorandum from J. H. Byrne to F.H.H. Williamson, October 2, 1940.

10 LAC, RG 84, file B39-5, memorandum from Wardle to R. A. Gibson, September 30, 1940.

11 LAC, RG 84, file B39-5, memorandum from R. A. Gibson to J. M. Wardle, October 2, 1940.

12 LAC, RG 84, file B39-5, Gaherty to R. A. Gibson, October 10, 1940; memorandum from J. M. Wardle to Gibson, October 25, 1940, marked "Confidential"; Gaherty to C. C. Camsell, November 11, 1940.

13 LAC, RG 84, file B39-5, memorandum from B. F. Haanel, Chief, Division of Fuels, October 29, 1940; Camsell to Gaherty, November 1, 1940.

14 LAC, RG 84, file B39-5, Gaherty to R. A. Gibson, October 10, 1940.

15 LAC, RG 84, file B39-5, memorandum from R. A. Gibson to James Smart, October 15, 1940; Charles Camsell to H. J. Symington, October 18, 1940.

16 LAC, RG 84, file B39-5, memorandum from R. A. Gibson to James Smart, October 31, 1940; Camsell to Gaherty, November 1, 1940.

17 LAC, RG 84, file B39-5, Howe to Crerar, November 12, 1940.

18 LAC, RG 84, file B39-5, memorandum from Gibson to James Smart, November 12, 1940; memorandum from Gibson to Camsell, November 22, 1940.

19 LAC, RG 84, file B39-5, Crerar to Howe, November 13, 1940.

20 LAC, RG 85, 734, memorandum from R. A. Gibson, Director, Lands, Parks and Forests Branch, Department of Mines and Resources, to J. M. Wardle, December 2, 1940.

21 LAC, RG 84, file B39-5, memoranda from R. A. Gibson to Charles Camsell, November 14 (quoted), November 27, 1940.

22 LAC, RG 84, file B 39-5, Walker to James Smart, September 4, 1940. On Walker's activity, see S. E. Markham-Starr, "W.S.J. Walker and the Canadian National Parks Association," *Leisure/Loisir* 32 (2008): 649–80.

23 LAC, RG 84, file B39-5, Walker to James Smart, October 1, 1940 (quoted); Walker to R. J. Jennings, October 3, 1940; P. J. Jennings to James Smart, December 2, 1940.

24 LAC, RG 84, file B39-5, R. A. Rooney to R. A. Gibson, November 22, 1940; Gibson to Rooney, November 26, 1940. The writing paper of the Alberta Fish and Game Association was festooned with cartoons of wildlife, and at the bottom appeared this memorable bit of poesy:

Dad, your gun is in its case,
Your rod is on the wall.
Daddy, when you shooted ducks
Did you shoot 'em all?
When you killed the deer and fox
And cut the balsam tree
Couldn't you have left a few
Fer Billy and fer me?. . .

Daddy, wouldn't you suppose
That if you really tried
You could save a little woods
And fields and countryside?
Kinda keep a savin' up,
You and Uncle Len,
Just a little out-o-doors
Fer Billy and fer me?

25 LAC, RG 84, file B39-5, mimeographed letter from Banff Advisory Council to Alberta MPs, November 27, 1940; R. J.

Jennings to James Smart, December 2, 1940.

26 LAC, RG 84, file B39-5, V. Meek to J. M. Wardle, November 26, 1940; Gibson to Camsell, November 29, 1940 (quoted).

27 LAC, RG 84, file B39-5, clipping from *Calgary Albertan*, November 26, 1940; Crerar to Howe, November 30, 1940.

28 LAC, RG 84, file B39-5, W. S. Edwards, Deputy Minister of Justice, to Charles Camsell, November 26, 1940; Howe to Crerar, December 3, 1940.

29 LAC, RG 84, file B39-5, W. S. Edwards to Charles Camsell, December 10, 1940; Aberhart to Crerar, December 5, 1940; Crerar to Gaherty, December 16, 1940, enclosing PC 7382, December 13, 1940.

30 LAC, RG 84, file B39-5, R. A. Gibson to James Smart, December 7, 1940; G. A. Gaherty to Charles Camsell, January 2, 1941.

31 LAC, RG 84, file B39-5, memorandum to R. A. Gibson, January 3, February 27, 1941; memorandum from James Smart to Gibson, January 13, 1941. Departmental officials became concerned, however, when the Nakoda brought their families into the park with them, because they did not want to permit them to establish permanent residence in the town of Banff. Eventually, the Indian Agent for the band agreed to assume responsibility for supervising the Indian workers and for seeing that they did not remain once the job was completed. See LAC, RG 22, 238, file 33-4-4, memorandum from Gibson to J. M. Wardle, March 3, 1941.

32 LAC, RG 84, file B39-5, press release, April 10, 1941.

33 LAC, RG 84, file B39-5, Walker to Crerar, March 13, 1941, marked "Confidential"; Walker to F.H.H. Williamson, March 18, 1941.

34 LAC, RG 84, file B39-5, Walker to James Smart, April 25, 1941.

35 Canada, House of Commons, *Debates*, June 4, 1941, 3578.

36 Canada, House of Commons, *Debates*, June 4, 1941, 3763.

37 *Statutes of Canada*, 1941, 4-5 Geo VI, c. 22, An Act to Amend the Alberta Natural Resources Act. This short three-clause statute, assented to on June 14, 1941, formalized the memorandum of agreement (included in the act as a schedule) permitting the development of the Lake Minnewanka project. Clause three squared the legal circle: "The Minister of Mines and Resources shall have authority to grant the license referred to in the said agreement, notwithstanding the provisions of The National Parks Act, chapter thirty-three of the statutes of 1930 (First Session)."

38 LAC, RG 84, file B39-5, Smart to Gibson, October 21, 1941; LAC, RG 22, 238, file 33-4-4, memorandum from Gibson to J. M. Wardle, October 28, 1941. Matthew Evenden explores the implications of drowning a landscape in "Immersed: Landscaping the Past at Lake Minnewanka," in *Placing Memory and Remembering Place in Canada*, ed. J. Opp and J. C. Walsh (Vancouver, University of British Columbia Press, 2010), 247–70.

39 LAC, RG 22, 238, file 33-4-4, Charles Camsell to G. A. Gaherty, March 20, 1942; memorandum from J. E. Spero to James Smart, April 2, 1942; memorandum from R. A. Gibson to C. W. Jackson, April 2, 1942.

40 LAC, RG 22, 238, file 33-4-4, Charles Camsell to Gaherty, January 21, 1943.

41 LAC, RG 22, 238, December 4, 1941, Charles Camsell to Gaherty, December 4, 1941; memorandum from J. M. Wardle to Camsell, December 18, 1941; LAC, RG 84, file B39-5, memorandum from J. E. Spero to file, July 9, 1943.

42 LAC, RG 22, 238, file 33-4-4, Gaherty to J. M. Wardle, April 24, 1944;

memorandum from Wardle to Charles Camsell, April 28, May 3, May 20, 1944.

43 LAC, RG 84, file B39-5, Smart to Professor F. Webster, April 13, 1942.

44 LAC, RG 84, file B39-5, memorandum from Smart to R. A. Gibson, April 30, 1942.

45 LAC, RG 84, file B39-5, memorandum from James Smart, October 6, 1942; J. M. Wardle to G. A. Gaherty, October 14, 1942.

46 LAC, RG 84, file B 39-5, no. 21, J. A. Harrison to J.R.B. Coleman, November 10, 1955.

47 LAC, RG 84, file B39-5, memorandum from Gibson to James Smart, December 13, 1944.

48 LAC, RG 84, file B39-5, memorandum from James Smart to R. A. Gibson, August 21, 1946; memorandum to Smart, September 9, 1946.

49 LAC, RG 84, file B39-5, J. A. Mackinnon to James Smart, April 8, 1947. The company had $8 million worth of 5 per cent debentures, payable in US funds, which it desired to replace with "Canadian-pay" securities, saving foreign exchange.

50 LAC, RG 84, file B39-5, A. G. Mackinnon to James Smart, April 8, 1947; R. A. Gibson to Smart, May 2, 1947; final licence for storage and development of water power, Lake Minnewanka and Cascade River, Banff National Park, Alberta, May 14, 1947. The rental payments varied according to how much the value of the lands was depreciated by commercial use from that which they would have as parklands.

51 Ironically, the drowning of a townsite, the old dams, and Devil's Canyon created a new recreation attraction in the park, scuba diving. At a depth of approximately twenty metres in clear cold water, divers explore foundations,

chimneys, bridge piers, a concrete dam and other relics. See R. W. Sanford, *Lake Minnewanka: The Spirit of the Waters* (Banff: Lake Minnewanka Boat Tours, 1999), 44–45. See also the Banff National Park website, http://www.pc.gc.ca/pn-np/ab/banff/natcul/natcul4m1.aspx, for detailed descriptions of the diving sites and a map.

CHAPTER 9: PUBLIC POWER

1 See Brian Brennan, *The Good Steward: The Ernest C. Manning Story* (Calgary: Fifth House, 2008), for a full treatment of Manning's political counterrevolution, although Brennan does not present it as such. For a review of *The Good Steward*, see H. V. Nelles, "That Old-Time Religion," *Literary Review of Canada* (January–February 2009). Most of the literature on Social Credit deals with its early insurrectionary phase; the Manning years are curiously understudied. J. J. Barr, in *The Dynasty: The Rise and Fall of Social Credit in Alberta* (Calgary: McClelland and Stewart, 1974), briefly discusses "How Manning Used Power" (132–48) and his free enterprise ideology (135–38). Alvin Finkel, in *The Social Credit Phenomenon in Alberta* (Toronto: University of Toronto Press, 1989), deals with the early phases of the Manning government in a chapter entitled "Hot Economy and a Cold War" (99–140), in which Manning's anti-socialist views are elaborated and the potential nationalization of Calgary Power is briefly treated (126).

2 This figure is drawn from PAA, Premiers' Papers, acc. 69.289/1437, Premier E. C. Manning to G. A. Gaherty, July 11, 1947. Presumably, the figure was actually lower in 1945.

3 PAA, Premiers' Papers, acc 69.289/794, memorandum re: meeting of Alberta Power Commission, December 15, 1944.

4 PAA, Premiers' Papers, acc. 69.289/1347, Ora B. Moore, MLA, to E. C. Manning, February 15, 1946, enclosing letter from Glenn F. Pauk, Ponoka, February 11, 1946; memorandum from A. Bradshaw, Director of Technical Development, to L. D. Byren, Deputy Minister of Economic Affairs, April 17, 1946, re: "Ownership of Hydro-Electric Power Plants."

5 PAA, Premiers' Papers, acc. 69.289/1347, W. D. King, Deputy Minister of Trade and Industry, to G. A. Gaherty, August 1, 1946; Manning to Gaherty, October 8, 1946.

6 Cottingham's report is quoted in PAA, Premiers' Papers, acc. 69.289/1437, report of the Alberta Power Commission to E. C. Manning, October 22, 1947.

7 LAC, RG 22, 126, file 99-2-93, G. A. Gaherty to J. A. Glen, April 30, 1947; memorandum from W.J.F. Pratt to J. M. Wardle, May 2, 1947.

8 John Richards and Larry Pratt, *Prairie Capitalism: Power and Influence in the New West* (Toronto: McClelland and Stewart, 1979), 81–82.

9 PAA, Premiers' Papers, acc. 69.289/1615, report of the Alberta Power Commission, Plan for Rural Electrification, March 15, 1947.

10 PAA, Premiers' Papers, acc. 69.289/1437, Manning to G. A. Gaherty, July 11, 1947.

11 PAA, Premiers' Papers, acc. 69.289/1437, Gaherty to Manning, July 25, August 28, 1947.

12 PAA, Premiers' Papers, acc. 69,289/1347, Milner to Manning, December 5, 1947, marked "Personal and Confidential."

13 PAA, Premiers' Papers, acc. 69.289/1437, report of the Alberta Power Commission to E. C. Manning, October 22, 1947.

14 PAA, Premiers' Papers, acc. 69.289/1615, Reid to E. C. Manning, March 14, 1948.

15 Richards and Pratt, *Prairie Capitalism*, 82; PAA, Premiers' Papers, acc. 69.289/1615, "Financial Counsel" (mimeographed), November 26, 1948.

16 PAA, Premiers' Papers, acc. 69.289/1615, memorandum re: electrification plebiscite, August 17, 1948. Most rural constituencies favoured public ownership, and Edmonton turned it down only by 21,478 to 22,351. However, Calgary went against the proposal 26,325 to 11,478, Lethbridge by 4,237 to 2,291, and Medicine Hat by 5,186 to 1,214. Manning is quoted in PAA, Premiers' Papers, acc. 69.289/1615, "Financial Counsel" (mimeographed), November 26, 1948.

17 PAA, Premiers' Papers, acc. 69.289/1615, N. A. Shandro to E. C. Manning, September 14, 1948. The founders of the association came from Stettler, Acme, Swalwell, Three Hills, Ponoka, LaGlace, Drumheller, Shandro, Cochrane, and Calgary.

18 See, for example, PAA, Premiers' Papers, acc. 69/289/1615, text of "This Week" commentary on radio station CFCN, November 20, 1948.

19 PAA, Premiers' Papers, acc. 69.289/1615, resolution passed by first annual meeting of Alberta Rural Electrification Association, July 7, 1950; text of articles in *Farm and Ranch Review*, 1951; PAA, Premiers' Papers, acc. 69.289/1677, notice of motion by A.J.E. Liesemer, February 25, 1952.

CHAPTER 10: REVERSING RIVERS

1 LAC, RG 84, file B39-8, memorandum, April 13, 1928; Charles Stewart to John Brownlee, April 14, 1928; G. A. Gaherty to J. A. Mackinnon, May 26, 1948. In 1928, Gaherty had, in fact, "stated that in his opinion the release of any water from the storage reservoir for scenic purposes at Banff would imperil the whole project," adding that a flow of 425 cfs at the Spray mouth was "utterly out of the question." See LAC, RG 84, file B39-8, memorandum from J. M. Wardle, April 13, 1928.

2 LAC, RG 84, file B39-8, R. A. Gibson to F. R. Burfield, October 1, 1942; Superintendent P. J. Jennings to James Smart, September 24, 1942.

3 LAC, RG 84, file B39-8, memorandum from James Smart to J. E. Spero, October 30, 1942.

4 Parks Branch director Roy Gibson observed, "I do not think that our officers should discuss even informally with the officers of the Calgary Power Company, or for that matter any other company, schemes to alter the watercourses in National Parks. Most of these schemes have very far-reaching effects." LAC, RG 84, file B39-5, memorandum from Gibson to James Smart, December 13, 1944.

5 LAC, RG 84, file B39-5, memorandum from James Smart to R. A. Gibson, November 30, 1945; LAC, RG 84, file B68, memorandum from Smart to Gibson, December 3, 1945.

6 See GA, "Highlights in [Calgary Power] Company's Growth," in the finding aid to company papers.

7 LAC, RG 22, vol. 238, file 33-4-10, H. L. Keenleyside to G. A. Gaherty, June 23, 1947; W.J.S. Walker to Keenleyside, August 16, 1947.

8 LAC, RG 22, 238, file 33-4-10, W. M. Neal to C. D. Howe, September 4, 1947; Keenleyside to Neal, October 13, 1947, marked "Confidential"; Neal to Keenleyside, November 7, 1947, marked "Private"; RG 84, file B39-8, memorandum from J. E. Spero, April 22, 1948.

9   LAC, RG 84, file B39-8, V. A. Newhall
    to W.L.M. King, May 6,1948; Manning
    to Mackinnon, May 21, 1948.

10 LAC, RG 84, file B39-8, Gaherty to J. A.
    Mackinnon, May 26, 1948.

11 LAC, RG 84, file B39-8, memorandum
    from R. A. Gibson to James Smart, May
    27, 1948.

12 Mackinnon's predecessor, J. A. Glen,
    a Manitoban, had a heart attack in
    the summer of 1947; first C. D. Howe,
    then Mackinnon acted in Glen's stead
    for a number of months. The deputy
    minister, H. L. Keenleyside, had moved
    over from External Affairs in 1947
    to replace the long-serving Charles
    Camsell at Mines and Resources. See
    H. L. Keenleyside, *On the Bridge of
    Time*, vol. 2 of *Memoirs of Hugh L.
    Keenleyside* (Toronto: McClelland and
    Stewart, 1982), 281–89.

13 LAC, RG 84, file B39-8, Mackinnon to
    Gaherty, May 31, 1948.

14 Robert Bothwell and William
    Kilbourn, *C. D. Howe: A Biography*
    (Toronto: McClelland and Stewart,
    1979).

15 LAC, RG 84, file B39-8, Howe to
    Mackinnon, June 15, 1948.

16 LAC, RG 84, file B 39-8, memorandum
    from T. E. Dunn, June 1, 1948.

17 LAC, RG 84, file B 39-8, Mackinnon to
    Manning, June 12, 1948; memorandum
    from Ben Russell to Manning, June 18,
    1948 (quoted); LAC, RG 22, 238, file
    33-4-10, Manning to Mackinnon, June
    18, 1948.

18 LAC, RG 84, file B 39-8, W. A. Mather
    to Mackinnon, June 22, 1948; A.D.P.
    Heeney to Mackinnon, June 23, 1948,
    marked "Confidential"; Mackinnon to
    Manning, June 23, 1948; LAC, RG 22,
    238, file 33-4-10, Manning to W.L.M.
    King, June 23, 1948; King to Manning,
    June 28, 1948.

19 LAC, RG 22, 238, file 33-4-10,
    memorandum from acting deputy.

minister to Sinclair, July 26, 1948
(quoted); memorandum from R. A.
Gibson to H. L. Keenleyside, July 28,
1948.

20 LAC, RG 22, 238, file 33-4-10,
    memorandum from acting deputy
    minister to minister, July 21, 1948;
    LAC, RG 84, file B39-8, R. A. Gibson to
    James Smart, August 9, 1948.

21 LAC, RG 84, file B39-8, memorandum
    from Gibson to V. Meek, August
    31, 1948; memorandum from J. A.
    Hutchison to Mackinnon, August 21,
    1948; R.E.W. Edwards to Mackinnon,
    August 17, 1948.

22 LAC, RG 84, file B 39-8, memorandum
    from R. A. Gibson to V. Meek, August
    31, 1948.

23 LAC, RG 84, file B39-8, J. A.
    Mackinnon to E. C. Manning,
    September 9, 1948; A.D.P. Heeney
    to Mackinnon, September 10, 1948,
    marked "Confidential"; LAC, RG 22,
    238, file 33-4-10, Fraser Duncan to
    Mackinnon, August 31, 1948, marked
    "Personal".

24 LAC, RG 84, file B39-8, memorandum
    from Gibson to James Smart,
    September 30, 1948; Gibson to C. W.
    Jackson, November 2, 1948. Within
    the Alberta provincial government,
    fisheries officials raised only tepid
    opposition to the Spray Lakes project,
    mainly on the grounds that raising
    water levels would drown shallow
    fish-spawning beds. See PAA, acc.
    72.302, Minister of Agriculture Papers,
    box 7, file 341, correspondence of E. S.
    Heustis, Fish and Game Commissioner,
    with Ben Russell, Director of Water
    Resources, 1947–49; memorandum
    from Heustis to N. E. Tanner, Minister,
    August 29, 1949. Heustis wrote the
    following to Tanner:

    It would appear necessary that power
    development proceed as the demands
    of the province require, but it would
    also appear desirable that before

any project of this kind is allowed to proceed, that an opportunity be given to this department to make and investigation to determine just what influence the project will have on the stream concerned and its tributaries. The Government would then be in a position to decide whether the project is doing sufficient harm to warrant requesting its discontinuance, or whether the company having disturbed or destroyed the fishery in a certain stream, should be required to reimburse the fishery interest to the extent of supplying fish hatcheries, and rearing ponds for the introduction of sport fish into these streams on an angling basis and of sufficient size to allow for angling during that particular season.

Included with the memorandum was a report by R. B. Miller and W. H. MacDonald entitled "The Effect of the Spray Lakes Development on the Sport Fishery," June 21, 1949.

25   LAC, RG 84, file B39-8, James Smart to Devereux Butcher, June 9, 1949.

26   LAC, RG 84, file B39-8, Walker to R. A. Gibson, November 15, 1948; LAC, RG 22, 89, file 560, Mackinnon to Walker, November 22, 1948.

27   LAC, RG 84, file B39-8, memoranda from James Smart to R. A. Gibson, September 30, November 2, 1948; LAC, RG 22, 89, file 560, memorandum from Gibson to James Smart, January 18, 1949. Typical of this material was a lengthy summary by T. E. Dunn dated January 14, 1949, also preserved in RG 22, 89, file 560, which listed all the *"Intrustions* [sic] *Calgary Power Limited"* and concluded: "In the last thirty-six years the Calgary Power Ltd., has continually brought pressure to bear to establish storage reservoirs, power plants, canals and transmission lines within the park area, or to have further areas removed from the park. Other corporations may well press

for concessions. And why should they not?"

28   LAC, RG 84, file B39-8, Mackinnon to David A. Ure, January 25, 1949; Gaherty to Ure, February 7, 1949 (quoted); Ure to Mackinnon, February 9, 1949. For the other side of the correspondence, see PAA, acc. 72.302, Minister of Agriculture Papers, box 7, file 341, Spray Lakes 1949, Manning to St. Laurent, March 2, 1949; A. F. Duncan to David Ure, March 16, 1949. Premier Manning's letter impressed the prime minister, who, according to the minister of agriculture, pushed the bill in cabinet.

29   Canada, House of Commons, *Debates*, March 23, 1949, 1910–11; LAC, RG 84, file B39-8, J. A. Mackinnon to D. A. Ure, March 30, 1949.

30   LAC, RG 84, file B39-5, James Smart to R. A. Gibson, September 14, 1949; Norman Marr to Smart, December 2, 1949.

31   LAC, RG 84, file B39-5, Gibson to A.C.L. Adams, August 30, 1949.

32   LAC, RG 84, file B39-5, memorandum from W. Nason to Gibson, September 7, 1949; James Smart to Gibson, September 14, 1949; Nason to Gibson, October 3, 1949; memorandum from Smart to Gibson, November 28, 1949.

33   LAC, RG 84, file B39-5, T. D. Stanley to J. A. Hutchison, November 22, 1949.

34   LAC, RG 84, file B39-5, J. A. Hutchison to James Smart, November 23, 1949; memorandum from Smart to R. A. Gibson, December 9, 1949; Gibson to G. A. Gaherty, December 9, 1949.

35   LAC, RG 22, 316, file 33-4-10, memorandum from James Smart to J. M. Wardle, May 22, 1951; Harold Riley to the Deputy Minister of Justice, October 24, 1951; PAA, acc. 72.302, Minister of Agriculture Papers, box 10, file 488, Spray Lakes 1950; box 14, file 641, Spray Lakes 1951.

36 LAC, RG 22, 316, file 33-4-10,
    memorandum from J. M. Wardle to
    the Deputy Minister, July 25 1951;
    memorandum for the Deputy Minister,
    January 19, 1952.

37 LAC, RG 22, 316, file 33-4-10,
    memorandum from Deputy Minister
    Brigadier General H. A. Young
    to file, January 30, April 21, 1952;
    memorandum from James Smart to
    Young, March 4, 1952; G. A. Gaherty to
    Young, May 9, 1952; Young to Gaherty,
    May 27, 1952.

38 LAC, RG 84, file B39-5, T. D. Stanley
    to J. A. Hutchison, February 2, 1951;
    Robert H. Winters to G. A. Gaherty,
    February 9, 1951.

39 LAC, RG 84, file B 39-8, R. A. Mackie
    to J. A. Hutchison, October 23, 1952;
    memorandum from H. A. deVeber
    to Hutchison, November 4, 1952;
    Hutchison to James Smart, November
    14, 1952.

40 LAC, RG 84, file B39-5, memorandum
    from J. A. Hutchison to file, September
    9, 1955; T. D. Stanley to Hutchison,
    September 22, 1955.

CHAPTER 11: LEAVING THE BOW

1   In 1928, Calgary Power leased the
    City of Calgary's Victoria Park steam
    plant to meet peak winter demand but
    owned only hydroelectric generating
    stations.

2   PAA, acc. 90.618, Public Utilities Board
    records, Calgary Power, waterpower
    leases, 1909–72; PAA, acc. 72.302,
    Minister of Agriculture Papers, file
    46, Ghost Dam 1947, and file 47,
    Kananaskis Development. For a
    discussion of the impact of these hydro
    developments on the fish of the upper
    Bow watershed, see C. Armstrong, M.
    Evenden, and H. V. Nelles, *The River
    Returns: An Environmental History
    of the Bow* (Montreal and Kingston:
    McGill-Queen's University Press,
    2009), ch. 8.

3   The provincial government had
    inserted a clause in the earlier Spray
    Lakes licence requiring the company
    to build flood-control works before
    it undertook further storage work if
    called upon by the government. See
    Armstrong, Evenden, and Nelles, *River
    Returns*, 265–66.

4   This additional capacity was made
    possible by raising the level of the
    water stored behind the dams in the
    headponds at the Spray and Rundle
    plants; see PAA, acc. 90.618, Public
    Utilities Board records, Calgary Power,
    waterpower leases, 1909–72.

5   Ibid.

6   Calgary Power Ltd., *Annual Report*,
    1954; report to shareholders, March 24,
    1955.

7   Calgary Power Ltd., *Annual Report*,
    1955, 1956.

8   Edmonton's municipal generating
    system is now called Epcor.

9   Average sulphur content of Canadian
    coal ranged from 3 to 5 per cent; see
    TransAlta Utilities Corporation,
    Some Facts 1985 (Calgary: TransAlta
    Utilities, 1985), 7.

10 Calgary Power Ltd., *Annual Report*,
    1956.

11 The tie line also permitted Calgary
    Power to begin selling wholesale power
    to the City of Red Deer.

12 Calgary Power had constructed
    additional tie lines after signing
    interchange agreements with
    Lethbridge in 1927 and Medicine Hat
    in 1953.

13 Calgary Power Ltd., *Annual Report*,
    1954–58; quotation from Gaherty's
    report to shareholders, April 3, 1957 in
    the 1956 report.

14 Reports to shareholders, March 26,
    1959 and April 4, 1960, in Calgary
    Power Ltd., *Annual Reports*, 1958–59.
    The contract specified a firm price for

the first 240,000 kw, with the charge for the remainder to be negotiated.

15 Report to shareholders, March 28, 1961, Calgary Power Ltd., *Annual Report*, 1960. Doubling the scale of Wabamun # 3 meant that with the strip mine producing one million tons of coal annually (with an eventual capacity of 2.5 million tons), the smaller, older units #1 and # 2 would require 5 per cent more fuel per kwh, making the cost per kilowatt 20 per cent higher than a proposed unit # 4, which was to have almost 300,000 kw of capacity; see report to shareholders, March 25, 1963, Calgary Power Ltd., *Annual Report*, 1962. Time passes. After fifty-four years of producing, on average, 3.7 million megawatt hours of electricity, the four units of the Wabamun facility reached the end of their useful life early in the twenty-first century. They were decommissioned beginning in 2002 in a long-running process that culminated in the 2011 toppling of the candy-striped smoke stacks. See the TransAlta website, http://www.transalta.com/facilities/plants-operation/wabamun/decommissioning.

16 Report to shareholders, March 26, 1959, Calgary Power Ltd., *Annual Report*, 1958.

17 See PAA, acc. 90.618, Public Utilities Board records, Calgary Power, waterpower leases, 1909–72; reports to shareholders, March 28, 1961, March 21, 1962, Calgary Power Ltd., *Annual Reports*, 1960–61.

18 Report to shareholders, March 25, 1963, Calgary Power Ltd., *Annual Report*, 1962.

19 Calgary Power Ltd., *Annual Reports*, 1963–69.

20 Calgary Power Ltd., *Annual Reports*, 1969–72.

21 PAA, acc. 90.618, Public Utilities Board records, Calgary Power, waterpower leases, 1909–72. As at Bighorn, the company would pay the province a water rental of $40,000 annually plus a sliding scale of $1.30 per horsepower per year at 40 per cent load factor, $1.25 for 40–45 per cent load, $1.20 for 50–60 per cent load, $1.15 for 60–70 per cent load, $1.10 for 70–80 per cent load, $1.05 for 80–90 per cent load, and $1.00 for 90–100 per cent load.

22 Of course, the company did not have sufficient stored water to produce this wattage on anything close to a continuous basis.

23 Report of president A. W. Howard to shareholders, February 16, 1973, Calgary Power Ltd., *Annual Report*, 1972.

24 Calgary Power Ltd., *Annual Report*, 1968.

25 The Alberta licence to divert the upper Ghost into Lake Minnewanka was revised in 1947 to increase the size of the diversion for another fifty years.

26 PAA, acc. 990.618, Public Utilities Board records, Calgary Power, waterpower leases, 1909–72.

27 Report to shareholders by president A. W. Howard, February 19, 1971, Calgary Power Ltd., *Annual Report*, 1970.

28 PAA, acc. 90.618, Public Utilities Board records, Calgary Power, waterpower leases, 1909–72. These two volumes commence with the agreement between the company and Environment Minister William J. Yurko, September 28, 1972, and the changes to the various agreements are interleaved in them on sheets of yellow paper bearing that same date.

29 LAC, RG 85, vol. 734, memorandum from R. A. Gibson to J. B. Challies, March 15, 1923; RG 84, file B39-5, V. M. Drury to Minister of the Interior, April 12, 1923.

30 Reports to shareholders by president A. W. Thompson, March 6, 1970, February

19, 1971, Calgary Power Ltd., *Annual Reports*, 1969–70.

31 Cold precipitators used at the Sundance plants were supposed to eliminate 99.5 per cent of the solid particulates, but differences between the mineral content of the coal from the Highvale mine and that produced at the Whitewood mine used at the older Wabamun units required the installation of hot precipitators at the latter, a first for any Canadian utility.

32 TransAlta Utilities, *Some Facts 1980* (Calgary: TransAlta Utilities, 1980).

33 Calgary Power Ltd., *Annual Reports*, 1972–76. The quotation is from the report to shareholders by the chair, A. W. Howard, and the president, M. M. Williams, February 20, 1975.

34 Calgary Power Ltd., *Annual Reports*, 1975–76.

35 In 1975, the company also received approval from the Alberta Electric Utility Planning Council for construction of a two million kw plant near Camrose, forty miles southeast of Edmonton, where it controlled substantial coal reserves, but the provincial government ultimately withdrew this permission owing to doubts that the land mined could be successfully rehabilitated for agriculture afterwards. See Calgary Power Ltd., *Annual Reports*, 1974–76.

36 TransAlta Utilities, *Annual Report*, 1982. The company's application to build two more units at Keephills was refused in 1982.

37 TransAlta Utilities, *Annual Reports*, 1982–84.

38 TransAlta Utilities, *Annual Reports*, 1983–85.

39 In 1985, TransAlta's customers were divided as follows: retail (residential, commercial), 15.3 per cent; industrial, 43.8 per cent; wholesale (Calgary, Lethbridge, Red Deer), 35.4 per cent;

farms, 5.5 per cent. TransAlta Utilities, *Some Facts 1985* (Calgary: TransAlta Utilities, 1985).

40 TransAlta Utilities, *Annual Report*, 1982. In 1982, TransAlta's average cost of production was $1.98 per kwh versus $3.87 for Edmonton Power and $4.73 for Alberta Power's less concentrated system, producing a provincial average cost of $2.74. TransAlta Utilities, *Some Facts 1984* (Calgary: TransAlta Utilities, 1984).

41 By 1986, TransAlta's predicted average costs were $3.12 per kwh versus $2.71 for Edmonton Power and $4.20 for Alberta Power, yielding a provincial average of $3.12. TransAlta Utilities, *Some Facts 1987* (Calgary: TransAlta Utilities, 1987).

42 TransAlta Utilities, *Some Facts 1990* (Calgary: TransAlta Utilities, 1990).

43 TransAlta Utilities, *Some Facts 1985*.

44 Alberta Water Resources Commission, South Saskatchewan River Basin Planning Program, Hearings, Strathmore, Alberta, December 4, 1984, II, 148–63, transcript, Legislative Library of Alberta, Edmonton.

45 Alberta Water Resources Commission, South Saskatchewan River Basin Planning Program, Hearings, Strathmore, Alberta, December 4, 1984, II, brief of TransAlta Utilities, 182–224, transcript, Legislative Library of Alberta, Edmonton.

46 Alberta Water Resources Commission, South Saskatchewan River Basin Planning Program, Hearings, Calgary, November 7, 1984, I, 322–25, typescript, Legislative Library of Alberta, Edmonton.

47 Jennings admitted that the Bow River Protection Society numbered only a dozen or so persons because it was believed that this was more effective for highly informed lobbying than a mass movement.

48 Alberta Water Resources Commission, South Saskatchewan River Basin Planning Program, Hearings, High River, Alberta, November 8, 1984, 43–47, transcript, Legislative Library of Alberta, Edmonton.

49 Calgary Power, *Some Facts about Calgary Power Ltd. 1960* (Calgary: Calgary Power, 1961); TransAlta Utilities, *1994 Some Facts* (Calgary: TransAlta Utilities, 1995). Between 1990 and 1992, hydro production declined from 2.051 billion kwh to 1.502 billion kwh, while thermal output rose from 27.635 to 29.311 billion kwh.

50 Alberta Water Resources Commission, South Saskatchewan River Basin Planning Program, Hearings, Strathmore, Alberta, December 4, 1984, 110–21, testimony of Alberta Weather Modification Co-Op, Red Deer.

51 Alberta Water Resources Commission, South Saskatchewan River Basin Planning Program, Hearings, Calgary, November 6, 1984, 89–90, testimony of Mark Schmitke.

CHAPTER 12: CONCLUSION

1 Thomas P. Hughes, in *Networks of Power* (Baltimore: Johns Hopkins University Press, 1983), uses the phrase "technological momentum." Paul David develops the theory of path dependence in a much-debated essay, "Clio and the Economics of QWERTY," *American Economic Review* 75, no. 2 (1985): 332–37. As the phrase among the defenders of this concept goes, "history matters."

2 TransAlta Utilities website, www.transalta.com/facilities, and Bow River Basin Council, *The 2005 Report on the State of the Bow River* (Calgary: Bow River Basin Council, 2005), 28–29.

3 Alberta Utilities Commission, *Alberta's Hydroelectric Energy Resources* (Edmonton: Hatch Engineering, 2010). The likeliest site was downstream from the point at which the Highwood River joined the Bow near Dalemead; this would create a huge reservoir which would back up the water as far as the eastern suburbs of the city. Mainly for irrigation purposes, this dam might also permit an interbasin transfer as part of a larger scheme to redistribute water supplies across southern Alberta.

4 Richard White, *The Organic Machine: The Remaking of the Columbia River* (New York: Hill and Wang, 1995).

5 The raw data records the mean streamflow in cubic metres per second (m^3/s) for the week at Calgary. For example, in 1912, in Week 4, mean streamflow came to 37.5 m^3/s; in the same week in 1962, the recorded mean was 74.7 m^3/s. Similarly, in 1914, the mean flow in week 24 came to 316.8 m^3/s; in 1964, the number was 278 m^3/s. There could be substantial variation in flow, night and day, even hour to hour, as water was released for power generation. The mean simply notes the midpoint of readings. And there could be annual variation as well: the week 4 average flow was 37.8 m^3/s, but during the period 1912 to 1919, that week's flow reached a maximum of 39.9 in 1917 and a minimum of 23.5 in 1914. The data are derived from Alberta Environment, Water Management Division, South Saskatchewan River Basin Historical Natural Flows, 1912–95, Version 2.02.

6 William Cronon, in *Nature's Metropolis: Chicago and the Great West* (New York: Norton, 1996), loosely defines *first nature* as "original, prehuman nature" and *second nature* as "the artificial nature that people erect atop first nature" (xix). He explores the interaction of the two natures (in the hinterland and in the city) under the dominion of urban capitalist commodity flows in separate

chapters devoted to grain, lumber, and meat.

7   The phenomena discussed in the following paragraphs are explored in the last three chapters of C. Armstrong, M. Evenden, and H. V. Nelles, *The River Returns: An Environmental History of the Bow* (Montreal and Kingston: McGill-Queen's University Press, 2009), to which interested readers are referred for greater detail.

8   Alberta Forestry, Lands, and Wildlife, Bow River Recreation Survey, 1987, vol. 4, University of Calgary Library. This survey concluded that 70 per cent of Calgary households used the Bow Valley for recreation during a twelve-month period, representing an estimated 3.48 million user days.

9   Two recent reports summarize this ecological analysis: Banff-Bow Valley Task Force, "Trends in Aquatic Ecosystems," sec. 4.4.3 in *Technical Report*, 101–10, and Bow River Basin Council, *The 2005 Report on the State of the Bow River Basin* (Calgary: Bow River Basin Council, 2005), 22–28.

In the latter report, each of the eight chapters that follow on each reach of the river contains a section describing ecosystem changes. Both reports have extensive bibliographies.

10   This position is advocated by the Heritage River advocacy group in Canada, American Rivers in the United States, and some fishers and biologists attempting to restore the native species in the Bow watershed.

11   Jennifer Earle, a fisheries biologist with Alberta Sustainable Resource Development, quoted in "Species Recovery Plan in Motion for Alberta's Cutthroat Trout," *Globe and Mail*, August 5, 2011.

Index

Belcourt, Senator N.A., 37
Bell, Helen "Nellie", 75
Benjamin, Jonas, 49
Bennett, R.B., xi
   advisor to Max Aitken, 28, 30–31, 40
   Calgary lawyer, 17, 23, 25
   Kananaskis negotiations, 43, 45, 50, 54
   Spray Lakes negotiations, 105–6, 114, 119, 129
Bennett, Rosamond, 75
Bennett, W.A.C., 206
Big Bend project, 188, 200
Bighorn River, 190–91
Big Stony, Amos, 20, 22 (photo)
Blake, Jim, 199
boating, 199, 201, 218
Borden, Robert, 40, 41
Bow Falls, 11, 12, 13, 14, 75, 215
Bow River, vii, viii, x, xvii, 2, 4, 6–8, 10, 13–14, 100, 109, 113, 120, 151, 165, 183, 188, 195, 200
   changes in, 214, 218, 219, 222
   description, 11–12
   flow, 11, 12 (graph), 29, 30, 35, 52, 53 (graph), 58, 61, 77, 167, 185, 199, 200, 201, 209–14, 211–13 (graphs)
   Horseshoe Falls development, 17–23
   Kananaskis development, 35–50
Bow River Water Quality Council, 220
BC Hydro, 197
Brazeau River, 188, 200
Brewster Brothers, 87
British High Commission, 137, 151
British North America Act, 21
Brownlee, Premier John, 95, 97–100 (photo), 105–6, 107, 108, 111–13, 121, 124–26
Budd, W.J., 17–18, 20, 22–23, 54
Byng, Lord, 105
Byrne, J.H., 137

C

Calgary, Alberta, City of
   electricity, 2, 7, 9–10, 14, 35, 54, 70, 74, 203, 219, 222
   growth of, 7, 8, 15–16, 39, 60
   municipal electric system, 10, 16, 26, 204
   Max Aitken, 24–25
   power contracts, 17, 22–23, 25–26, 28, 30–31, 33, 44, 46, 57, 60, 68, 71, 78, 102, 105, 121–22, 125, 187, 189

power shortages, 19, 68–69, 78–80, 95, 101, 103, 105–7, 110–11, 113, 116, 121, 123, 145, 150, 161–64, 165–69, 172, 176, 179, 181, 185
sewage, 200–201
Calgary Automobile Club, 81
Calgary Board of Trade, 80, 101–2, 123–24, 128, 129
Calgary Electric Commissioner, 168
Calgary Electric Company, 7–9
Calgary Power Company, vi (map) vii, viii, ix, x, xii, xvii, xviii, 6, 27, 36, 46, 51, 54, 60–61, 73, 76, 159, 204–6
   Alberta negotiations, 99–116
   Depression, 119, 127, 133
   dividend, 122, 195
   generating capacity, 160, 184–85, 188, 200, 208, 225–26 (chart)
   Horseshoe development, 28, 30–33, 54
   Kananaskis development, 35, 44, 45–46 (photos), 47–50, 54
   Minnewanka storage,1912, 54–55 (photos), 56–58, 59 (photos), 60
   North Saskatchewan developments, 191
   park boundaries, 97–117
   power contracts, 17, 22–23, 25–26, 28, 30–31, 33, 44, 46, 57, 60, 68, 71, 78, 102, 105, 121–22, 125, 187, 189
   profitability, 71, 157, 161, 207 (graph)
   public ownership, 125–27, 155–64
   rates, 192–93, 195
   rural electrification, 157–59, 163
   Spray Lakes, 74–96, 99–117, 120–23, 136–37, 142–43, 165–81
   storage negotiations 1920's, 61–78, 82, 95, 103, 119, 127–31
   thermal generation, 136–37, 173, 183–201, 204–5, 208, 221
   water levels, 152–54, 165–67, 176–80, 193, 201, 217
   WWII dam, 133–37, 139–42, 143 (photo), 144–46, 148–49, 150 (photo)
Calgary Trades and Labour Council, 128
Calgary Water Power Company, 8, 9 (photo), 16, 17
camouflage, 151–52
Campbell, Glen, 43–44, 47–49
Camsell, Charles, 134, 138
Canada Cement Company, 26, 57
Canadian National Parks Association, 74, 121, 215
   Spray Lakes, 89, 90–91, 97, 106–7, 109, 112, 115, 129

Progressive Party, 98–99, 105
public ownership, 73, 93, 124–27, 155–64, 168, 189, 191, 206–7

Q

Quebec, 99
QWERTY, viii

R

Radnor, Alberta, 26–27, 38, 121, 131
ranching, 10–11
rates, electricity, 192–93, 195
Red Deer, Alberta, 93, 103–4, 189, 198
Reid, Ken, 161–62
resources, transfer, 97–116, 193
riparian rights, 19–22
River Returns, The, xvii, xviii
Roche, Dr. W.J., 44
Rocky Mountains National Park, xvi, 12–13, 28, 36, 40, 52, 56, 62, 66–67, 70–72, 73–74, 79, 82, 84, 91, 94, 95
 boundaries and Spray Lakes development, 97–116
 See also Banff National Park and Lake Minnewanka
Royal Securities Corporation, 23, 24, 27, 60, 76, 123
Rundle, power station, 184–85, 208
rural electrification, 124, 156–63

S

Saskatchewan River, 104
Scott, Duncan, 46, 48–50
second nature, xvii, 212–13
Shawinigan, 3–4
Sheerness coalfield, 197
Sibbald, A.S., 89
Smart, James, 149, 151–52
Smith, C.B., 23, 25–28, 30, 52–53
Social Credit, 155–56, 157, 159, 160, 191, 206
South Saskatchewan River, 11
South Saskatchewan River Basin Planning Board, 198
South Saskatchewan River Basin Study, 220
South Saskatchewan Water Basin Council, 220

Spray Lakes, xvii, 74, 185, 193, 204
 in Alberta resources transfer negotiation, 97–117
 park boundaries, 119, 120, 143, 153
 storage debate 1920's, 74–78, 80–84, 88–96, 119–31
 storage 1950's, 165–73 (map), 174–81, 184–85, 200, 208, 217
 WWII, 134, 136, 137, 140, 142
Spray Lakes power stations, 184–85, 187, 193, 200
Spray River, 120–22, 122 (photo), 166, 168–69, 172, 174, 176–77, 179, 217, 218
Stairs, Denis, 76
Stairs, John F., 24, 60, 75–76
state, the, 215
Stevens, H.H., 92–93
Stewart, Charles, Minister of the Interior, 65–68, 70, 74, 77, 80–81, 91, 93–94, 97–100, 105–8, 108 (photo), 109, 111–16, 120, 122–23, 128–29, 166
Stoney Indians. *See* Nakoda
Stoney Plain Fish and Game Association, 198
storage, hydroelectric, vii, x, xvi, 52–72, 208, 215, 216, 218
 See also Minnewanka and Spray Lakes
street railway, 17, 25
Stronach, R.S., 86
Sundance power station, 190–91, 193, 195
Swampy, James, 20, 22 (photo)
Symington, H.J., 135, 138

T

Tarr, Joel, xvii
Tennessee Valley Authority, xi
Tesla, Nicola, 2
Thermal electricity, 136–37, 173, 183–201, 204–5, 208, 221
Thompson, G.H., 187
Thompson, Stanley, 146
Three Sisters power station, 208
Toronto Field Naturalists, 91
tourism, 12–13, 56, 63, 70, 78, 83, 104, 116, 139, 216
TransAlta Resources Company, 196
TransAlta Utilities Corporation, xviii, 196–200, 219, 220–21
transmission lines, 68
Treaty 7, 21
Turner Valley, 107, 136, 143

WILDERNESS AND WATERPOWER

U

United Farmers of Alberta, 81, 92, 97, 113, 124, 126–27
use and enjoyment, 223

V

Van Horne, William, 12

W

Wabamun Lake power station, 186–89, 190 (photo), 191, 193–96
Waddy, J.W., 43, 47, 49
Walker, J. Selby, 90, 106–7, 112, 142–43, 146–47 (photo), 148, 176
walking tours, 85–86
War Measures Act, 135, 145
Wardle, J.M., 134–35, 137
washout, 179–80
Water Power Branch
  Horseshoe Falls negotiations, 22, 41, 48, 60, 61
  Lake Minnewanka storage, 62, 64–68, 70, 74, 79
  Spray Lakes storage, 98, 102–4, 110–11, 121, 130

waterpower, defined, xv–xvi
  development of 1–3
  on the Bow, 3, 6, 11, 16
water rental, 21, 23
Webster, George, 81, 101, 108
weeds, 194–95
Wesley, Chief Peter, 20, 22 (photo)
Western Canada Coal Operators Association, 90–91
Western Canada Power Company, 25, 76
Wheeler, Arthur O., 83–88, 85 (photo), 90
White, Arthur V., 3, 11, 14
White, Richard, xvii, 209
wild rivers, 221
wilderness, debated, xiii–xv
Wildman, Dan, 49
wind power, 221
Wood, E.R., 26
woodpeckers, 152
World War I, 61, 65, 74, 76
World War II, 6, 133–55, 159, 207–8
Worster, Donald, xvii

Y

Yellowstone Park, 12
Yoho National Park, 115
Young Man, Chief Jonas Two, 20, 22 (photo)